Individual Preferences in e-Learning

Individual Preferences in e-Learning

HOWARD HILLS

GOWER

Published by
Gower Publishing Limited
Gower House
Croft Road
Aldershot
Hants GU11 3HR
England

Gower Publishing Company
Suite 420
101 Cherry Street
Burlington, VT 05401-4405
USA

Howard Hills has asserted his right under the Copyright, Designs and Patents Act 1988 to be identified as the author of this work.

British Library Cataloguing in Publication Data
Hills, Howard
    Individual preferences in e-learning
    1. Open learning – Computer network resources 2. Individualized instruction – Data processing
    3. Internet in education 4. Curriculum planning
    I. Title
    371.3'58

ISBN 0 566 08456 2

Library of Congress Cataloging-in-Publication Data
Hills, Howard
    Individual preferences in e-learning/Howard Hills.
        p. cm.
    ISBN 0-566-08456-2
    1. Distance education -- Computer-assisted instruction. 2. Internet in education. 3. Individual differences. I. Title.
    LC 5803.C65H53 2003
    371.3'58 -- dc22
                                                                                2003049373
Printed & Bound in Great Britain by MPG Books Ltd, Bodmin, Cornwall

Contents

List of Figures

List of Tables

1 *Perspectives on Learning*

Why read this book?

This book gives designers and implementers of e-learning a learning model that will allow them to design and implement for the preferences of individuals. The reported research indicates that the majority of the population prefer to learn from examples and practical detail. The same research shows that intuitive and rational personalities are attracted to the computer profession and that these personality types are likely to prefer theory and conceptual topics. By inference, the majority of creators of e-learning prefer concepts and theories. The assumption is that the majority of creators of e-learning will not naturally create material that is a preferred learning activity for the majority of the population. This book therefore provides a theory and concepts that will enable all e-learning material to be in a form that enables each individual to learn from their preferred activity. Along the way it presents a model for learning based on the Myers Briggs Type Indicator (MBTI)® functions. If all you want to do is use that model then read Chapters 5 and 6. A brief conclusion at the end of Chapter 7 might save you reading the book. Each chapter has a summary that allows you to see if that chapter interests you.

This book presents an individual view of the usefulness of e-learning, which is the communication and information processing combination represented by a PC and the Internet, not what it means to an individual but from the perspective of individuals. The book draws on research into individual differences in learning that are rooted in personality. The premise of the book is that by understanding the learner, and to some extent the learner's environment, we can create e-learning that is more appropriate for the individual. The purpose is to give designers of learning material and users some simple rules that produces learning that can be tailored by the individual in ways that best suit their individual preferences. The learning model proposed is based on MBTI theory, specifically the MBTI functions.

The book focuses on the individual and the preferences he or she has for interaction with others, for concrete examples, abstract theories, objective decisions or subjective choices. An understanding of these preferences gives simple guidelines for improving e-learning, indeed for improving learning. This book does not focus on IT or on the tools of design. These are not irrelevancies, but will change rapidly and should not determine long-term decisions made about the use and deployment of e-learning.

Assumptions have been made that the reader understands e-learning technology and terminology. Many of the terms in use today have different meanings for different individuals and where this is so I have provided my understanding of the term. This is not offered because I think it is better than anyone else's but simply to help you understand the ideas I have put forward. There are divergent views on what e-learning is and what it is not.

Within the book, a definition that includes all applications of Internet and web technologies that have the purpose of improving human competencies is put forward. The Internet will bring about a fundamental change in society, and has already started to do so.

The Internet changes everything and yet human nature remains the same. The purpose of this book is to reconcile the conflict in these two statements and develop approaches that blend human nature with the internet for productive learning. Human nature is individual. Each of us is different and this diversity is very valuable in helping others learn. We are all social animals and our learning is social. We are cooperative as a species at the team level because that helps our survival, but perhaps we still have to learn to be cooperative at the global level! E-learning has to make allowances for individuality, diversity and socialization. The Internet changes everything, the way we work together, the way we trade with each other and the nature of the work we do. The impact it has had and will have on us and society will change what and how we learn. Trainers are interested in working out what these changes will be and how they might take advantage of them.

The questions trainers ask me are:

- What topics is e-learning good for?
- Which learning styles does it suit?
- Who likes e-learning and who doesn't?
- How do we encourage people to get the best out of it?
- Where is it best used and in what sort of surroundings?
- When, if ever, will it be appropriate for behavioural learning?
- Why should we use it? (Perhaps the most fundamental question of all).

This book attempts to answer some of these questions. It is based on practical observation of deploying electronically-delivered learning in large organizations. This has been called many things in the past: phrases such as *embedded CBT*, *EPSS* and *CDROM* were used. Many of the lessons learned with these technologies are applicable to e-learning now.

This book is also based on a theoretical understanding of learning and its implementation in organizations and with individuals. Our understanding of learning has improved significantly over the last century. The acquisition of mental skills (cognitive learning) was the province of the classroom. Vocational and behavioural skills were mainly acquired in the workplace. The experiential-learning model demonstrated the importance of experience in all learning. The application of learning has become more important than the acquisition of knowledge. By its nature, on-line learning, with the exception of PC psychomotor skills, is cognitive. It may therefore easily become theoretical in nature. We risk losing the ideas of Dewey and Kolb (1984) that encouraged a 'progressive' and pragmatic approach to learning. I intend to explore ways that we will not.

What is in this book?

The book makes extensive use of previous observations of learners and draws on the discussions I have had with large organizations on the deployment of e-learning. In the first part of the book, I establish the lessons we can learn from developments in training, learning and technology and the training methods that have responded to changes in society. The application of the Internet to training is another example of this happening.

There are also factors in the growth of the Internet that are relevant to e-learning. The nature of work and of organizations is subtly changing, although the changes are continuous rather than discontinuous. Any industry or service where information moves, sees a radical simplification of work, and in this context, money and orders are information rather than currency.

The introduction of the PC gave a huge boost to the games industry. It was apparent that this would happen when software engineers used mainframes to play maze-style games in text. I remember being hooked on such a game in the early 1980s. Before that, games were played with cards and boards and counters of various types. Likewise the Internet has not created a brand new industry other than that of itself. It has created a fundamentally different way of doing what we have done in the past and that also includes learning.

Our approach to learning has also changed as we understand more about the process. Chapter 2 reviews the growth of the Internet in relation to personal preferences in its use. The chapter explores the e-learning market place, infers from history what are the most likely developments for its use in relation to learning and the impact culture has in its use and the impact e-learning may have on corporate culture. Chapter 3 focuses on the emotional and social aspects of learning as these may be the areas where e-learning will have its weaknesses. These three themes – training, technology, and learning – form the first three chapters of the book, partly a historical perspective, but using history to draw inferences about the future. The chapter also lists the different reasons why a learner needs to interact with others in the context of e-learning and, by inference what e-learning may lack. The role that e-learning may have in replacing or replicating the reasons for these interactions is described. I explore the individual differences each of us brings to the learning process, whether as tutor or learner. As part of this chapter, there is a brief mention of the ways in which e-learning can give feedback of cognitive skills. This draws on the work of Bloom (1956) and relies on his well-developed taxonomy. This theory is well understood and is merely related to the e-learning context.

The next part of the book focuses on the individual learner and is research- and observation-based. It uses the research findings associated with education and the MBTI®, observations of learners of computer systems, observations of learning in education that were managed by a pseudo-computer system and, briefly, some of the research findings of Kolb (1984). Chapter 4 begins with a summary of the research of Carroll (1990). He observed how people actually use computer systems when they are learning. The chapter continues with the work of Pask (1976a, 1976b, 1988). Although Pask's observations predate desktop computers, the learning he studied, delivered learning chunks where an electro-mechanical system monitored progress and restricted learner choices and is wholly relevant to on-line learning. Chapters 5 and 6 are based heavily on an understanding of MBTI preferences.

A significant body of research exists that identifies individual preferences in learning. These preferences relate to the MBTI personality types. There is a wealth of material indicating the extent to which personality drives our choices, for learning approaches as well as other activities. The research is used to understand the type of activities that learners prefer, what percentage of them are likely to do so and what activities we may design into e-learning to take account of personal preferences. Chapter 6 presents the learning model that I believe is helpful to the designer and to the on-line tutor and to others who help in the learning process. Much of the chapter describes the preferences of individuals in relation to learning. Every reader should be able to recognize themselves at some point in this chapter.

Readers who have some understanding of their personality type and their learning preferences will gain most from these chapters.

Pask felt that it is helpful to look at the nature of the topic when assembling learning materials. A learning model based on MBTI functions enables us to characterize learning activities against those functions, rather than the nature of the topic. You may notice that I have changed learning material to learning activities: there is a close link between the two. Interaction with others is a essential part of the learning model I propose. The role of an on-line tutor is growing in prominence. Some remain as subject specialists available to answer questions, others provide a more facilitative role of encouragement and motivation. As the complexity of society increases, the amount of knowledge available to us also increases. No one tutor can keep up-to-date with all the knowledge pertaining to their topic, the tutor and the learner frequently have to explore topics together. The tutor has moved from being the source of knowledge to being a facilitator of a process and to becoming a learner at the same time. The learning model is proposed to help the tutor to identify the interactions for which their role is most appropriate. I do not believe there are any surprises at this point. The tutor helps learners make subjective decisions about their learning activities and the learning content, they provide energy and excitement for some and to others, motivation to explore activities they might prefer to avoid or, at best, pay scant attention to.

The final part of the book attempts to make sense of the preceding chapters and provide practical guidance on making e-learning work in relation to individuals. Chapter 7 revisits the functional learning model presented in Chapters 5 and 6 from a practical viewpoint. It futher describes examples of design solutions for specific topics. All solutions include exercises and activities that will appeal to some facet of every personality type, none requires advanced technology. If a designer and a tutor use their own preferences in creating learning activities then they will find that natural, a bit like wearing a comfortable shoe. Since we are all different some learners may need material and activities that the designer and tutor will be uncomfortable creating and providing, the functional learning model and the examples in Chapter 7 gives a guide as to what they need to create. This helps the designer and tutor make allowances for the preferences and learning styles of others.

It will be apparent in Chapter 1 that training methods have responded to changes in society and technology. Chapter 2 shows that the Internet heralds significant changes in both. It is inconceivable that training functions will remain unaltered in the future. The trick will be to guess the changes and to take some practical actions to prepare for these. The examples indicate the sort of practical actions, trainers and training functions might have to take. It is important that the book is not a dry textbook, so I will illustrate the text with some examples and stories, and I would like to start with a story.

A mouse and a hamster

This is a story about a couple of animals. Imagine if you will a mouse and a hamster in a maze, a particular sort of maze. This maze is composed of rooms, not corridors, and each room has many rooms opening from it. There are signs on the doors and sometimes maps in the rooms. Neither the mouse nor the hamster know how many rooms are in the maze. There is a sign they come across that says '500 rooms in this section', or '400' or '100' or '25'. They know what one room looks like and they can imagine what 10 rooms look like, but how can they understand what 100 rooms are like, when they can only ever see one room?

Could you do any better? They cannot go outside the maze and see the maze as a whole; there is no outside, as far as they are concerned.

The rooms in the maze have food in them. Sometimes the food is stale and boring, many rooms have food that is rotten or no food at all. A few rooms have wonderfully tasty food for either the mouse or the hamster and sometimes for both of them. They spend all their time looking for this particular food. The mouse is very happy in the maze, leaping from room to room, spending just a few moments in each room and moving on through an interesting door. The mouse is called 'Hurry' and every few moments Hurry's claws make a little click on the threshold of each door. Sometimes, Hurry stops and munches a bit of food in a room, but quickly runs on, searching for that perfect little titbit. The hamster, who is called 'Steady', spends longer in each room, sniffing around the corners. Steady often picks up morsels of food in his cheek pouches and runs along to the next room, getting slower and slower as more food is carried from room to room.

Both Hurry and Steady frequently get lost and wonder where they are: that is a feature of mazes, especially when you can never, ever see them from the outside. Fortunately, each time they leap over a doorway, their claws leave a little mark as they click on the threshold. This means that they can always find their way back. Hurry finds this boring, although Steady likes the feeling of a safety net. Life seems much more secure when you can find your way back: the trouble is that many of the rooms look strange when you enter them backwards. That changes their appearance. Some rooms are so tall that you only ever see the bottom or top half and both Steady and Hurry find this confusing. Hurry does not mind, thinking of it as a separate room and runs on elsewhere, seeking that elusive perfect little titbit. The maps are useful, but so often the maps and signposts are put up by the rats who built the maze. They know the maze very well and it is difficult for them to imagine themselves as mice and hamsters, for whom the maze is a strange place, full of exotic food and unexpected doorways.

Hurry visits many more rooms than Steady, but takes just as long to find that perfect little morsel, sometimes running straight through a room with a titbit, in too much of a rush to sniff everything in the room. Sometimes, Hurry gives up and lies panting in the corner of a room. Steady visits fewer rooms and collects much more food on the way. The hamster thinks more in each room and tries to sniff out the best next step for finding that tasty titbit. Steady sometimes runs round in circles between a few rooms, somehow stuck in a loop.

Sometimes, Hurry and Steady come across a well-organized maze. Food is neatly piled on shelves in each room, seven shelves with seven spaces. There are never too many exits. Some exits are to cul-de-sacs, sort of like a cupboard in the main room. If the maze is too simple, Hurry gets bored. Hurry likes to rush about and a small tightly controlled maze is too limited. This type of maze makes Steady much happier. The big haphazard mazes make Steady nervous and worried. Although they both enter the maze to find food, their reactions are different because they have different personalities. We might expect other animals to react differently in other similar mazes. Perhaps a lion might lie around and expect other lesser animals to find food in the maze and then lay it out carefully on a desk in front of the lion; then wait patiently to follow instructions from the lion. The lion never appreciates the significance of the maze, how much work it takes to find the right food or how much rubbish and rotten food the maze contains.

I have presented this story to help you think about web-based material in relation to its users. Similarity with people you know is intended. Hurry and Steady represent two approaches to learning and the maze is the Internet (or Intranet). An e-learning component in the maze may be well organized, signposted and well-structured, but will still have the attributes of a maze. Relating the personality of an animal to a human being is not a new trick in the training community. A frequent team-building ploy is to ask team members to describe themselves as an animal and then explain why they have chosen that animal. This is done as a way of increasing the insight others in the team have about the personality of individuals in the team.

This need for insight into others is an important building block in working and learning with others. Insight helps us to understand that others will behave differently from us and have different reasons for doing so. We may expect two different species of animal to behave differently and that is why I chose a mouse and a hamster, similar but different, which is very like the situation with humans, similar but different. As a result, individuals will use web-based material in different ways. Those differences are based on personal differences. They are based on personality, preferences for learning styles, attitudes to others in the workplace, what is considered acceptable locally, fluency of web familiarity, keyboard dexterity, command of literacy and numeracy.

E-learner and non e-learners

E-learning is very good for learners who are motivated and understand how to get the best from learning material. They also need to know how to get the best out of the Internet. The ideal e-learner is digitally literate, probably self-sufficient, intuitive and self-motivated. The ideal e-learner is probably the ideal book learner. Where does that leave those who are reluctant learners, who need others to help their motivation, for whom the computer represents an artificial way of communicating, and those who seek help and reassurance while learning?

Heavy reliance on e-learning creates the risk that the work force, indeed the population at large, will divide into competent e-learners who race ahead and those less than competent who find the experience lacks personal reward. Will this lead to a greater division between the skilled and the non-skilled? It is important to ensure that it does not. The performance of any group of people is dependent on the performance of everyone, not just a select few. Everyone is important and everyone contributes. At an early stage in my career I was advised to ensure that I knew the names of our cleaning staff as they were important. I did and usually had a brief chat before going home. The result was that they were a little bit more considerate to me, left me alone when I worked late, left my room that bit tidier. Looking back now, I am sure that improved my day so that I was more organized and performed better. At the time, I was just treating others as people, without making a special fuss. The consequences of everyone doing their job well, whatever their role, is that organizations function more efficiently. This means that everyone has to be a competent learner and in the new digital economy: a competent e-learner. That may not mean an individual studying at a PC working through material on a screen. It does mean that the communication aspect of the Internet and the processing power of the PC are harnessed to deliver learning to individuals and small groups. There is an expectation that there will be certain common features about those who prefer a particular type of e-learning solution. If we can understand these common features we can begin to design for those preferences.

Each of us is unique and yet e-learning seems to present a 'one size fits all' solution. It is true that virtual classrooms (or collaborative working tools) give the opportunity for human interaction. This, in turn, introduces a flexibility that makes some allowance for differences. The personal control that each of us can exert over our use of a PC also gives flexibility. However, this flexibility can only be exploited by individuals for e-learning where the learning material and any learning support is presented in a way that makes full allowance for individual preferences. This is not something that is particularly prevalent in much electronically-delivered learning support, or in most learning packages.

Books and e-learning styles

In writing this book many ideas and concepts are presented in a serialistic way; that is the nature of books. I have tried to use signposting and summaries. Those in a hurry for a titbit of knowledge can rush through the book, flicking over pages. Those of you who prefer a steady approach can read the book from cover to cover. I have used diagrams to convey information and stories to provide light relief. An e-learning solution would give me an opportunity to provide multiple ways of accessing the material, allowing for a variety of individual preferences. An e-learning product carries a cost and time penalty in development which may explain why I have written this as a book as I cannot justify the extra cost of an electronically delivered product. At least everyone who might be interested in the topic can use and operate a book. I cannot yet guarantee that for e-learning. By the end of 2002 48 per cent of the adult population used the Internet (MORI Technology Tracker, 2003) with a survey by OFTEL in the same period reporting that 42 per cent of households had access to the Internet. The figure from the July 2002 National Statistics Omnibus Survey reports that 55 per cent of adults have used the Internet at some time or other. Projections for 2005 indicate that the figure for regular use will rise to 68 per cent of the adult population. It is likely that those interested in this book title will have access to the Internet and therefore to an e-learning product. If I could guarantee a large enough audience, what factors might persuade me to present the material as e-learning? The most persuasive factor is the ability to connect to examples of best practice and excellence.

There is a vast amount of material available to anyone through the World Wide Web. Much of this material is of outstanding excellence, and much of it is unmitigated rubbish! Think about Hurry and Steady – how can they tell the difference? Some food may taste really nice, but many of us know that tasty food is not always good for us, and some food that tastes awful, may be very good for us.

If I produced this book as an e-learning product, I would choose for you which examples of other material to include, perhaps in a similar way that each book has a bibliography. Of course, not everything I refer to is on the web and where it is a cost may be incurred. A really good web product has a whole host of complexity added. This is one reason why most e-learning products are fairly self-contained. The packaged material is just that – a package and the virtual classroom session is a closed community. Perhaps chatrooms and discussion boards are the most open and free-flowing e-learning environments. My definition of a discussion board is a tool that enables an individual to enter text that is read by others a short time later. They may then respond with an entry that is also read by others. The difference between chatrooms and discussion boards is that chatrooms are simultaneous in that others read your input as you type it. They are both closed communities in that entry is restricted. The barrier to entry may be very low, just a requirement to register in some cases. In the e-learning environment they are usually restricted to co-learners of the same topic.

The other overriding reason for this restriction is financial. Most adult learning is not provided free at the point of use – someone pays. In the UK public-funded bodies like the BBC do make high quality material available at no cost to the user, other than through the license fee. But this is a rarity.

There are thus two reasons why this is a book. One is financial. You (or someone) bought it, the publisher and I get our reward for writing and publishing it. I avoid a high number of complexities in my inter-relationships with other material as much as in the design of the product. I am able to say what I want to say straightforwardly and easily. Why then has the training industry not stayed with books and tutors? A clue lies in the fact that I used the phrase 'industry'. If I belong to an industry or if I define myself as a professional, then I expect that industry or profession to change with the times and to progress. It is impossible to deny that some training professionals are in love with technology and have been so since the 1950s. Universities are, quite rightly, at the forefront of driving forward thinking in the application of technology to learning. I would like to place current e-learning and on-line developments into an historical context. Some themes will emerge that allow us to make more sense of on-line learning and get more out of it.

Historical perspective

THE APPRENTICESHIP

The adoption of new forms of training has been encouraged by the rise of the training department. A review of the historical development of training indicates that e-learning is one more step along the road of modernization. Prior to the Industrial Revolution, skills and knowledge were transferred on a one-to-one basis. Books and learned papers were used by academics but the acquisition of vocational skills was achieved by working alongside someone who knew how to do things, someone who could show the learner and explain things in a way that was directly relevant to the job. This became formalized as the apprenticeship scheme. At a very early stage the state intervened in apprenticeship schemes, not always with the result desired.

Apprenticeship schemes were started by the élite guilds of the Middle Ages, such as goldsmiths and ironmongers. In many cases these schemes protected the profession as well as providing a means of entry. These schemes were established by the fourteenth century. In the sixteenth century they were extended as a means of improving the economic well being of the community. Parishes and towns were able to pay for poor children to be apprenticed into trades and crafts. This was a direct recognition that helping someone to acquire a vocational skill would move them from being a drain on local taxes to being a productive member of society and able to contribute to those same taxes. For example, Norwich set up a scheme where women were paid twenty shillings per annum to take up to a dozen women and children and supervise their work in the cloth industry. The system was abused, with many parents who were members of guilds and trades seeking payment from the local parish to take their own children into an apprenticeship scheme. Some of the commercial schemes had significant rewards in the final years. For example, as a mercer (a commercial trader) an apprentice would be set up with a stock of £50 during the last two years of an apprenticeship. Another apprentice was to have the benefit of the commission on the goods traded, which would be guaranteed at a minimum of £20 per annum (Jewell, 1998,

p. 85). By the eighteenth century the apprenticeship scheme was well-established as a means of providing vocational education for the poor. In 1733 some 20 000 children passed through English charity schools, of those some 8 400 were placed into apprenticeship schemes. It has to be said that the majority (7 000) of these were boys (Jewell, 1998, p. 91).

The typical learning strategy for most of these apprenticeship schemes would be drill and practice; watch me and I will explain, do and I will give you feedback, correct your errors and reward your successes. The pairing of an expert with a novice produced a simple pragmatic learning strategy for individuals. Skills were acquired at an early stage in life and tended to remain relevant for a lifetime. The master benefited from cheap labour at an early stage of the apprenticeship and the apprentice gained a marketable skill for the rest of their life.

THE INDUSTRIAL REVOLUTION

The advent of the Industrial Revolution meant that a generation went from farm and field work into factory work. Suddenly, a whole group of adult learners had to reskill themselves. Fortunately, many of these adult learners had achieved a minimum standard of literacy. By 1750 between 30–40 per cent of the population of Britain was regarded as literate (Stevens, 1998, p. 56.) There is a point of view that this standard of literacy was not essential for fuelling the Industrial Revolution. For many of the skilled trades of millwrights and mechanics, a high standard of numeracy and a grasp of fundamental scientific principles was much more important, although literacy may have been a key in helping the worker become numerate and understand the necessary scientific concepts. The industrial developments that led to the rise of Britain as an economic power were based on the achievements of highly-skilled craftsmen and mechanics, using the scientific method of rational analysis (Stevens, 1998, p. 68).

A skilled workforce was needed by firms to enable them to expand and innovate. The workers themselves benefited economically as well, as rural wages near industrial areas were higher than elsewhere as a result of factory wages being higher than farm wages. In 1830 field labourers south of the Thames rioted in an attempt to get a wage of half a crown a day (12½p) (Trevelyan, 2000, p. 484) but no such riots occurred in the 'industrialized' north of Britain. Factory owners gained from skilled workers even more so. The initial Spinning Jenny could do the work of eight people in spinning threads. Later machines spun 80 threads simultaneously. Machines could be bought or built, but experienced operators did not exist; they had to be trained. It might be logical to assume that the factory classroom arose out of this business need. In fact, Government legislation played a significant part. The Factory Act of 1802 required children to be taught reading, writing and arithmetic during their first four years of any factory apprenticeship. Adult training on the other hand seems to have been more available outside the factory rather than inside. The need for skilled workers was met through the foundation of Mechanics Institutions early in the nineteenth century. Each institute was an independent organization created by its local community. Members typically paid a guinea (£1.05) to become a member. Many of these mechanics institutes have gone on to be the modern institutions of further and higher education today. Some companies extended this concept and set up classrooms in their factories.

For adults the classroom was a revolutionary approach to learning. However, the main method of acquiring vocational skills was working on the job with an experienced colleague. The classroom backed up this training. Even as the Industrial Revolution progressed, the classroom was used for academic skills rather than work-related ones. Although the pace of change gradually accelerated, training methods did not. Even the First World War did not produce significant change in training methods. The soldiers who returned from the war at demobilization returned to jobs that had changed little. In fact, the economic downturn meant there was a surplus of workers. In part, this was because business leaders reinvested in the same technology as existed before the War (Taylor, 1992, pp. 139, 145).

THE SECOND WORLD WAR

After the Industrial Revolution the next major impact on the need to reskill individuals came at the end of the Second World War. Technology developments were forced in the hothouse of war while a large percentage of the normal working population were away fighting. In the UK, four and a half million men and women left the armed forces in the eighteen months immediately after the end of the Second World War. They all wanted jobs. They all wanted the same jobs they had had before, but the workplace had changed radically since the 1930s. For example the employed population in the UK was 3 million greater than in 1939 (Taylor, 1992, p. 599). If all of them were to acquire jobs, then they needed skills they did not possess and the economy would have to expand fast. Some of that expansion was fuelled by the innovation brought about by the war, 'unlike the First World War the Second stimulated and created many new industries and new working practices', (Taylor, 1992, p. 600). The demobilized servicemen and women came back to a radically different workplace. The armed forces played their part, with a rapid expansion of service education. For example, every soldier received 6 hours of compulsory education a week, either vocational or cultural depending on their choice. 'In about thirty industries free training was provided in government training centres' (Addison, 1995, p. 24). There were grants for those who wanted to be self-employed, together with a three month training course. This explosion in government-funded classroom vocational training was mirrored inside large companies. Many companies set up, or enlarged, their training functions. Classroom training was more efficient than asking those working to train someone else alongside them. That required a one-to-one relationship whereas a one-to-twelve, or even one-to-twenty ratio allowed one expert to train many more.

In 1948, Lloyds Bank opened its staff college at Eyhurst Court in Surrey. The first training course for aspiring bank managers lasted 11 weeks and covered the complex techniques of banking law and practice, customer relations, business development, organization and staff control, balance sheet analysis and appraisement, judgment in lending and business statistics (The Dark Horse: June 1948 – Lloyds Bank Staff Journal). Later, Lloyds Bank established a comprehensive training scheme for boys and girls joining the bank and in 1950 established a training centre. In the immediate post-war years many organizations recognized that not only had young people to be attracted to join organizations but retained once they were in it. 'One of the ways of trying to keep them on the staff was to ensure they received adequate and systematic training' (Winton, 1982, p. 152).

These developments were mirrored in countless other organizations. The increased investment that organizations made in training meant an increase in the number of people who regarded themselves as professional trainers. This in turn led to the establishment of The British Institute of Training Officers in 1964 which became The Institute of Training and Development in 1979, now merged into The Chartered Institute of Personnel and

Development. The thinking of academics and thought leaders also became focused on training as an activity, differentiating it from education. Robert Mager (1972) and Peter Pipe (1999) encouraged trainers to be much more specific about what they wanted to achieve and in defining performance problems that were amenable to training solutions and those that were not. Increasing effort went into designing training sessions that were efficient and structured. The expert was in short supply and was needed doing their work, so trainers became adept at capturing the knowledge and skills of experts and transferring them to others

THE DEVELOPMENT OF THE TRAINING PROFESSIONAL

The job of the trainer and the designer began to become differentiated from that of the subject expert. The work of Mager (1972) had a major impact on the way trainers approached design. The systematic approach to training demonstrates a business-like approach: the debate is no longer about curriculum but focuses on output. The format of objectives, conditions and standards has enabled the trainer to articulate to business what people can do as a result of training. This discipline has enabled trainers to exert more control over the means used to help people learn. It is ironic that this discipline may inhibit some of the more exciting developments in e-learning.

The creation of the classroom for adult learning was a response to a business issue arising from the Industrial Revolution. Likewise the creation of the systematic management of training, objective setting and programmed learning was a response to a business issue arising from the immediate post-war years. as large numbers of people had to be trained rapidly and quickly. That need has not diminished. Although the pressure for new skills was acute after the Second World War, it has been increasing at an every greater rate throughout the twentieth century, a trend that is likely to continue during the twenty-first century.

The very first application of a systematic approach to training actually happened during the First World War with a need to train workers in the shipping industry, but more widespread use did not occur until the Second World War. The Second World War also saw an increase in access to education. The British army introduced education and debating sessions for 'other ranks', a social grouping that would not previously have had access to adult learning, other than that needed for army training.

LESSONS WE MAY LEARN FROM A REVIEW OF THE PAST

This brief review of the changes in vocational education reveals a number of themes:

(1) State intervention does not always produce the desired results. Individuals always seek an opportunity to manipulate that funding into ways that it was not intended. This does not mean that State funding does not achieve its objectives, it does mean that there is a certain amount of leakage in any State intervention process. The twenty-first century example of individual learning accounts is very similar to the way in which the parish apprenticeship schemes were taken advantage of, by those they were not intended for.
(2) Businesses respond to a lack of skills in the labour force by creating training opportunities for individuals. Recently, this is more likely to occur inside an organization rather than outside. Historically, many of our educational foundations

were established by business leaders who wanted a better-educated workforce to draw on. When companies were forced to provide education by the State they would then direct this into areas they felt beneficial. The factory schools that employers were compelled to set up by the various Factory Acts seemed to exist more to encourage obedience than to educate. Such a repressive and focused school regime is described in the opening sequence of *Hard Times* by Charles Dickens. If Charles Dickens described a similar repressive regime for Hurry and Steady (the mouse and hamster from earlier in the chapter) this would be like enclosing them in a cage so that they can turn neither to the left nor to the right. One might almost imagine Mr Gradgrind (the School Inspector in *Hard Times*) saying 'Hard cheese, hard cheese, that is what these animals need and that is what they will have, soft cheese is wrong and a lie, any animal that likes soft cheese is lying'. The compulsory aspect of education portrayed in *Hard Times* is one that eliminates enquiry and where there is only ever one answer, that of the teacher.

(3) There have been many occasions in the past when adults have had to retrain to remain in employment. The frequency with which this is required has increased. It is no longer possible for job-related skills to last for an individual's working life. Companies have responded, as they did in the 1940s and 1950s, by expanding and creating training functions.

(4) In turn that has led to the creation of the training professional. Professionals of all disciplines seek to improve the way in which their profession works. It was (and is) quite natural for trainers to seek out new ways of working. Technology developments have been one of many changes that the profession has introduced over the last 50 years.

This brief historical perspective highlights that training functions are relatively new on the scene and those working within them will seek to change and progress the way their work is done. Two of the most significant changes in adult learning, the classroom and the systematic model, were responses to key business issues both created by significant change in society.

The introduction of technology

THE TEACHING MACHINE

The second change in training that I would like to reflect on, is the impact of technology on training. The use of the application of technology to learning originates in the 1920s, with the invention of the teaching machine by Samuel L. Pressey. This thinking and experimentation was in advance of significant improvements in the theory of training. The most sophisticated ideas on training were based on drill and practice ideas; show, tell, do and monitor. Teaching machines were introduced commercially in the 1960s. By this time, Skinner's ideas on behavioural learning were being taken up (Skinner, 1968). Mager's work on objectives had yet to be published, although trainers were aware of the requirement to define precisely, a learning outcome in either cognitive or psychomotor objective terms. Teaching machines presented a frame of information through text, pictures or graphics. Multiple choice questions enabled either different routes of study to be selected or answers to be judged. Learning was essentially sequential with very little flexibility. Teaching machines provided a mechanistic approach to programmed learning (PL), itself a very mechanical view of the learning process. PL techniques closely followed the drill and practice approach but were used with cognitive objectives, usually just knowledge based. The PL concept is: break down a topic into very small discrete steps; introduce each step; test the memory of that step; and only continue to the next step when the question is answered correctly. The approach can be described as: tell; test; judge; retest until correct. PL applications were not exclusive to teaching machines and one of the more successful applications was a book aimed at teaching the rule of the road at sea, a purely cognitive knowledge-based requirement.

Teaching machines provided an ideal mechanistic environment for PL. Machines contained a roll of film that displayed a frame of information with a multiple-choice question. An answer was selected by pressing a button and the film rolled one way or the other a designated number of frame spaces and the appropriate answer displayed. The film was 35mm and, because of cost, most applications were monochrome. There was little visual stimulus and no audio. However, pictures and good quality graphics could be included. In the 1970s, technology advanced a little and tape-slide machines were developed. These were based around a random access projector, giving instant access to 80 separate images. Audio was added to colour, and design could be more flexible.

Applications were mainly in the defence and aerospace industries and usually for knowledge-based objectives. One notable example could be described as a part-task simulator. A slide projector was connected to contact points on a circuit diagram of a radar set. Touching a probe to the circuit diagram displayed oscilloscope pictures of the electrical waveform at that point in the circuit. Different slides demonstrated different fault conditions in the electronic circuit. The set up allowed electronic engineers to practice fault-finding on a radar set. A simpler technology was used by Lloyds Bank to train branch staff. This was based on an eight-track tape recorder. The equipment was used alongside workbooks. A question was presented either on the tape or in a workbook. This was a multiple-choice question with up to seven different responses. Learners selected their response by selecting a track on the tape recorder. The track played a response appropriate to their selected answer.

COMPUTER-DELIVERED LEARNING

At the same time, mainframe training or learning systems were introduced. Phoenix, Plato, Interactive Instructional System (from IBM) were examples, each with their own authoring systems. One of the most successful was at Barclaycard, which ran unchanged for 15 years. CBT programming languages were introduced, Microtext, Tencore, Pilot, for example. Each had their roots in a matching programming language such as Basic and Fortran. At this point in the history of technology-based training, the issues of conflicting standards had emerged.

Commercial opportunism and the expectation that companies would spend millions buying technology-based learning systems and products drove a proliferation of competing systems. Thankfully, this issue is killed stone dead by Internet standards, well almost, as conflicting IT specifications and configurations continue to bedevil the e-learning designer. However, matters have improved and there is little technical competition in fundamental operating standards across the Internet. Commercial and policy decisions may well create technical incompatibility but there is no technical reason why any training product or activity should not be available within any technical environment.

Throughout the last twenty years technical developments followed. The business argument was often based on lower cost of delivery of learning, but some instructional benefits began to appear. These were, the ease of displaying high quality visual information, record keeping and learner management, simulation (with the consequence of safe practice) of some part of the task, interaction between the learner and the machine (with some judging by the machine) and the introduction of learning support into the content. The 1980s saw the introduction of the desktop (or personal) computer, the genlock card (which allows computer images to be displayed on the same screen as video) and laser disc players. There was a proliferation of technologies with consequent casualties along the way.

THE PERSONAL COMPUTER

In the PC arena in the 1980s, Regency sold a computer specifically designed for screen-based simulation. This achieved some use in the defence and aerospace industries. The BBC microcomputer was used for the first large-scale interactive video (IV) – The Doomsday project developed in 1986. Lloyds Bank considered this for a large scale IV installation but eventually went for an IBM PC clone. There were casualties in the laser-disc player market but many of the technology issues of importance then are completely irrelevant now.

TECHNOLOGY INNOVATION DOES NOT EQUAL LEARNING IMPROVEMENT

One lesson that is apparent is that each advance in technology has been at the expense of a previously-gained instructional benefit. For example, most IV systems were stand-alone and the data capture and learner management benefit of mainframe systems was lost. Similarly the early moves to Internet delivery of learning packages meant we lost the video and audio enrichment of CD-ROM. This historical view does bring out some of the lessons learned from the application of technology to training. A word of caution – although the application of technology to training was relatively widespread, spanning the last fifty years of the twentieth century, its use has been restricted by topic and industry. Most learning is cognitive in nature, even that aimed at affective objectives or interpersonal skills. Uptake has been restricted to high-tech industries, such as defence and aerospace, or service sectors with large distributed populations such as banking. IT related topics dominate. This is still a very large domain both by topic and industry and does produce lessons that we can apply to the development of the Internet as a learning aid. From this historical perspective, what is important?

LESSONS LEARNED FROM APPLYING TECHNOLOGY TO LEARNING

The visual display of memorable graphics or pictures is an important aid to the learning process, more so for the 50 per cent of adults whose visual sense is their prime sense. Action and aural learners are not helped as much, although the addition of a sound track does help an aural learner. The sense of smell is not exercised, but then this is unlikely to be exploited by other means of learning. (A little known fact is that candidates perform better in exams if they wear the same scent or aftershave they used when revising, providing it is a distinctive fragrance.) The work of Buzan (1974) has made most trainers aware of the importance of the visual image in the learning process.

Simulation of the real task as closely as practical, in safe surroundings is a valuable aid to learning. Airline pilots go straight from flight simulators to fly aircraft on scheduled routes, although usually as second pilot. The predominance of IT and PC training in technology packages shows the advantage of this benefit. This is particularly appropriate for psychomotor skills, but can be applied to high order cognitive skills such as judgment. The communication aspect of the Internet really opens up some possibilities at this point. Complex synthesis tasks can be carried out in collaboration with others in an environment that simulates most aspects of the management environment, particularly in a world in which more and more management is conducted virtually.

Engagement and interaction with the machine is an important element in learning. However, this begins to introduce a barrier for some people. For those less proficient at interacting with a computer, engagement is more difficult. Lack of typing skills for example remains a barrier for many users.

The mainframe computer learning systems of the 1970s included record keeping and management information – indeed the term CML (computer managed learning) was coined to describe this function. While such an approach does induce a feeling of 'big brother is watching you', the learning advantages are considerable. Learning has to include an emotional content, even where the topic is cognitive in nature. Each learner requires Feedback from others, a sense of Achievement, personal Motivation as well as a source of Expertise (FAME). (See Hills, 2000, for more on FAME.) The record-keeping aspect provides a benchmark for each individual against which they can measure their Feedback and Achievement. Some people will require human interaction at this point, but others will be content with machine judgement and recognition. The absence of record keeping prevents either Feedback or Achievement being delivered or recognized.

A benefit of record keeping is that original plans and intentions can be monitored. What actually happened with a learner's progress through a topic may be compared with the intentions they had at the beginning. The machine can prompt a learner with comments such as: 'you planned to be on module 4 by the end of this week, which means you have to complete the following by then'. Learning may be planned on a personal basis, as in a diary of learning appointments and then the learner may monitor their progress against their plan. A feature of many successful distance learning academic programmes is that they run to a timetable and a group of students works to the same timetable. The timetable aspect forces a discipline on the individual learner. Learning must be planned and managed for now and in the future. This produces an interesting dichotomy with the concept of just-in-time learning, the byte-sized chunks that e-learning providers talk about. Maybe it does not have to be a dichotomy, the need for just-in-time learning would appear to arise spontaneously and therefore at odds with planned learning. Most business-focused adult learning is pragmatic in nature. It has a practical purpose rooted in the day-to-day job. Adults tend to learn because they want to do something different. Academic requirements broaden a syllabus beyond the here and now for the individual, but we can reconcile the split between planned and unplanned learning by focusing on the performance outcome.

Another aspect of learning-value that we can observe from past implementations of technology in learning systems is the opportunity for repeated practice. This is associated with either testing systems or simulators. Applications tend to be few in number but the opportunities they represent are not. First, let me describe a fairly typical approach that might be used by an instructor in a flight simulator. The instructor will take the student pilot through a number of standard manoeuvres. Anything they get wrong is seized upon and they repeat the task. There is a focus on mistakes, and constant practice to repeat tasks that contained errors. Tasks become more complex and challenging, always pushing the edge of individual pilot performance. Similarly with testing systems, the learner will request repeat tests for those topics where they make the greatest percentage of mistakes.

Current testing systems rely on random generation of questions from a question bank. With practice exercises, why should this be random? There is an example of a simulated testing exercise where examples were based on previous learner performance. The system analysed previous performance and generated problems for the learner to solve based on their problem areas. An example is a defence application in which individuals were required to recognize ships and submarines from the sound they make in the water. Simulation software generated sounds and was able to create a limitless variety of sound signatures. Operators classified these and their results were recorded. The simulation then began to generate sound signatures in which operators were making the greatest number of errors. This very simple idea focuses practice into the topics that are most prone to error.

Another lesson we can learn from the past, is that learners use computer-learning material in ways that might not be expected. An example is a simulation of a food-processing machine designed to train operators in the correct use of the machine. The systems suffered down time that was attributed to operator error mainly because the operators did not realize the consequences of some of their actions. The simulation was technically accurate. The maintainers of the processing machine used the training system to help them diagnose faults on the machine when it was down. This significantly reduced the time it took them to fix a fault. Another example is a multimedia product that included a pseudo-simulation of interpersonal interactions. Learners would select multiple-choice answers to achieve a successful outcome from a meeting or interview situation. Learners were far more likely to select wrong answers to see the consequences rather than the right answers to achieve a successful outcome.

Learner behaviour

If we cannot predict how learners might use material and systems made available to them, why should we design on the assumption that we expect a learner to behave in a certain way? The two examples I quote, allow users a lot of choice about how they work with the material. This has to be the case with a good simulation. It may be that with many other types of computer learning packages, freedom is not offered to the learner. But freedom is inherent in any genuine web-based learning material, a designer has to design it out, rather than build it in. The navigation functions of the standard browser for example may be disabled by some on-line learning products.

At this point I would like to revert to the story at the start of the chapter and introduce a friend for Hurry and Steady – remember them? Hurry rushes about from room to room sampling bits of juicy material, perhaps getting a quick overview. Steady methodically works through each room, thoroughly assimilating all the contents. Skippy the squirrel on the other hand has learnt that it is possible to go from any room to any other room anywhere in the known Internet Universe. Skippy jumps straight out of one room into another one miles away. Skippy can even keep two rooms open and hop from one to another. Perhaps there is a test in one room and the answers in the other. Skippy has learnt to hop backwards and forwards, carrying the answers back into the test. Skippy likes behaving in unpredictable ways. If you have a part to play in creating an e-learning system or package, then remember that the Skippys of this world exist and are agile and intelligent. Some learners will use your system or package in ways that you had not thought of. There are many more animals and they will all behave in different ways within a cheese maze. We cannot design a maze that caters for all and each of their preferences but we can design e-learning that gives an individual experience to the individual.

Summary

This first chapter serves three main purposes. I have identified the issue of individual differences in relation to e-learning. I have set the current issue of e-learning against a wider backdrop of developments in training in the past. I have looked at the more recent developments of technology in training over the last fifty years to ensure we capture the lessons that are useful for e-learning.

Many of the trainers I talk to express concerns about e-learning. While being excited about the future and keen to get involved, they are uncertain about the broader application of e-learning. These concerns are related to human issues and not technical ones. Human nature remains the same and sociability is a key part of that nature and of learning. There are two other key features of learning: everyone is different and learns in different ways; learning thrives when we value the differences of those around us and use those differences to learn. I describe the actions of a mouse and a hamster to illustrate these differences and how they might affect the way people use e-learning.

Methods of training have evolved and major shifts have been in response to changes in society. The introduction of the apprentice came about with the development of crafts (and craft guilds). The more complex tasks required novices to learn from experts on a one-to-one basis. The classroom (for adult learning) was a response to create a skilled industrial workforce from agricultural workers during the Industrial Revolution. Later, it become the tool to train large numbers of people during and after both world wars. The theories of systematic approaches to training arose when it became necessary to train people quickly. Speed in training became essential and those who instructed had to know exactly what they wanted to achieve and how to do it. In the mid-1940s, training departments were created to cope with the significant number of servicemen and women returning to civilian jobs. This in turn created the profession of 'adult trainer' and to further refinement of the systematic approach to training and training design, perhaps exemplified by Mager (1972).

E-learning can be seen as a response to the Internet and the impact it has on the business world. If the Internet changes the way we work and interact with others, it must change the way we learn. This change is likely to be as significant as the introduction of the classroom to adult learning in the Industrial Revolution.

Finally, I take a look back at the lessons we have already learnt from applying technology to learning:

(1) Each change in technology means we lose some functionality in the learning effectiveness of what we produce.
(2) The systems for which users express greatest preference are those which allow greatest flexibility in use.
(3) Material that makes full use of visual imagery to carry meaning and delivers an aural stimulus is more easily remembered.
(4) True interaction with the material involves the learner. This involvement introduces

kinesthetic learning and motivates. I exclude both page turning and navigation interaction from true interaction.

(5) The keeping of student records aids learning by providing a benchmark for the individual. This helps feedback and a sense of achievement, both key ingredients in the learning process.

(6) Recording of results enables learners to concentrate their learning on the areas of greatest weakness, either making the choice themselves or with the system guiding (or directing) them.

(7) Learners will use learning material, systems and packages in ways that designers never thought of.

(8) Computers aid planning and discipline in the learning task, but this must be balanced against the value of casual, unplanned and incidental learning.

2 Internet Growth and the Impact on Learning

Cultural aspects of Internet use

NATIONAL CULTURE

The Internet changes everything and yet human nature does not change. What evidence do we have that the first part of this sentence is true? There is a steady and rising increase in the number of people having access to the Internet. By April 2003 this was over 60 per cent of the population. The figures for November 2002 from the UK National Statistics office show that 45 per cent of households had Internet access and about 79 per cent of the population have used the Internet to order goods or services. Research conducted by the Chartered Institute of Personnel and Development in 2001 (available from the author) showed that among male professionals, some 50 per cent used the Internet every day; the figure is 38 per cent for female professionals. Growth in Internet access is sometimes described as exponential but it must be an 'S' curve, as there is evidence from economic trends that the rate of increase is reducing. A number of large companies who provide Internet-related equipment find that their sales forecasts exceed actual growth. The percentage of use also varies between nations, while the USA still has the largest number of Internet connections, other countries have a greater ratio per 1000 inhabitants, with Finland, Iceland and Norway leading the field in 1998 (Stroud, 1998, p. 45). Southern European countries have some of the lowest percentage penetration of Internet connected computers. There was a ten-fold difference between Spain and Norway, for example, in 1998.

Is there an inherent difference in the national characteristics that makes it more likely that Northern Europeans will embrace Internet use rather than Southern Europeans? If the answer is 'yes', then this has profound implications for e-learning. The stereotypical Southern European is sociable and the extended family is a strong unit. Business decisions tend to be made collectively with much debate and discussion (*Culturegram'98 Italy*) 'social life and interaction is very important'. The stereotypical Northern European is more reserved, although equally friendly and home tends to be a private place. Business decisions are more measured in nature with less debate (*Culturegram'98 Sweden*). Of course, cultural differences may have no relation to differences in Internet use. It may be that Northern Europe is simply colder than Southern Europe and people spend more time indoors in the North and therefore spend more time using the Internet for communication, entertainment and work. However, if not, there are cultural implications for organizations.

ORGANIZATIONAL CULTURE

Individuals will be attracted to organizations based on a number of personal preferences. Clearly salary, status and company image will be major factors, as will location. However the 'feel' of a company: what people are like, what behaviour is valued will play a part in attracting people to one organization or another. I will consider organizational culture in four groups (see Figure 2.1 on page 36). Organizations that appear to be people centred, focused on customer service and helping others are more likely to attract individuals who feel that other people are more important than ideas. Organizations that appear creative and spontaneous are more likely to attract individuals who think that new ideas are more important than structure and organization, who enjoy chaos and who value ideas more than people. Organizations that appear well-structured, disciplined and organized are more likely to attract individuals who value order and routine and are happy to subsume themselves within the role as a 'cog in a well-oiled machine'. Organizations that appear driven, competitive and target orientated are more likely to attract individuals who are competitive themselves and who feel that what people do is more important than who they are. In one sense, like tends to attract like, and as such company cultures develop for two reasons. Those within the company or organization behave in a way that conforms to certain norms of behaviour and others who like these norms of behaviour join that company or organization. Culture does not always operate on an organization-wide basis and there will be local variations.

The implications for e-learning are that local culture may influence the acceptability and take-up of the Internet for learning. Part of the evidence for this comes from wide variations of take-up of Internet connections in European countries. The current evidence I have mentioned is related to Internet connection rather than Internet use. It is unclear exactly what people use the Internet for. To understand what is happening, it will be helpful to review the history of the Internet and understand some of the principles behind its development.

The development of the Internet

The birth of the Internet owes much to the United States Department of Defense (DoD) that was concerned at the vulnerability of US defence systems to a few computer-processing sites. The need was to connect these sites together in such a way that the system would operate independently and survive the removal of one or more computers. The advanced research projects agency network was created. As the ARPANet grew, a set of protocols was developed that provided a uniform method of communication, this was transmission control protocol over Internet protocol (TCP/IP). The whole network is based on packet switching. Each packet of data that moves from one computer to another has an address as part of the packet. The packet may go by any number of different routes from one computer to another. This met the DoD's requirement that the network would still operate even when large chunks were removed by enemy action. The consequence of this is that the Internet is inherently uncontrollable. If you, as a user, access a website, you send a 'packet' with an address asking for a copy of that website. This packet can go by any route. The computer hosting the website will send your PC a number of packets back, all of which could go via different routes. All each computer needs is the address of the other.

The academic community picked up the ARPANet and the TCP/IP standards. They developed the joint academic network (JANET) that linked computer systems in most UK universities. This network was established on 1 April 1984. Academia, by its very nature, is open and thrives when ideas flow between people rapidly and easily. Researchers became used to publishing their findings on the Internet and academic websites are still some of the richest sources of information. The predominance of academic and research use has established a principle that the Internet should be open with little restriction on its use or access to material. In the early 1990s a World Wide Web program was developed at the European Centre for High-Energy Physics (CERN). Scientists at CERN wanted an easy way of accessing the huge range of data held on their computers. They used the object oriented technology of NeXT Software Inc to develop a browser which allowed *WYSIWYG* (What you see is what you get) editing of World Wide Web documents. CERN released the software to the public in 1991, designing it to run on a number of computing platforms. The components included: the server technology; the browser; the protocol used for communication between the clients and the server – hypertext transfer protocol (HTTP); the language used in composing web documents – hyper text markup language (HTML); and the universal resource locator (URL). This made it simple for any one user to access other host computers.

This development was followed by the design of Netscape and then Internet Explorer, two competing web browser programs. In the mid-1990s these two programs made it easy for the home user to access World Wide Web material. The majority of early users were professionals and their main focus was to use the web for research. Other early adopters were young IT professionals. Many of the IT-aware began to see the potential of the Internet as a commercial gold mine. Negroponte (1995) described a future where the Internet became a commercial and communication tool. In 1996 Clinton and Gore declared the goals of the next generation Internet initiative. These were to connect universities on high speed networks 100 times faster than current Internet speeds, develop new applications to connect doctors, schools and colleges, and the public with a huge range of information services, perhaps most significantly, information on health care. The eight years of the Clinton-Gore administration saw a massive rise in the use of the Internet in the US as an information and business tool. The number of Internet addresses went from 1.3 million to 93 million and there are estimated to be 100 million educational users in the US, business-to-consumer. E-business was estimated to be $61billion in 2000, 90 per cent of US schools were connected to the Internet in 2001 with 30 million children able to use it in 47 000 schools and colleges (White House Press Release, 2001). The stage was already set for an educational revolution.

Commercial exploitation of the World Wide Web

At the start of the dot.com revolution astute IT-aware individuals began reserving domain names that they felt might have commercial value in the near future. They believed, rightly, that every company would need a web presence as a means of communicating with customers, a more interactive alternative to traditional advertising on television, radio and in newspapers. Reserving a good catchphrase or a company name was felt to be akin to prospecting in a new and untapped gold field. Others wanted to set up new businesses. They prepared business plans for venture capitalists that led to many new dot.com businesses being founded, all based on a similar model:

(1) Product marketing and operation will be extremely cheap because the Internet and web databases will do all the routine work of both.
(2) Margins will therefore be very small and those companies will undercut other suppliers (even those suppliers who supply the dot.com in the first place).
(3) Prices to the consumer can be reduced and this will be sufficient to bring in large numbers of purchasers.
(4) In some cases, delivery can be electronic and hence prices reduced even further. In these cases a subscription service is the ideal financial model. E-learning appears to fit this business model perfectly.
(5) One added value that the Internet does bring is total availability of every item in a catalogue. Availability is never immediate and delivery times vary with the individual product. Because stock is held virtually it is possible for a website catalogue to hold an entry for every single product ever provided, one advantage that a virtual bookstore has over a real bookstore. E-learning portals apply this business model. Portals are one-stop shops reselling a range of other suppliers' products.

Very large sums indeed were (and are) put into new ventures of this type with travel-related services leading the field. Even by 2002, far too few companies had made money from these operations, although some early start-ups are no longer losing money. Again the various e-learning ventures are no exception. This drive for commercial exploitation of the Internet has been supplier driven, supplier led and, in most cases, conceived by IT-focused individuals. One of the early financial assumptions is that a commercial website could be set up and would then run itself, making money while its owner was 'asleep'. There is some truth in this, but there remains a considerable amount of maintenance required. Customers expect contact, albeit, e-mail contact with real people and answers to their questions promptly. The site will require updating and refreshing. Unless the transaction is routine (like a banking transaction) customers will expect new items to attract them back to the site. Any physical transaction, like receiving a parcel, must be on time. The lessons being learned by commercial suppliers about customer expectations have a direct parallel in learner expectations. The occasional (or frequent) access to real people to answer questions, prompt virtual service, timely delivery, something new to tempt the learner to return and a reliable and consistent interface (especially for frequently repeated tasks). A good learner site must supply all this.

Although commercial consumer sites are learning many lessons of use to the e-learning industry, the commercial motivation conflicts with the open and free ethos established (and assumed) by early users of the web. At the same time as new dot.coms were springing up, established companies developed websites that paralleled their other business activities, most noticeably in banking and finance. Some of them bought out the claimants who had reserved domain names of value. Three approaches were seen:

(1) Companies which replicate their normal activity but with a new brand name; this reflects an uncertainty about the new model. The existing brand name is not used in case the operation fails either through technical problems or lack of customer interest.
(2) Other companies developed a related activity as a website, establishing a completely new service, again with a new brand name.
(3) The third approach is for the website to provide the same service with the same brand name. This approach is becoming more common as companies gain confidence in the

ability of their technology functions to deliver the required standard of service and their confidence that existing and new customers will happily use the new media. This approach is seen in traditional learning companies that move to offering their products on-line. Within this group I will include companies which sold (and still sell) CDROM material that is now made available over the Internet.

The pricing approach being used differs between companies. Most companies use a transaction-driven pricing model. The consumer pays for an individual transaction, they have access to a free catalogue and buy items from it. All tangible products are sold in this way, be they travel services, CDROMs, books or clothing. This is the traditional mail order catalogue approach. The alternative is for users to pay for access on a subscription basis and then download material at no further cost. This is akin to a magazine where the contents are provided free with the subscription. E-learning providers are using both models. The advantage to the learner of the latter method is that shorter segments of learning are more likely to be used. The learner knows the site is constantly available. They will be more inclined to dip in and out seeking the immediate answer to today's problem. Rapid answers are wanted. The site that charges a subscription for access to its contents offers this rapid answer for the business user.

Hybrids are emerging in other industries. One or two travel service operations are appearing where access to the website is 'purchased' by the user in return for significant discounts on each holiday bought. The customer joins an exclusive club and then pays a transaction charge for items bought. So called 'book clubs' operate this way. The collective buying power of the club brings down the price on each transaction item. This is akin to existing organizations like unions and recreational clubs that are collections of consumers. These consumers join a club for a reason not connected with the wish to buy items. Perhaps an exception might be a share-buying club. By joining they become a group that can purchase in volume and generate discounts. The local gardening society that sells many gardening items at a discount, the union that sells insurance and the sailing club that sells equipment. Perhaps we may see a learning club that is able to bulk buy e-learning!

Access to the World Wide Web

At this point, I would like to return to an issue identified at the start of this chapter – there is an increasing percentage of the population who have access to the Internet although there are some indications that the rate of increase may be declining. What does 'have access' mean? How are people using the web and what are they using it for? In relation to understanding individual preferences, the latter question is more interesting. Let me, out of a sense of completeness if nothing else, deal with the first question. Both the UK and US governments have stated an aim that every school in their countries will have an Internet connection. Every child in school will use the Internet in some way during their education. The use they make of it, either in groups or individually, will increase. In 2000, 32 per cent of homes in the UK had access to the Internet with a predicted rise of 13 per cent per annum, by 2001 the figure was 39 per cent and by 2002, 45 per cent (Office of National Statistics, 2003).

The advent of more services will increase the percentage of home and regular users steadily. The UK government set some challenging targets in 2002 with 6 000 UK on-line centres to be up and running by the end of 2002 with some 70 per cent of government services available on-line by 2003. This move to on-line information services lags behind the US, but is mirrored in all other developed countries. The extent of the government commitment varies, as does the acceptance of the general population to Internet use, but the overall direction is consistent. Some fraction of the UK population will remain disenfranchised from the Internet and this will also apply in other countries. I can make that assertion based on other services. Not everyone has regular access to television; in some cases on grounds of cost, in others by personal preference, for others because they live in parts of the UK where reception is poor and for others because they have no suitable place to call home. The same is true of electricity, water and certainly gas supplies. Alternatively, we can look at percentages of households with ownership of satellite receivers and video recorders. We can use the same data to show that access to these services is increasing and has always done so. Therefore, we can expect the same steady increase in Internet access. We may assume that somewhere between 60 per cent and 95 per cent of the UK population will gain access to the Internet eventually, using it as a source of information and communication. This assertion is based on the premise that access to the Internet is a consumer purchase and past technologies are a good guide to future behaviour in consumer purchases and that it has reached a critical mass (so it will not decline and fade away). Already, almost 90 per cent of adults under the age of 25 use the Internet on a regular basis. That is not something they will stop doing as they get older.

Personal preferences and the Internet

It therefore becomes interesting to speculate as to how individuals will use the Internet and what for, how this relates to personal preferences and what part learning activity will play in this. Regrettably, 'speculation' is the word to use because there is little hard evidence. Let me remind you of some of the basic issues I have established about the Internet:

(1) A consequence of its design is that it is uncontrolled.
(2) Early users established an ethos of open and free access to material.
(3) Early use is based on free research and the Internet is still full of material to which users have open and free access.
(4) Commercial interest conflicts with this earlier ethos.
(5) Internet-only business models rely on attracting customers on price or availability.
(6) Many suppliers offer free training material as enhancements to existing non-training services.
(7) Subscription services for electronically-delivered information and images represent a successful financial model that makes money while the supplier sleeps.

From this list, it is apparent that it will be difficult to track down the use that individuals make of the web. The vast majority is free or part of a pre-paid service. If we consider those companies with active websites, we can draw some inferences about use now. Professional people use it for research and professional activity. Several 100000s in the UK use it for financial transactions. (For this source simply look at the customers claimed by the various banking and financial sites, including on-line trading sites.) Small numbers of mostly busy people use it for shopping. Large numbers of people use the Internet to obtain information on sports, leisure activities, travel arrangements, entertainment and corporate brands. The Internet appeals to those who are interested in those activities. It also appeals to busy people.

One concept of e-learning that is described that also appeals to busy people is the just-in-time byte-sized learning component. The concept is elegant. At the time you need to know how to do something, tap into the e-learning site and find the answer to your question. The concept may be elegant but implementation may not. Any successful e-learning site will need to make allowances for individual preferences. We may see if that is possible by considering how the use of the Internet may develop in the future.

Possible futures for the Internet

Many of us are aware that the Internet is changing the nature of society and the way we work. Such change is not necessarily rapid or taking an obvious direction. A technological innovation that ought to be similar in its direction is the introduction of television. First, there was a lapse of ten to fifteen years between its invention and its first use as a broadcast medium to the general public. At an early stage, its use drew heavily on techniques used on the stage and radio and to a lesser extent on film. The synchronous nature of the medium influences where that design inspiration came from. The asynchronous nature of cinema meant that design principles from film were less relevant. Early television used lengthy shots. Film techniques became more relevant as recording medium for television became, firstly available and then cheaper. There has been a steady evolution of design coupled with a significant increase in content. Early on, TV was a status symbol and at the start of the twenty-first century it is a status symbol not to watch TV! Programming content has also changed. The quiz show is largely an invention of the television age. This may be as much a product of increased leisure as it is of the broadcast medium. TV has been evolving for 60 years and the World Wide Web for 10 years. In the UK it remains a mystery to perhaps 40 per cent of the population. However, for the sub-group who applied for University places in 2002 almost all used the Internet to process applications. If we isolate the patterns and trends, how might the Internet look in another ten to twenty years? Now the use of the PC as a gaming device is a growth industry and is one new industry created by the existence of the PC in the home. Collaborative gaming is one small step away from collaborative learning.

If the Internet is to become truly universal, it must provide tasks, activities and events that will appeal to all, including those who have the time to use more traditional means of communication and investigation. The use of multi-site quiz shows in which a thousand participants start and progressively knock each other out is an obvious possibility. Those thousand participants might be involved in a learning exercise. Flight simulators are (or were) a very popular PC-based game. Why? First, they were easy to program. Flight characteristics of aircraft are well understood and computer models already existed before the introduction of the PC. Second, the role of pilot is challenging and glamorous. Most of the early simulations were based on military aircraft and therefore inherently competitive. This introduces the third element. Feedback is simple and performance levels are easily measured and compared. A sense of achievement can readily be gained. The future use of the Internet for learning is likely to replicate those characteristics. PC-based flight simulators were modelled on large mainframe computer models so we should look at existing applications to see how they might develop.

Shared computing and parallel processing are existing features of the net. Screensavers are used by university research teams as a means of harnessing the processing power of thousands of PCs. The screensaver is copied to individual PCs on the Internet. While the PC is idle, the screensaver processes the data that came with it. After processing, the data is sent back to the parent application which then sends more data for the screen to process the next time the PC is idle. Complex business simulations exist that work from large databases or objects. Human interaction changes the contents of the database and thus the behaviour of the simulation. Existing games allow users to play against a computer or a computer and other users. It now becomes possible to envisage a number of e-learning situations in which participants can play within a safe environment with others. All that is necessary is for this environment to be modelled in some way. An example might be a project in which a number of different people are involved. The progress of each task or activity may be modelled by computer software but each player would receive only a partial picture of the changes taking place in the project. The impact on the wider organization may be modelled with different users playing different parts. Virtual meetings would take place and the skills of influence and persuasion practised. Because of the involvement of other players there would be an opportunity to practise some of the interpersonal skills required. The virtual nature of the interaction may inhibit some of the real world learning. In the future more business interactions will take place over the Internet. Virtual working will be a normal way of working for more people. Virtual learning will become just as natural as a way of learning. This will not be the same as self-study or distance learning. The best parallel for this type of learning is the action learning set, a concept originally developed by Reg Revans in 1937. The seeds of this type of learning are already being established on the Internet. Mutual interest discussion groups are emerging in the various chatrooms and discussion board facilities that are available. People are sharing information through the Internet because they find it mutually advantageous. I have describe this as a virtual learning set. The features of such a set is that members are able to share information on a one-to-one or one-to-many basis. Ideally the one-to-many discussion is synchronous. The virtual classroom (see later in this chapter) is the ideal vehicle for the virtual learning set.

Increased automation

Are there other ways in which the Internet will develop into new areas and, by extension, bring new e-learning activities? The trend that is emerging is one where individuals interact more directly with the original equipment supplier, rather than the local store. In many cases they work for the company they are buying from, doing work previously done by that supplier, or their representative. The classic example is travel purchase where the buyer enters all information about the trip and those going. Individuals do more work for themselves, whether as employees or customers. Customer service is increasingly automated with the human being as a cog in the machine. The profound impact of the Internet is only just beginning to make itself felt in these areas. The trends were apparent in the 1980s. The introduction of computer systems to deal with transactions and robots to deal with an increasing range of physical tasks indicated that machines could replace human beings in repetitive tasks. The link between the customer and the actual provision of the service is becoming shorter. The number of intermediaries needed is fewer. Let me give you an example. I order foreign currency through a call centre. The operator is perfectly civil and polite but she reads from a script. I know she does because of what she says and how she says it. I walk to the local bank branch to collect the currency. I am handed an envelope with the money precounted. The cashier is polite and we chat. She has no script but she does not need one. I could dispense with both of these people. I could talk to the computer, which would tell me everything the operator told me, and the postman would deliver. The package would contain a return envelope for when I want to sell the currency. I could negotiate the purchase price on the Internet the day before posting the currency back. Someone merely has to count the money against my entry in the website. However, I continue to deal with human beings because it is easier for me, usually, and I am not charged extra. But both jobs are now much less complex than they were. The trend is apparent in other industries. Car computer systems give you on-board information, television systems tune themselves, the travel agent is bypassed, hotel bookings can be made direct to a computer system. Anywhere that information flows from supplier to customer, the number of people in the loop is reducing.

Learning provisions as customer service

If customers have to do more, then they need more information and knowledge to be discerning customers. Previously, the intermediaries provided that knowledge to customers. If a customer buys direct, they need and expect more information from those suppliers. Companies are providing training and help material through their websites. Far more product information is available through the Internet than in brochures and pamphlets. Computer manufacturers, software companies, healthcare providers, financial service providers all recognize the advantage of helping a customer learn about their products. Product knowledge training that was previously available to front line staff can be available directly to customers. The beauty of the Internet is that this valuable commodity can be provided free to customers. This free training goes beyond product knowledge and may explain basic principles. For example a financial trading retail website might provide training in the stock market and the principles of buying and selling shares, commodities and even futures. Websites selling medicines may provide background information on disease and illness. Websites selling cars may explain the difference between aspirated and non-aspirated engines.

The role of professional institutes

It might be nice to think that employers would also increase the training available to their workforce. There is no immediate evidence that this is happening. For some jobs, there is more continuous support from systems (the script available to call centre operators above). Because of this increased support, there may be less training for the human operator. The irony of this is that these jobs are the ones that are the most vulnerable for the very simple reason that entry to deskilled jobs is easier. Just as during the Industrial Revolution, there are compelling reasons for individuals to acquire new skills. Simply put, if your skills are hard to acquire, your employability is more secure. If you took a month to master your job, then someone else on the other side of the world can do the same just as quickly. If technology makes your job easier, then it becomes increasingly vulnerable. This is the economic drive that is as real as the Industrial Revolution and as acute as the need to retrain five million men and women in the space of a few years. If we reflect back to the response during the Industrial Revolution, it was to create mechanics institutes. Now, as then the training response does not always come from the employer. In many cases, the employers who have need of skills in new media are desperately busy, too busy to train. The response to the need for skill development is coming from recruitment companies who offer free learning over the Internet and from professional organizations who offer more e-learning support to their members. The professional institute is able to make more of its services available over the Internet, at less cost than providing the same service by phone, or perhaps by conference. This trend is seen with more institutes adding material to their websites and developing extra on-line services.

The unique contribution of on-line learning

There is an area of skills where on-line learning is particularly useful. For many business functions the employee is part of a machine operation. The system supplies all the routine information and guides the user. What is left is the unusual and unpredictable. These are the very tasks that it is difficult to train for. A standard task analysis technique is to assess the difficulty, impact and frequency of tasks, this is a prioritization technique. Tasks included for training are those with high business impact and high frequency. More time is spent learning the more difficult tasks. Tasks which are not trained for are those which occur less often (lower frequency) or have low business impact. The rationale is that frequent and important tasks must be mastered quickly and because they occur frequently, employees will remain competent. Tasks that occur infrequently are more difficult to maintain at a high skill level. There is less opportunity to practise and keep the skill current. Unless the impact of a mistake is high, providing training for employees in infrequent tasks is not cost effective. It is better, more effective and cheaper to provide them with guidance at the time. If the impact is high, then as well as training, employees need an opportunity to practice. It is for this reason that pilots practice rare (hopefully never occurring) events in flight simulators. Although the frequency may be very low the impact is very high (unacceptable). This is the area where e-learning may come in useful, provided a cost analysis shows it to be worthwhile. On-line learning can be available at the time the employee needs to perform the task. There is a very narrow difference between e-learning used in this way and knowledge management. Indeed for the user the difference is irrelevant. The user has the equivalent of an on-line reference book designed so that a learner can access the right page of information and that page gives them a full picture of what to do.

For example, a rare event for many managers is the disciplinary interview, and normally one where they call in support from human resources (HR) or personnel. An e-learning website on this interview would include all the procedural and legal information, it would also include the soft skills aspect, appropriate interview techniques and how to be assertive without being aggressive, perhaps horror stories of what happens when it goes wrong and how not to do it. Notice that I am making an assumption that the disciplinary interview will remain a face-to-face exercise. I have two reasons for making this assertion. First, because of the legal framework within which we operate. The detail of employment law varies between countries, but the rights of the individual employee tend to be protected. Part of this protection is that an employee must be fully aware of any actions the employer is likely to take in respect of the employee. A documented face-to-face meeting is likely to remain a requirement of ensuring an employee is 'fully aware'. The second reason I have is my assertion that human nature has not changed with the introduction of the Internet. People still respond to people and while some of that response may be achieved virtually, the face-to-face meeting will remain a richer experience than any virtual meeting. Performance-related issues are therefore likely to need personal contact because of the need to motivate, even if negatively.

Learner choice

What emerges is that a learner is likely to have more choice. On-line learning will be available from more sources, because of cost. When it becomes cheaper to supply more people then suppliers broaden their market. More learning will be available from employers, from education, from professional bodies as customer support to other products and just-in-time support to users of machinery and computers. Computer chips are included in more and more pieces of machinery, it is a simple extension of function to add learning material directly relevant to the operation of the machine. Suppliers of non-learning products will realize the ease and cheapness of providing on-line learning as part of the support package. They will view on-line learning material like an extra sales support tool, a unique selling point their competitors do not have. With many more suppliers, the amount of material will increase. One would hope that the number of users and learners will increase to take advantage of the increased supply. The alternative is that the market reduces to its previous size as suppliers fall by the wayside through competition in a market that is not growing. Learners are driven to acquire new skills by economic necessity or curiosity but there is also resistance to e-learning, some of which is resistance to learning, to a large extent created by conditioning in schools. It is at this point that the effect of attitudes and personality begins to make itself felt. Different personality types will show a different preference for the type of learning that the Internet delivers. As well as personality, individual capability will raise or lower barriers to e-learning as they apply to individuals.

   I started this chapter with the assertion that the Internet changes everything but human nature remains the same. Let me review where we have got to so far:

- Every month more people connect to the Internet.
- Even so, it is still difficult to assess what people use the Internet for.
- Cultural differences may influence a propensity for using the Internet.
- The Internet is designed to be uncontrolled and there is an ethos that information is provided freely, although this conflicts with the commercial interests that have moved to exploit the Internet.
- All schoolchildren will access the Internet in some way or form.
- Interactive games and quizzes may become a new area of Internet (and e-learning) exploitation.
- The nature of work has changed with customers (including internal customers) doing work previously done by suppliers (including internal suppliers such as HR departments).
- Employees receive more support from the systems they use. This should include learning and performance support.
- Many tasks will continue to require personal contact. These are likely to be in the difficult human interaction areas such as customer complaints and employee performance issues.

Provided learners have time to prepare, full e-learning support (including both procedural and soft skills) is likely to be valuable.
- The majority of existing Internet use mirrors existing work and leisure patterns.
- Completely new ways to exploit the Internet may yet emerge.

The e-learning market place

THE VARIATION OF PRODUCTS

The previous section described the broad Internet scene. This section describes the e-learning market place. This enables me to differentiate the type of products on offer. I will then match individual preferences to types of products. Many people see the e-learning industry as an opportunity for investment and have expectations of making money. There are those companies that already had an established presence in the training industry and their product was probably technology-related. They have converted that product for use in a web browser environment and then may have added additional functionality. Their products may have been non-technology-related in which case the companies are converting material. There are those companies that perceive a brand new product offering and are developing that from the ground up. In the majority of cases, these companies act as resellers of other products. They add value with additional services. There is a circle of interest that drives interest in e-learning companies. Investment decisions are made, perhaps by a few, to deliver learning services via the Internet and web browser software. This interests the press who start to write about it. This generates interest from potential users and other investors and companies. This interest encourages others to invest, further fuelling interest from journalists and writers who write more about e-learning! Within the training community, interest is also generated by suppliers, vendors and consultants writing about e-learning (myself included), generating yet more interest. And all this can be achieved without a single user really learning anything! While there is evidence of considerable benefit being gained by individuals and organizations from e-learning, this is focused on particular areas of activity. It is therefore important to understand what type of products and services e-learning offers, how this affects individuals and what the outcome for them is or might be.

Let me briefly differentiate each product type and then discuss them in more detail:

(1)   Course offerings coming from institutions of higher and further education. In many cases the e-learning element is an extension of an existing course or the gradual conversion of existing distance learning text-based material. Tutor support, the marking of assignments and a qualification are usually part of the offering.

(2)   Course and study products coming from existing commercial providers of face-to-face courses. This may start either as enhancements to existing products or as stand-alone courses.

(3)   Courses from commercial suppliers that were originally CD-ROM or text-based that are being converted for web delivery.

(4)   New material specifically created for web delivery.

(5)   Software of varying degrees of complexity that allows learners to interact with each other at the same time as if they were in a classroom together. The content is provided

by a facilitator and will be in a standard computer application such as PowerPoint or Word. These are referred to as virtual classrooms or collaborative learning tools.

(6)   Integrated learning websites that offer services to the learner that include chatrooms (for synchronous typed discussions), discussion boards (for asynchronous typed discussions) and e-mail facilities to contact tutors or co-learners. Such websites are part of the offering that includes the provision of learning material in one of the forms listed above (1–4). Many of these websites resell products from elsewhere. Most virtual classroom software offers similar functionality.

(7)   Learning management systems that offer a variety of functionality. With one or two exceptions the majority of LMS products have been created from existing products that were based in related activity.

(8)   There is an increasing number of companies that offer integration services. They will pull all this together for a client and implement it within their organization. This service can include the change management implementation that impacts on the individual.

(9)   Although well outside the scope of this book, there are those companies that offer to host all this material externally. All potential learners have to do is to type in the URL and then they can access material held for them.

(10) Again out of completeness, it is necessary to mention the many companies that offer bespoke development services and create specific e-learning packages for clients.

Because this activity is driven by commercial interests, almost any company will offer any combination of these services and there is really only one caveat, if qualifications are going to be awarded, then a certain amount of rigour is required. The requirement of a standards board will dictate the amount of study and assessment conditions. This applies to universities, professional institutions and any examining board that an FE college might use.

COHORT-STUDIED COURSES

I shall start by looking at this market in more detail with a specific focus on the UK. However, this market is international and some of the most respected names are entering it. Products from higher education institutes may be accredited or may not be. Management education material is included on a website that is available as ongoing support. This is a popular offering for a business school to make. The individual manager can access the site whenever convenient. There will be various supporting functions that enable an individual to plan what they will read and look at. E-mail support from real tutors may be available. The learner has the advantage of control, but requires considerable self-discipline and motivation. The reputation of the brand name helps the motivation. Such sites depend on providing answers that are relevant to the immediate problem faced by the individual. Professional Institutions are developing similar sites packed full of resource material. The appellation 'learning' is rarely used. Information tends to be very concrete and specific. All the above sites are usually based on material that has previously existed as text. This is reflected in the design and appearance. In the UK, FE colleges are beginning to enter this market with short introductory courses in a variety of topics. There are an increasing number of qualifications that can be gained through on-line study.

The trend is most apparent in the US with universities offering degrees through on-line study, but courses are appearing in the UK. The existence of the qualification imposes a number of differences that impact on the individual. Courses usually have a start date and an end date. Learners are placed into cohorts and everyone is expected to start and finish at the same time. There is far more of the traditional feel to these courses. There are assignments to be done and marked. The tutor is more involved with the study material. Learners progress through material that is presented as a syllabus. Material is not presented in bite-sized chunks, this is in no sense just-in-time, neither is the content under the control of the learner. The advantage comes from communication with other learners and the tutor with access from the study material to reference sources. Much of the material could be in book form and indeed may be printed out by many learners. The discipline imposed by the need to study for a qualification motivates people, as it would do for a more traditional text-based course. However, for the individual there is a much greater sense of belonging to a group of co-learners. The design and content may be the same as a course that is posted to you but this is more remote. For most of us this little difference can be very significant. Most of us get our motivation from those we are in direct contact with: it is for our colleagues we go to work for in the morning rather than our employer. It is the co-learners we know well we will want to help and appreciate them helping us. Remote co-learners are not as important to us as those we see every day, nevertheless, the feeling that we will let someone else down by backing out of a course will push each of us to continue and complete the course. This mutual encouragement can be significantly reinforced if a cohort has to tackle a project as a team. Learners not only rely on others but are relied on themselves. This reinforces the sense of belonging.

Some commercial providers are developing courses that have some of the features of academic providers. Courses use learning sets for shared tasks and the members of the set are drawn from the same cohort, or if the cohort is small in number, the learning set will be the full cohort. Assignments and tasks are set that are completed outside the course. Current examples are mostly in management and executive development topics. Content is based mainly in existing face-to-face material. Indeed, the ethos and attitude of face-to-face training comes through in the design of the course. Courses are shorter and, without the need to satisfy academic requirements, more flexible. FE colleges and commercial training groups fall into this group and many of them produce web packages designed for self-study on an individual basis rather than group study by a cohort.

SELF-STUDY STAND-ALONE COURSE

This is a product area that is full of material. Courses are shorter and deal with specific skills. There is an overt commercial nature to these courses. For the individual they are usually paid for by the employer, except perhaps in the current market IT courses. This is the market in which providers of CD-ROM and text-based material have competed for a number of years. The origins of this material can usually be seen in the design. Material originally presented on a CD-ROM (or even originally on interactive video) is likely to contain 'story' segments with text and graphics replacing audio and video. Material is likely to contain more examples and less text than a product that was originally a book or distance learning text. The perceived difference in selling web-based material over CD-ROM or text courses means that material can be segmented. At this point, things may become very confused for the individual. Lists of courses available are longer, titles are very similar. What slowly emerges is a similarity with the book market. The way individuals select books may well become the way we will select e-learning. People select books by author, by topic and by recommendation. We also go into book shops and browse, picking books off the shelf, perhaps reading the first few lines and then opening pages at random. A book is also tangible and can be lent to others. There are differences in the way men and women look for books, directly related to shopping habits. If I am buying (or borrowing) fiction, I rapidly scan the shelves trying to spot an author's name or a title that looks interesting. I have been known to be in and out of the local library in less than five minutes with two or three books. My wife on the other hand has a totally different approach, browsing much more thoroughly, looking at more than the outside cover, description and title. Individuals are likely to want to select e-learning in either way, by browsing or hunting.

E-learning delivery software

This brings me to two related e-learning developments, those I describe as the integrated learning websites (unlike a portal, the integrated learning website offers contact with other learners, a curriculum rather than a lot of courses, time management help for learners and tutor support) and learning management systems (LMS). From the perspective of the individual learner these two products blur. I will deal with LMS first.

LEARNING MANAGEMENT SYSTEMS

There are aspects of their functionality that are irrelevant to a learner and there are also aspects that support the integrated learning website. There were in 2001 several hundred LMS of varying degrees of complexity. Any academic establishment that aspires to being an e-learning provider will probably have developed its own. This is certainly true in the United States where there is the greatest proliferation. Many large organizations will have developed their own and many are taking their systems into the commercial market, as are academic institutions. While this may be confusing for an organizational purchaser, the proliferation is largely irrelevant to the learner, except that this means functionality varies between systems. What one learner finds useful in one system may not appear in another. Many of the differences in functionality are due to the different origins of these systems. What were these origins? Most relate to the work of IT functions and administration product management. Several started life as tools to help organize the development of multimedia. They include databases of video, audio and programming objects that can be re-used and assembled in different ways.

Curriculum management
A related functionality is the ability to organize modules, lessons, topics, subjects and faculties. Again, primarily a database requirement to meet the needs of the subject organizers, training management, teachers and lecturers.

Catalogue
It is the front end of the above activity that is of most interest to the individual learner. The learner will be able to browse by subject or hunt for key words. Individual components will be described, be they lesson or module or course, and links to related topics, either

prerequisites, further study or parallel components, shown. The catalogue is there to aid the individual in selecting what they need. They may do this on their own or with the support of others. The catalogue may recommend alternative courses and prerequisites, it may provide comment about suitability and study times.

Web launch tool

This part of the functionality allows a learner to click on the selected component and this will either download a course component to the learner's PC or gives access to a website on which the course is held. The sophistication of this tool will depend on whether record-keeping or a charging mechanism is involved. (The implications of this are described in the following section on administration.)

Classroom and course administration

Some LMS started life as training centre administration tools. The software is designed to allocate courses and tutors to classrooms and to book learners on to the courses. Bills are sent to individual learners automatically. A small extension of this functionality will enable the same process for learning packages and for web-based learning components delivered directly to the learner's PC by a web launch tool. Part of the launch process will be to check that the learner is entitled to access the component (are they registered for it and have they paid?). The administration system will also keep a record of their use of the material and, perhaps, their progression through it. Several LMS are designed from the start to do this as part of an integrated website. This makes possible both a learning record and a learning plan for an individual.

Learning plans

If the system records all this information about the learner and the use they are making of the material and resources, then it makes sense to provide them with both the means for future planning and a record of what they have achieved. Either with help or on their own, the learner can browse a catalogue and select material that will help them achieve some goal. Catalogue entries will recommend study times and the order in which material should be studied. Learners may begin to allocate dates to courses. The system may do this for them once they have agreed an average time allocated to learning each week. Alternatively, the system may tell them the average weekly study time required given a target date for a learning goal. Having provided all this information the system can help the learner construct this into a plan relevant to them as individuals with target dates and sequences. The system has information about what the learner plans to do and can monitor what they actually do. The user can compare their plans with their progress. This can mark the achievements of the learner as a record to be reviewed.

All this order and structure is a world away from just-in-time byte-sized learning that many e-learning professionals extol as one of its virtues. E-learning can achieve both, but the differences to the individual are profound. An LMS which includes a learning plan will also be able to have a learning record and monitor progress against the plan.

Human resource systems

Many HR systems already have a functionality that borders on that available in complex LMS. The ability to provide a catalogue, a learning plan and learning record is designed in.

In addition, the system may include a competency framework against which individuals may assess themselves or be assessed by others (including 360° appraisal). The individual learner can review their own competencies (with or without help): identify gaps in their competencies either in their current role or one to which they aspire: be advised (by the LMS) as to which courses, lessons or components will help to plug those gaps; construct a plan, perhaps including non-learning activities; and then start to execute that plan.

The rationale for an LMS

Most LMSs seem to be based on a commercial need for administration and charging. Students, or their employers, have to pay for access. The other rationale is the need to monitor activity within organizations. Classroom management automatically generates information about usage, occupancy and who does what courses. An e-learning website can operate without this functionality as delivery costs are effectively zero. However, this denies the organization information that will help in making decisions about investment and helps them to understand what is happening.

Integrated learning websites

This type of functionality may be offered by a commercial provider or internally within an organization. They are unlikely to include competency assessment tools, but will certainly enable an individual to go from the selection of appropriate material through to the construction and execution of a learning plan. Authorization will be, and payment may be part of the functionality of the system. However, once the learner has access to the course, a whole range of additional functionality becomes available. They may be part of a cohort and have access to e-mail contact with tutors and co-members of the cohort. There may be a discussion board shared by that cohort. Chatrooms may be open at specific times. All this functionality will be available to a course that completes with a qualification. Several commercial integrated learning websites do not operate cohorts (with their restriction on start times) and tutors, discussion board and chatrooms are available for anyone using the course at that time. By means of a subscription service, these sites can begin to provide the continuous support that enables just-in-time and byte-sized learning. Learners are not constrained by courses or topics but perhaps by the total time they spend using the site.

Implications for the individual in the organization

Individuals will be attracted to organizations based on a number of personal preferences. Clearly salary, status and company image will be major factors, as will location. However the 'feel' of a company, what people are like, what behaviour is valued, will play a part in attracting people to one organization or another. I will consider organizational culture in four groups, see Figure 2.1. The top half of the diagram includes organizations in which ideas are more important than tasks, concepts are valued more than procedures. The lower half includes organisations that focus on process and procedure. Safety or operational efficiency may be an issue in such organisations. There is a need to be sure that what is done is done right. The vertical axis is concerned with the type of tasks that are valued by the organization, conceptual or procedural. The horizontal axis is concerned with how people

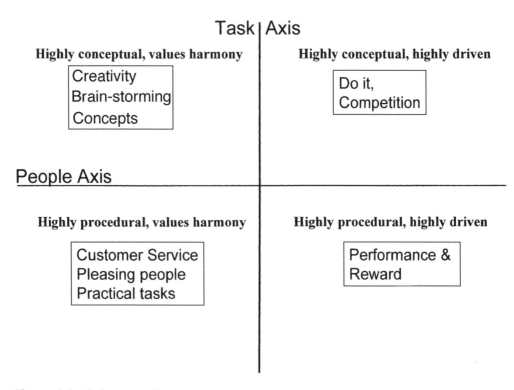

Figure 2.1   Culture matrix

are valued; are the valued because of who they are, or for what they can do. Organizations found in the left half will be concerned with harmonious relationships, those on the right hand side will value a competitive spirit more. People will be attracted to, and comfortable within, organizations with which they feel an affinity. In the bottom left quadrant we find organizations that are people centred, focused on customer service and helping others. They will attract people who feel that other people are more important than ideas and who value an ordered existence. Organizations that appear creative and spontaneous (the upper left quadrant) are more likely to attract individuals who think that new ideas are more important than structure and organization, who enjoy chaos and who value ideas more than getting things done.

Organizations that appear well-structured, disciplined, organized and with clear goals for individuals (as in the lower right quadrant) are more likely to attract people who value order and routine and are happy to subsume themselves into a role; achieving recognition for the job they do rather than who they are. Organizations that appear driven, competitive and target orientated (as in the upper right quadrant) are more likely to attract individuals who are competitive themselves and who feel that what people do is more important than who they are. In one sense, like tends to attract like, and thus company cultures develop for two reasons. Those within the company or organization behave in a way that conforms with certain norms of behaviour and others who like those norms of behaviour join that company or organization. Culture does not always operate on an organization-wide basis and there will be local variations.

The implications for e-learning are that local culture may influence the acceptability and take-up of the Internet for learning. Managers exert the biggest influence on that culture. We can relate management style to this culture model and from that understand how e-learning might be used by individuals.

LAISSEZ-FAIRE MANAGEMENT

For many organizations the degree to and direction in which employees develop themselves is a matter of indifference to managers. For these managers, individuals and the skills and attitudes they possess are synonymous. They fail to appreciate that skills and attitudes can change without the need to change the employee. Perhaps no manager would overtly make such a statement but an example of their ethos is 'If you can't do the job I will get someone who can'. They abdicate from their responsibility. E-learning can empower the individual in these circumstances. Empowerment is a two edged sword in that it further relieves managers from their responsibilities. Some individual learners will welcome both. Learning will be free range and the individual can peck and scratch wherever takes their fancy. Without direction, such development may not become of value to the employer and without guidance it may be without value for the individual. The empowerment of e-learning enables well motivated and discerning individuals to seek out development for roles they may aspire to. E-learning deployed in this way (empowered employees, abdicating managers) will increase the divide between good and adequate performers (on the assumption that adequate performers are less likely to seek out learning opportunities in a free range environment). The existence of e-learning, by reducing the incremental cost for individuals, increases the availability to all. Fewer employees find themselves on the left-hand side of the vertical division in Figure 2.2. This applies even in an organization that provides little, if any, learning support. The cost of e-

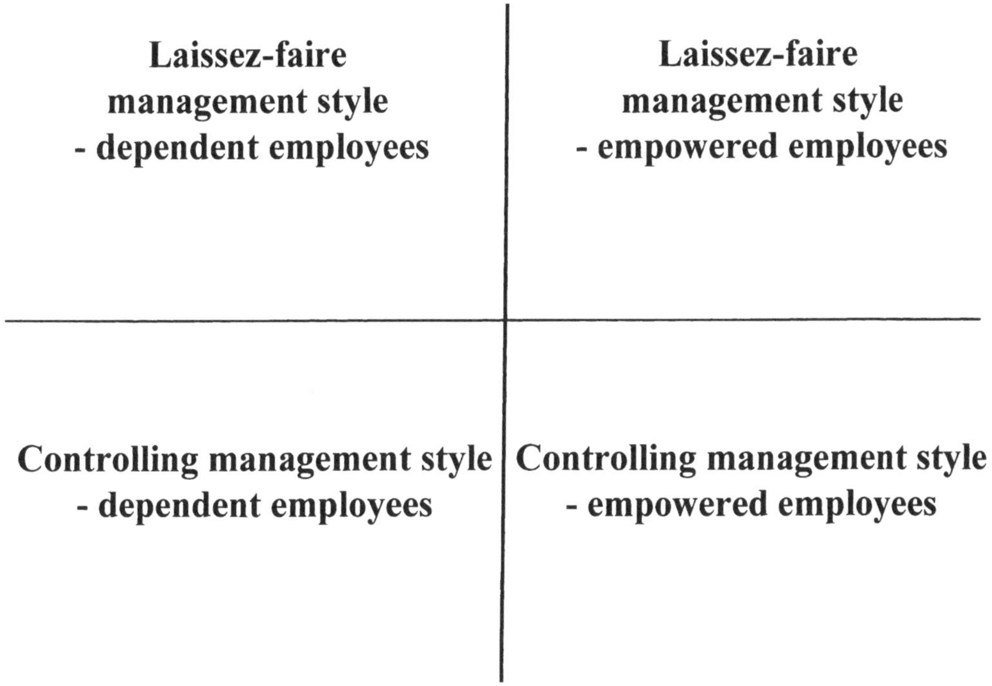

Laissez-faire management style - dependent employees	**Laissez-faire management style - empowered employees**
Controlling management style - dependent employees	**Controlling management style - empowered employees**

Figure 2.2 Management/subordinate relationship

learning from a commercial provider is approaching that of books and is within the financial reach of many individuals in employment. The division between those who use e-learning to develop themselves and those who cannot, becomes one of access on price and availability. E-learning should imply empowerment but may not. Lack of access to the Internet and other controls may prevent individuals from acquiring access to learning and, crucially, information about learning. It is here that Government intervention is making itself felt in most developed countries. Public provision of information about learning and of learning itself is increasing.

CONTROLLING MANAGERS

Some managers will dislike the lack of control that this empowerment brings. This might be in a negative sense because they feel that employees should focus on the job in hand or feel that it is their responsibility to provide learning support in ways they feel appropriate. This management role is widely recognized by employees. Many employees feel that the provision of training is one employment benefit that managers have greatest control over and is the best indication of a good and supportive employer (Eisenberger *et al.*, 1997). This perception means that training is top of the list for support that employees expect from their managers. The appraisal process identifies areas for development (areas of weakness) and allocates training to those areas. The existence of an e-learning delivery system makes it difficult for the manager to be seen as the arbiter as to who gets what training and development. If the training is always available then employees may exercise their own control over what learning they do. The extent to which they actually exercise that control or not is a function of their preferences which I argue are as much personality based as

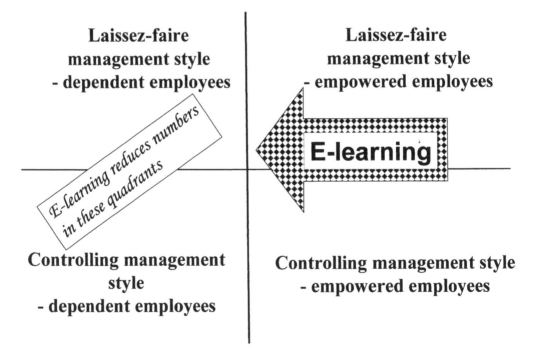

Figure 2.3   Effect of e-learning on management/subordinate relationship

intellectual or attitudinal (bearing in mind that attitude itself is also influenced by personality). The presence of a learning management system may bring that control back into the hands of the manager. An LMS can have the functionality of requiring authorization from a third party (for example, a manager) before giving access to a learner. This requires managers to assume responsibility for the development of employees and forces a discussion based on available learning opportunities. Such an approach encourages responsible behaviour on the part of both manager and employee. This may reduce the number of managers who abdicate from the role reducing the number of employees above the line in Figure 2.2. This reduces the likelihood or organizational culture being to the left of the line in Figure 2.2. Thus e-learning pushes the dividing line between supportive and non-supportive cultures as indicated in Figure 2.3. Many personality types will prefer this environment. Decisions are not made in isolation; there is an opportunity to talk to someone else and perhaps assess emotional as well as intellectual needs. There are risks with an environment where managers exercise too much control. This may foster a patronizing culture in which managers make decisions for employees because they retain the information that enables them to do so. The partial solution is to make information widely and freely available but to manage the access to learning material in a way that encourages dialogue between manager and subordinate. I use the word partial because managers have to be ready and willing to take on this role.

E-learning types and reactions of the individual

Let me summarize the types of e-learning we can expect with particular relevance to individuals and their likely reactions.

TUTOR-SUPPORTED GROUP STUDY

Academic and professional institutions are providing on-line courses, usually supported by tutors. Learners work in cohorts and gain a qualification. Learning is planned. There is virtual contact with co-learners. The individual has a low (or lower) cost entry route to some form of qualification. The cohort and the need to progress with others provides order, discipline and structure. Access to the material is almost always asynchronous so individuals can choose their own time to study. World wide cohorts are perfectly possible. This is like any other correspondence or distance learning course with the added convenience of electronic communication. This convenience should not be understated. Unlike correspondence courses, learner to learner dialogue is the norm. This establishes a social context. Many learners express surprise at the extent to which email and discussion forums actually generate a feeling of community. If the topic is IT-related, then it may include real assignments and performance exercises. Individuals will miss personal contact and the rich debate that comes from conversations with others. The extent to which this is important depends on what each individual gets from this interaction. This is where personality and learning styles become important. For some of us the buzz of debate in the learning context is tiring and we would prefer to sit and observe, for others such debate increases energy and stimulates. Some of us are active in such debates even if they are tiring and participating in the debate stimulates the thought processes, others prefer to reflect on the debate when it is over and review the discussion and draw conclusions from it. Some people find the virtual interaction better than face-to-face and others find it more sterile and less helpful. What is likely is that there will be less incidental learning. Replies are more considered and tend to be more focused on the topic. Actual conversations are freer ranging as it is easier to interrupt and bring in knowledge and opinion irrelevant to the immediate topic. Virtual interactions reduce the opportunity for incidental learning. There is no reason why the drop out rate should vary from traditional methods of learning. Indeed since the tutor is more involved with people rather than the topic, retention may be higher than an equivalent part-time traditional course. Learners always drop out of courses and more drop out of part-time courses than full-time courses. E-learning is always part-time and learners may underestimate the work required, personal circumstances may change during the course, their personal motivation may not be sufficient for the study involved, they may prefer the company of people and find the isolation of distance study tiring.

PACKAGED LEARNING

Commercial providers may provide similar (although shorter) courses with the range of support similar to academic providers, cohorts, tutors and virtual contact. Similar personal factors will apply to these courses. The lack of a recognized qualification will reduce motivation for many, although the much shorter course length will make completion quicker (and therefore emotionally easier). If the content is IT-related the course will include real practice, sharply increasing its relevance to immediate problems faced by the individual. These courses will be related to immediate business issues. The individual who likes their own company and who has intellectual rather than emotional needs is likely to prefer this type of course.

INTEGRATED LEARNING WEBSITES

Integrated websites and learning management systems represent two related products or services that utilize the database and communication features of the Internet and PCs. Both of them provide support to the learner. Support tools of specific relevance to the individual include learning plans, monitoring of progress, e-mail to tutors and co-learners, bulletin boards shared by co-learners of the study group and a catalogue organized directly relevant to the learners' job skills (or those of a job that is aspired to). Some individuals will relish the control and access to information this brings them. Other individuals will miss personal contact and the reassurance they get from discussing decisions with others. Both these products meet the management needs of learning and content is added into the framework. During the writing of this book it would appear that the popularity of these products has reduced, perhaps because content delivers benefit, rather than authoring or delivery or management software.

VIRTUAL CLASSROOMS

As with many forms of e-learning, there is a wide variance in what people may describe as a virtual classroom. In the context of this section, I want to confine myself to synchronous sessions where participants can talk and be heard by others. It may include a level of technology that allows the presenter or facilitator to be seen by others. This is unlikely to be Internet-delivered and the basis of this book is to explore learning issues specifically in relation to the Internet. I therefore assume a level of technology that is web-delivered, allows audio to be transferred and enables all participants to view the same screen. Interaction is somewhat mechanical in that the facilitator controls who is enabled to talk (and when) and what is seen on the screen. A participant may present material they have prepared themselves. The technology is appropriate for meetings and that is likely to be where its greatest use will be.

The virtual classroom or collaborative learning space is, in my view, one of the more interesting developments in e-learning. Contact with others is immediate and by voice rather than keyboard. Interaction lacks the spontaneity of face-to-face groups and incidental learning is less likely (although more likely than with any other form of e-learning). People – other learners – are much more part of the learning process. Many visual and kinesthetic cues are missing. A learner who needs movement and action will find the virtual classroom constraining – they may feel chained to their keyboard, which in a very real sense they are, particularly if they are using headphones. The ease of meeting others combined with the discipline of timing, makes them ideal for learning sets with short sessions.

There are some features that are similar to classroom learning. An event has a start and stop time, everyone is expected to be present and someone is expected to run the meeting. There are many drawbacks, participants cannot interrupt each other, the mood or feelings of others cannot be read by body language, empathy between participants is difficult, fun is difficult, relaxing is difficult and there is no opportunity for physical movement. Why should these things matter? A clue to the importance of fun is to observe children learning. Most of the time children learn through play. Adults lose this relaxed approach to learning. Competition with one's peers becomes an issue early on in school. Feedback from others verges on disapproval which introduces a negative emotion to 'being wrong'. Adult learning does not have to be like this and a good classroom trainer can bring relaxation and fun into adult learning. It is more difficult to bring relaxation and fun into the virtual classroom. The advantage of a learning set is that participants will all be dealing with a related work problem. Trust between participants can be established by face-to-face meetings before the virtual sessions. Alternately, participants may be encouraged to talk about themselves and perhaps some of their preferences for learning and those based on personality. The importance of these latter preferences will become much clearer in Chapter 5.

Virtual classrooms lack the capability for learners to move around. This is important for those who prefer kinesthetic learning. Although all of us learn with all our senses each of us has a sensory impact that we prefer. Smell is an important memory trigger for all of us and a particular aroma may remind us of events from long ago and not always pleasant events. The smell of Dettol^{TM} for example always reminds me of being looked after in bed when feeling ill. In the learning situation the visual, aural and sense of feeling (kinesthetic) provide most learning input. An individual's preference can be seen in meetings. I have been in meetings with a pacer. Just as the meeting gets to a critically important point, this individual leaps out of their chair and paces the floor, maybe gesticulating wildly as they talk, or maybe just thinking furiously. I have known colleagues who, when they wanted to think, would walk. For these people, the sense of movement and feeling is part of the learning process. This is missing from the virtual classroom. Another meeting type I have worked with, indeed I am one myself, is the sketcher. She or he leaps up and dashes to the flipchart or whiteboard. They draw and sketch and scribble. More covert displays of these preferences are the doodler and the pencil fiddler. Those whose preference is for aural learning and interaction, are less obvious in meetings. Perhaps the clearest evidence is their preference for listening closely to what others actually say. Virtual classrooms can help the visual and aural learner, but not the kinesthetic, unless the skill is that of using a PC.

So far I have stressed the negative aspects of virtual classrooms. In my view they are a valuable e-learning tool that we still need to work out how to use. The most appropriate use is likely to be work groups or learning sets where participants work together collaboratively outside the virtual classroom sessions.

Summary

Research shows that the take up of Internet access and technologies varies greatly across Europe. The more sociable Southern Europeans use the Internet less than the Northern Europeans. This raises the intriguing possibility that the willingness to use the Internet, for whatever purpose, is cultural. It could also be that it is colder more often in the North and surfing the net in the warm is preferable to trudging in the snow in the freezing cold. The growth of the Internet as a communication channel for all is a new phenomenon, less than 10 years old. Its roots go back further into the academic community and this encourages a freedom in its use. Experienced users have a whole range of different expectations to its use than what actually happens. This has established an expectation that information and knowledge will be freely transferred through the Internet as a medium. New developers of websites, on the other hand, have an expectation that the Internet will give them a commercial advantage and provide income streams. This would certainly appear to be the case where the product or service delivery is one fundamentally based on information: banking is one such example. The provision of these increasingly commercial services has led to a steady rise in the number of people whose homes are connected to the web and to the number of people who use the Internet. We have reliable figures for the percentage of the population who are active users (approximately 50 per cent in the UK in 2002), but it is less clear how particular individuals use the Internet, or how it will develop. In much the same way that television drew on past experience of the stage and then film making, the Internet has drawn on past experiences of the music industry, the film industry and the computing industry.

Within the provision of learning some trends are becoming apparent. Product and service providers find it cheaper to add learning as a free service that is part of the product or service purchase. Professional institutes see it as a means of adding value to membership services. Additionally, employers may find it easier to provide just-in-time training, particularly in infrequently performed tasks. This is blurring the division between computer help, knowledge management and learning. The increasing choice and the changing shape in the provision of learning will increase the choice available to the individual.

The e-learning market place has displayed the typical entry-cycle of a new technology. Initially, a considerable amount of froth is created driving up expectations. This is followed by the period of realism as both suppliers and products are consolidated. Two broad types of content products have emerged. There is the self-study stand-alone course, perhaps with some face-to-face training, which in essence replaces the CD-ROM, albeit with increased communication between learners and tutors. The other main product range is the cohort-studied course, where a group works collaboratively through a website studying a course over an extended period of time leading to some type of qualification. Other products in the marketplace are software-driven, for example authoring systems and learning management systems. These offer increased operational efficiency within the training function; they do not, of themselves, offer learning content. These various software tools increase the accessibility of learning for the individual. The manager who likes to control, whether they are supportive or not, will value the existence of a learning management system because it places the control of who gets learning in the hands of the manager. However, what e-learning will do within the management/subordinate relationship is to decrease the number of employees who have to feel dependent on their managers for meeting their development needs.

Individuals will react differently to the various methods of e-learning. Although some of these differences will be due to their skills and competencies, by far the greater impact on their preferences is that of their personality and learning style. The virtual classroom is an interesting subset of e-learning. It has very close parallels with the real classroom but it is a very different experience and virtual classroom sessions need to be designed in ways that are significantly different from standard classroom sessions.

CHAPTER

3 *The Case Against e-Learning*

This chapter focuses on those aspects of successful learning that e-learning might be expected to be deficient in. It might well be trivial to say that e-learning lacks human contact and humanity and just leave it at that. This chapter will try to identify those factors that the involvement of others brings to e-learning. Two things will emerge, there are ways in which we can design in some of what is missing and how important it is to different individuals. Human involvement meets the emotional needs of learners and we may expect to gain from those around us, not just in our involvement with a tutor. These needs are emotions associated with motivation, a sensitive understanding of our needs, encouragement for development and, of course, praise for our achievements. Self-sufficiency in learning is a necessary attitude for everyone to have, however, people still need some reassurance that they are successful, that they are doing the right thing and doing things right.

Another emotion important in learning is 'excitement'. Learning is always about something new; doing something you have not done before. If we are willingly to tackle learning, the excitement must overcome the trepidation. The simplest example I can give is of myself at the top of a steep ski run. I know that I will be able to practise and refine physical skills that I am not very good at. I know that I run the risk of hurting myself: either my pride or my body! Every instinct that I have tells me that the slope is impossibly steep and slippery, that I could not walk down it, let alone slide on two bits of plastic! And yet something always forces me over the edge. It is not intellect that drives me at that point, I have to be driven by emotion. Creating that emotional drive comes from my relationships with others, not wanting to let others down for example. It also comes from the exhilarating experience that is my reward. Computers are unlikely to generate the same kind of emotional drive.

There are other aspects of learning where we might expect a human being to have superior performance to a computer. One area is the ability to observe and interpret human behaviour. Human beings are very good at sifting and recognizing patterns, particularly of behaviour. It is now possible for a computer to recognize a face, but this requires considerable computing power and yet is something a human being does effortlessly. Much more important, from a learning perspective, the human being can attribute meaning to the expression on the face. We can identify uncertainty, confidence, fear and aggression along with a wide range of other emotions. Our ability to do this is significantly increased when we take account of body posture. Our ability to do this is based on excellent visual acuity and a lifetime's experience of relating to others, as a child ensuring we get what we want and as an adult probably trying to achieve the same but in a less selfish way. There are situations where our unconscious dependence on interpreting body language will lead us to incorrect conclusions. This inherent risk is our interpretation of facial expression and body posture based on an understanding of our own upbringing. Cultural differences will confuse us. For example, in some cultures lowered eyelids are a sign of respect but in others may be interpreted as insolence.

Another aspect of learning where we may expect humans to do better than e-learning is the ability to answer questions. The addition of the Internet to an e-learning package means that it is theoretically possible to find an answer to any question and yet it remains easier to ask the person next door! From a very young age we use questions as a means of understanding the world around us. Our experience in education extends this dependence on others. There is an implicit acceptance that not only is asking questions of adults the way of finding answers but that the adult is capable of giving us the right answer. One of the processes of maturing as a learner is the realization that there is rarely one right answer, that there are many answers, some of which may be more appropriate than others. It is, however, no surprise that most of us find it easier to revert to childhood behaviour and ask others to provide answers rather than looking for them ourselves.

Social aspects of learning

We know that learning is largely social. Why is that? What is (or are) the key ingredients of that social context? Perhaps by understanding the answer we can go some way to ensuring that e-learning provides some of that social support.

ROLE MODELS

From a young age, we observe those around us and mimic their actions. Walking and talking skills are acquired by watching, experimenting and responding to feedback from those who are expert in those skills. Perhaps this last statement is not totally true for the skill of walking, or indeed skiing, where most of the feedback comes from the ground and gravity. Mimicking others remains an important way of learning. For example, do you watch others before crossing the road at a strange junction or in a foreign city? As children get older their range of role models to mimic becomes greater. A very young child will accept their parents and perhaps those adults with whom they are familiar as role models. As a child grows, other role models are mimicked, many of those being media figures through television and, increasingly, other media. The approach used by Sesame Street™ has been an enduring design feature of educational programmes since the early 1970s. Puppets are used to encourage literacy and numeracy skills in children. The method is, and has been, very successful in achieving its goals. Children are happy to repeat what Big Bird or Kermit has said. Television has broadcast hours of television aimed successfully at the same goal – that of encouraging children to speak and read. Role models do not have to be flesh and blood, virtual role models are acceptable to children. We can replace an adult role model with a puppet, then show an image of that puppet and get a child to learn. Another area where virtual role models are widely used is with the training video. An individual demonstrates the correct way in which to carry out a certain task. The contrast may be used as an individual demonstrates the consequences of carrying out a task incorrectly. The training industry has produced a huge variety of such materials. Topics include how to operate a piece of machinery safely, how to take it apart, how to make a presentation, how to conduct a meeting or interview. Both hard (that is, technical) and soft (that is, interpersonal) skills are presented. Viewers watch and then practice.

IDENTIFYING WITH THE COMMUNITY

There are many examples of role models that are used in non-social settings. That is, learning from a virtual person. Most of us are very happy to mimic a phrase that we hear repeated on the television (and the same is true of radio). Catchphrases first used by television personalities become part of everyday language use. But why do people repeat catchphrases? They repeat them to others, and in this sense, learning is social. People use catchphrases to be part of society. They are willing to mimic someone they have never met so that they can feel part of a group of people they meet regularly. This need to belong is a powerful human motivator. We can see the impact it has by observing behaviour. The clothing worn by football supporters is an obvious sign of our collective need to be part of a group and to display that membership. Language is another sign of membership, perhaps of a trade or profession. Jargon is adopted by groups of people for two reasons, one is to simplify communication but a second reason is to signal membership of an elite group. Jargon is also one means by which those in the group who have not met can introduce themselves. In primitive societies individual tribes would have secret signs and membership rituals to mark members from non-members. This need to belong may well be a survival trait, primitive humankind found it advantageous operating collectively. This could explain why individuals are essentially gregarious. Being part of a class learning the same thing satisfies that need to be gregarious. It would seem that the act of learning does not need to be social in this context but rather that every individual wishes for as much of their activity as possible to be with others. A point to emerge later is that this need varies between individuals. It would appear from this that a real life role model is not necessary to our learning and that various virtual role models will serve just as well.

FEEDBACK

It is possible to copy the behaviour of a role model that is only seen at a distance. It is possible to repeat and practise that behaviour on one's own but something else is needed if the practice is to be a learning experience. Learners need feedback on how well they are doing. In some cases that feedback comes from the environment. Many psychomotor skills have in-built feedback, for example walking and cycling. If the learner falls down or falls off it is obvious that some aspect of the skill needs to be improved. Learning to type is another skill where the feedback comes direct to the learner. The typist must be observed and feedback given by that observer. Consider a more complex skill like ballet, not only is a coach on hand to comment on a performance but mirrors are used. These mirrors give immediate feedback. An effective tool in helping someone acquire other advanced psychomotor skills, for example, skiing and golf, is the video camera. The video camera gives objective and accurate feedback on the behaviour of the learner. In this context, the video camera allows learners to be observers of their own performance serving the same function as the mirror in ballet. Judgments (or feedback) on the quality of our actions or behaviour may come from ourselves or from someone who watches the video with us. This is frequently used in sports training and for behavioural skills like presentation and interviewing. Learning has to be social at this point. Performance can only improve when we get feedback and for most learning activities feedback is best provided by someone else, although some feedback can be machine delivered. Knowledge and some of the more advanced cognitive skills can be tested by computer-delivered tests.

BLOOM'S TAXONOMY

With a little care and thought e-learning can be used to assess the full range of cognitive skills. Work started in 1948 to classify cognitive skills. A group of educators set out to classify objectives in the cognitive (thinking), affective (behavioural) and psychomotor (action) domains. The thinking domain was completed first and is referred to as Bloom's taxonomy (Bloom, 1956). For designers, instructors and educators it provides a classification of instructional objectives, specifically the verbs that describe the actions that learners take. These apply to the style of questions that designers use, most significantly those amenable to computer delivery. Briefly let me remind you of the levels: knowledge; comprehension; application; analysis; synthesis; and evaluation. For example the verb 'list' applies to a thinking action that applies to knowledge retention, 'describe or paraphrase' applies to an action of comprehension, 'solve' to one of application, 'categorize' to one of analysis, 'develop or create' to one of synthesis and 'recommend' to one of evaluation. The taxonomy helps educators think more carefully about the learning outcomes they are seeking to develop or test. It is a very valuable tool for the e-learning designer.

Multiple-choice questions to assess knowledge retention are straightforward to design. There are various rules to follow to ensure that hidden clues are not provided in the question, for example grammatical constructions and word choice in the answer and stem. These basic principles apply to all multiple-choice questions. Free text questions, where specific words must be entered correctly, can also be used to test knowledge. At the next level, the assessment of comprehension, multiple-choice and similar computer-driven questions will need to present information and require people to demonstrate an understanding of some underlying theories and procedures which are not presented in the question. A useful addition to question style would be to present a diagram, perhaps a flow diagram, and ask the learner to identify points at which particular things happen.

At the application level, learners have to apply a concept, theory or principle to a practical situation. A typical e-learning example of an assessment at this level would be the presentation of a problem for which the learner had to work out the answer. Simulations, working diagrams and multiple-choice questions of various types can all be used to assess cognitive application at this level.

The next level of cognitive reasoning is that of analysis. The mental skill required is that of structuring material (information, data and knowledge) into its components. This is likely to include the relationship between components and an example might be of an analysis of why a machine does not work. This contrasts with the cognitive level of comprehension, which requires an understanding of how a machine works. Testing at this level by e-learning is very feasible. Problem solving questions are typical. There is a narrow dividing line between analysis and evaluation (or judgment). Faultfinding might use either or both of these skills. For example the skill of selecting a component that causes the type of fault seen is analytical but determining to replace it is evaluative. One of the factors that mark this level of assessment is the requirement to present the learner with significant amounts of information in various forms. The learner's task is to break this information down into component parts and determine the relationship between those parts.

The next level of cognitive skill is that of synthesis. It is perhaps at this level that the capability of e-learning falters. Synthesis is concerned with the assembly and putting together of information, data and knowledge; for example, developing a plan. As there are usually many ways to create or produce something, assessment at this level inevitably has to be completed by another human being. The highest order of cognitive skills as defined by Bloom, is that of evaluation or judgment. In much the same way that the assessment of analysis skills requires the presentation of a significant amount of information, so it is with judgment skills. The key criterion of assessment, at this level, is the requirement for the learner to make some value judgment on the information presented. In this sense evaluation goes beyond analysis. A typical type of multiple-choice question that can be used is the assertion/reason question, which will be familiar to many students of the Open University in the UK. This question style presents a causal statement. That is a statement in two parts, one of which is a cause and the other is the effect. Learners are asked to assess whether the cause and effect are correct or incorrect and whether the link is valid or is invalid. Knowledge is usually tested to show whether either the cause or the effect is true, but the learner must make a judgment as to whether they are linked appropriately. An example of such a question would be: 'Apples fall to earth because Newton discovered gravity'. Clearly the first is true and the second is not. Newton postulated the theory of gravity and might be said to have discovered the laws of gravity rather than gravity itself. There is, of course, no causal link between Newton's endeavours and what happens to apples when they fall from a tree. Given thought in the design, it is perfectly practical for e-learning to enable individuals to learn all the advanced cognitive skills except that of synthesis or creation.

INDIVIDUAL REACTION TO FEEDBACK

There is another limitation to machine feedback, although this may be both an advantage as well as a drawback. Feedback comes in many forms and is the key to improvement, the same feedback is received very differently by different people. There is a relationship between various personality traits and reaction to feedback. There is also a relationship between the effectiveness of feedback and an individual's preferred learning style. Some, but by no means all, human observers are perceptive enough to vary the way in which they give feedback to allow for the individual. Ironically the mechanical nature of machine feedback may be such that some personality types prefer its impersonal nature.

This may be the important element that makes learning social. Feedback is more attuned to the needs of the individual when it is given by another individual. What is more, the 'tuning in' is most effective face-to-face. The 'tuning in' is vital in achieving a positive outcome from the feedback. There are only three outcomes from feedback, be it complex, such as an appraisal interview, or simple, such as the results of a test:

(1) Acceptance of the feedback but no willingness to do anything differently, normally associated with sadness, or at the extreme, depression.
(2) Denial of the feedback, normally associated with anger at anyone who might have the temerity to find fault with one's performance.
(3) Positive acceptance that the feedback is accurate and that something can be done to correct and improve one's performance.

Most human beings have the expertise to steer a favourable course between the rocks of rage and the sands of despair when talking to others. This is why learning is social. The responsibility to get a good response to feedback is not solely due to the giver of the feedback it is also a responsibility of the receiver. Competency as a learner may have a lot to do with the way a learner can deal with feedback and ensure a positive outcome. This concept is encompassed by the general acceptance that mistakes present the ideal learning opportunity. An individual's capacity to use mistakes positively is influenced by the culture they find themselves in. A positive rewarding culture where people are valued for what they can do increases the probability that a mistake will be treated positively. A procedurally-focused culture in which people are valued more for who they are, rather than what they can do, is one in which blame is allocated and mistakes are less likely to result in positive outcomes. In a culture where blame is allocated, learners will hide their mistakes, perhaps from themselves as well as from others. Culture generates this attitude. Culture is another aspect of social involvement. Culture influences the success of learning and this is another reason why learning is social, although there may be some cultures where an absence of people produces a better learning environment.

PRAISE

Praise is related to feedback and is also a product of culture. Praise is more than positive feedback, it is a recognition of achievement. Praise should always be part of the learning loop, with positive and pleasant experiences. Therefore we will naturally repeat those things that others praise us for. Praise is another aspect of the learning experience that is social. Praise is recognition by others but the extent to which we value praise from others is related to the importance with which we rate the person giving that praise. I would like you, the reader, to reflect for a moment and consider situations in which you have received feedback from your peers and from your boss. Which had more importance to you? You can place other individuals on a rating scale of importance to you. The higher up the scale they are, the greater the importance of what they say (or do) is to you.

Cats and bosses

Consider for a moment the comparison between the relative importance to you of your family pet and a senior colleague at work, perhaps your boss. Which has greater power to make you change your behaviour? I expect your cat (if you have one) demonstrates displeasure if you buy food it detests. The behaviour may be aggressive; the cat curls its lip at you and bares its teeth or it may be assertive: the cat walks away from the food in that disdainful way that cats have and goes and purrs at the next door neighbour who may have something better on offer. Perhaps your boss (if you have one) demonstrates displeasure if you act in a way she or he does not like. The behaviour may be aggressive in that your boss shouts at you or it may be assertive in that your boss explains calmly why she or he wants you to do something different. What impact does the feedback from your boss and your cat have on you and how do they compare? What is the probability that you will change your behaviour as a result of that feedback? It may well be that the feedback from the cat has less of an impact, although you are more likely to change your behaviour. Maybe your wish to respond to your cat's needs is greater than your wish to respond to your boss's needs! Your emotional links with your cat are greater than with your boss although your intellectual links with your boss may be greater than those you have with your cat. How we respond to situations is a product of both emotion and intellect. Even in work situations and certainly in learning situations, we are likely to respond more to an emotional stimulus than to an intellectual one. How you feel about praise has the same degree of complexity. Intellectually we will value praise from an expert, someone whose opinion we respect, emotionally we will value praise from someone who is close to us, someone we like or have an emotional attachment to. As with most human behaviour the emotional response takes precedence over the intellectual response. The emotional response operates at a more basic level.

Given that praise is a part of learning and that praise is more effective when we have intellectual respect and an emotional link with the giver of that praise where does praise from a computer fit into the scheme of things. Where does an e-learning website fit? Where do co-learners who have never seen each other fit? Where do participants in a virtual classroom fit (where you can at least hear the other person)? The probability is that the more remote the individual is from you, the less important their feedback is. Feedback from a computer may only be relevant to you in the context of someone else observing that result. While this diminishes the importance of praise it also diminishes the impact of corrective feedback. This may help many learners. One of the arguments put forward to justify computer application training via e-learning is that individuals (perhaps, particularly the more senior and inevitable older employees) may practise using the application in privacy where mistakes will matter less. If only the machine knows you have got it wrong then this almost eliminates the emotional impact of mistakes. We dislike mistakes primarily because we do not wish to lose face with those around us. This may make e-learning feedback less stressful for some people since there are no human observers. This also reduces the feeling of success when you get it right. After all if no one knows you got an answer right or wrong why bother to get it right, especially as many people say that you learn from your mistakes. Perhaps I will maximize my learning by only making mistakes!

The ability to give praise is a vital human factor and the incapability of e-learning material to give valued praise, without human support, is a drawback that cannot be overcome. However a point that will emerge very clearly from the research reported in Chapter 5 is that we all have a different level of need for praise and some of us need very little.

DIFFERENCES BETWEEN INDIVIDUALS

The social elements of learning are based on the relative importance of others to you and their ability to observe, record and comment on your performance. An essential consequence is that you, the learner, will feel good about yourself when others praise you for doing well. You will also respond positively to corrective feedback recognizing that it is given to help you improve, rather than allocate blame. The need for praise from others is rooted in our childhood and our relationships with adults. Circumstances vary greatly for children dependent on family circumstances. Therefore, each of us will have different needs for praise and different responses to feedback. Some individuals will have high self-sufficiency in achievement while others will have a dependency on approval from others. The latter seek to measure their own performance always in the eyes of others and the former take little account of the views of others. Successful e-learning will meet the needs of individuals for praise and personal feedback in ways that are appropriate to the individual. Furthermore that feedback will come from a source that the learner respects intellectually and values emotionally. This means that achievement is rewarded in ways that are appropriate and important to the individual. The implication is that, for some learners, a human element has to be included in e-learning.

HUMANS AS INFORMATION SOURCES

Another social element in learning is the ability of human beings to answer questions and interactively problem-solve. Computers are a long way from being able to do this. A good example relates to the training of office staff in a new computer system. This is a commonplace and frequent activity. Let me describe an actual case study from the late 1980s. Members of staff, who needed to learn a new system, were used to some interaction with computer systems, but the majority of their job was conducted on paper. The company developed and implemented new system changes and applications regularly, with minor changes every month and major new processes every quarter. All the system changes were supported with workshops for local 'champions', embedded computer-based training (CBT), and workbooks and job performance aids. The local 'champions' were people who worked in each location, were enthusiastic about the change and had more than an average system expertise. The embedded CBT was always instantly available to every employee. Great care was taken to ensure that any part of the material could be reached quickly. If a complete course was studied, it rarely took more than fifteen minutes. The vision was that employees in local offices would work through the training just before the system was upgraded. They would then quickly revise the training as and when they were uncertain about a particular point. But what happened? The vast majority of employees studied a couple of sections in the CBT and read a bit of the workbooks. They rarely worked through to completion. Sometimes they felt under too much time pressure, sometimes they were driven by a strong desire to get on with the real thing and, perhaps, sometimes they became bored with studying on their own. After all the organization attracted gregarious people-centred individuals who liked talking to, and serving customers. Invariably, employees would start using the new and upgraded applications before having really grasped the essentials. If they became stuck they rarely clicked 'Help'. Usually, the first recourse was to shout a question across the office – 'Hey, I'm on screen so-and-so: what do I do?' The CBT had the information readily available, but not specifically in response to that question. However, a human being could instantly sort through the information in their head and come back with an answer. If they could not do so by shouting back across the office, they could do so from one glance at the screen. There was usually at least one individual in each office who knew more than the others, by design the local 'IT Champion' who had attended a workshop to be introduced to the changes and new applications. Perhaps given these circumstances and environment, it was only to be expected that learners would ask each other rather than look up the answer to their question.

There are a number of reasons why learners prefer to ask others rather than working things out for themselves:

(1) It is easier. The onus on getting the right answer is placed on the person asked rather than remaining with the learner. The person asked has to come up with the right answer rather than for the learner to come up with the right question. Or rather the question that gets them the right answer. Computer search facilities are a big step forward in enabling an e-learning website to respond to a question, but rarely will such a system come back with one reference; it will usually have at least two or three,

sometimes many more. The human will come back with one response, even if incorrect because their natural inclination is to help. Even when a search facility identifies what you want to know, the information is not organized in a way that answers your question. This is not a question of natural language interfaces, although they will help as they are improved. (A natural language interface is one where the input from the user is in normal language, the computer is able to parse the input sentences, applying a recognized syntax and convert the sentence to a command on which it can take action). The principle issue is that a computer will be programmed to give an answer, or if it is not sure, list options. The computer may come back with a message akin to 'I do not understand' or 'Please give me more information.' A human being is more likely to respond with another question if they cannot immediately answer yours. Humans have a natural tendency to problem-solve and a questioner will always get a simpler response from a human being than from a computer with less effort on the learner's part, provided that the human being actually knows the answer and the question is not so completely unambiguous that the computer system has only one simple choice. Even then you are likely to get extra information you do not need or do not want.

(2) It may be faster. It may seem highly ironic that a human being can provide a faster answer than a computer. There is the obvious drawback that the e-learning material may not be immediately available. This applies to learning any task where the computer is not part of the task or co-located. It may even apply where the learning task is a computer application, exactly as in the example discussed here. Perhaps the search facility of the e-learning website takes time to open and operate. For a poor typist it may be much quicker to speak to a person rather than enter text. A human being is also more capable of making associations and has a greater tolerance for ambiguity. Another human will recognize that you have mispronounced a word because it becomes misplaced in context. A computer rarely recognizes that you have mistyped a word. It will not recognize that 'saw' meant 'was' for example.

(3) It is a rewarding experience for both parties. The person asked feels good about themselves, they have been important to someone else, they have shown their knowledge, the person who asked now has an extra nugget of information and some of the stress (albeit very little stress) has been reduced since they are now more capable than before. It is perhaps for these reasons that asking questions becomes a social experience. All of us enjoy being needed and useful. What could be more useful than helping someone else learn? Asking someone a question related to learning a topic enhances their self esteem because the learner is making a statement about them. If you are asked a question the learner is saying that they respect your knowledge and judgment and wish to make use of it. This is a very sincere form of flattery. The learner in turn feels valued and appreciated because you, from your position of superior knowledge, take the time and trouble to help someone out. The transaction of imparting knowledge in response to a request enhances both parties to the transaction.

So another reason learning is social is that both parties get emotional value out of the exchange. Also from an intellectual perspective human beings are better at answering questions than computers.

HUMANS AS SOUNDING BOARDS

Human beings are also able to modify their responses to questions to take account of any emotional undercurrents the learner may have. Human beings are equipped to recognize and respond to emotion. Learners may be under a number of different pressures. They may lack confidence about their ability to learn a topic, they may be under time pressure to complete a task and they may be confused. All these states generate internal feelings that may interfere with learning. Questions sometime carry a hidden meaning reflecting uncertainty or impatience in the questioner. A human respondent will detect subtle changes of tone. This may indicate the best response is a rapid 'do it this way' or a lengthy explanation of why. People can vary their response to a question to take account of these emotional needs. Not all do so but computers can never do so. The human being who is insensitive to these nuances may appear either unfeeling or a bore or patronizing.

Although computers are inanimate objects, we may react to answers produced by software in much the same way as we would to a human who patronizes or bores us. It may seem illogical to take personally the response we get from the software but I have seen otherwise sane people talking to their computers in rage or irritation. Computers have no flexibility in the way they respond and take no account of an individual's feelings at the time. A similar aspect to this is that computers take no account of the personality of the learner. Personality affects feelings about learning in much the same way that surrounding events will do so. Some people are habitually more anxious than others for example. Anxiety inhibits learning and it may be more important to relieve the anxiety in a learner than to supply material to be learned.

THE SOCIAL RESPONSE TO MISTAKES

The classic ingredient in our ability to learn is how we learn from mistakes euphemistically described as 'learning opportunities' by many. I have described the impact on the way individuals feel about the mistakes they make. Feedback, in one form or another, tells the learner they have made a mistake. The way in which the learner reacts to that feedback is vital. It may well be that electronic learning, in its various forms, has an advantage over learning from others in the neutral and impartial manner of feedback. A significant proportion of the population prefers to make mistakes in private. They may have felt humiliated in a classroom situation because they made a mistake and do not wish to repeat the experience. They may work in a culture that likes to allocate blame. This encourages mistakes to be hidden. The private, impartial and impersonal nature of electronic feedback may well be ideal. However, it also lacks compassion and consideration. Although better than insensitive feedback, the electronic form can never be as good as sensitive, well-delivered human feedback. A good tutor or mentor is able to turn feedback into a motivational experience. The focus shifts to 'What can you do differently as a result of an objective understanding of your performance?' It is quite simple for a computer tool to ask this question and also remember the answer. The ability to remember information and reflect it back to people later is a powerful advantage of e-learning, but I would like to concentrate on how people work out answers to the question: 'What will I do differently?' The question is challenging to anyone. Good quality feedback will have helped through the emotional and intellectual realization of a need to change but a hurdle still remains. Making that change requires effort and a move away from what is familiar. Helping someone through the emotional barrier so that they make the effort to learn is more of a counselling role than a teaching role. Many teachers will argue that their job description includes counselling and I agree. I use the definition 'teaching' in this context to include only the imparting of knowledge and skills not motivating the individual to acquire that knowledge and skill.

Motivating someone to learn from their mistakes is a vital contribution that people can make and computers cannot. Of course, different people will react differently to their mistakes – that is the point. A human tutor can recognize and understand this. E-learning has to make allowances for those differences. Counselling and motivating a reluctant learner is something that has, up to now, required human intervention. Many of us will leap at an opportunity to learn something new but some of us may be reluctant. From a very young age we are likely to classify ourselves as good at some things and not so good at others. It is typical that people may feel themselves to be artistic or scientific but rarely good at both. The education system encourages this division. As a matter of record many geniuses were adept at both logical and creative skills. Buzan (1989, pp. 18, 19) gives examples of scientific geniuses who were musicians and great artists and adept at mathematics. But for most of us there will be some skill that we feel is not for us. It may be a creative skill, artistic, intellectual, or a physical skill. We are reluctant to learn this skill, it is not for us. If we make mistakes; perhaps sing a wrong note, add a column of figures incorrectly, fail to read a map: then we label this mistake as something we will always do because we are not singers, or mathematicians or map readers. We come to believe that the innate ability to do these things is not within us. My premise is that most of us are reluctant to learn something but all of us have the capability of learning anything. Motivating us to learn something in which we feel inept, requires support from another person. Motivating the reluctant learner is a human skill. It may be that the label we carry within us as 'not musicians', or ' not scientists' was given to us by another person when we were at a very young age. I was labelled a non-musician at a very young age, by a very scornful teacher, a belief that has become firmly rooted.

THE ROLE OF SOCIALIZATION IN LEARNING

I have discussed the social aspects of learning: that is those activities I might describe as the specific human contribution made to learning. If we can understand these, then it may be possible to structure e-learning to either deliver these ingredients, or to replicate them. Table 3.1 lists these human contributions and summarizes those which are exclusively human and which can be replicated by e-learning.

THE CHARISMATIC TUTOR AND ENTHRALLING MATERIAL

The tutor brings another dimension to learning, that of enthusiasm for the subject. The successful learner is one who becomes interested and enthusiastic in what is being learned. This enthusiasm may rub-off from a charismatic tutor, perhaps someone who can hold you enthralled by the passion they have for the subject. Many of us will be able to remember a good teacher from school who was able to interest us in a topic by their personality, their turn of phrase and their speaking-style. All these combined to enthrall and entertain, to help you learn what they were teaching. Good adult educational television programmes will have

Table 3.1   Reproducing the human contribution to learning with e-learning

Contribution made to learning by people	Opportunity for replicating this in e-learning
Role models	Replicated by cartoon characters and video films – many examples of how this is done.
Being part of a community	E-learning discussion boards and collaborative learning spaces encourage a feeling of belonging for the individual learner. Being part of a cohort helps further and is similar to being in a class.
Feedback	Simple feedback on the lower order cognitive skills can be given. Performance in a simulation gives objective feedback. (for example, problem solving in a management game). Feedback for more complex cognitive skills (for example, synthesis or evaluation) only comes from another human being. Sometimes self-observation can be used to give this feedback and the computer may be used as a recording tool. Feedback for affective objectives relies on observation of behaviour. Video can be used to record this observation so that the learner can use self-assessment. This stretches the definition of e-learning beyond PC and Internet use only.
Varied feedback (the need to respond to different emotional states in the learner)	An individual's emotional state influences their receptiveness to feedback. Anxiety or anger both generate a block to an individual giving a balanced response to feedback. The perceptive tutor or co-learner recognizes this and modifies their comments accordingly, perhaps delaying comment until a more appropriate time. However e-learning is less likely to generate strong emotions in a learner. E-learning can respond by ensuring that any feedback is highly factual and neutral in tone.
Discussion and debate	An Individual needs to organize and reflect on their thoughts for learning to take place. Discussing these with another person is a helpful way of clarifying thinking.
Praise	Appropriate praise from a valued source contributes to a sense of achievement. This may be a coach who is with the learner and or a manager. It does not have to be a subject tutor.

a presenter who is not only knowledgeable and enthusiastic about their topic but is articulate and talks in a way that makes them easy to listen to: e-learning can make a contribution that is similar.

Material which entertains and excites also motivates. A gaming approach may replace the charisma of the good teacher. Graphics, video clips and simulations may appeal. The response needs to be at an emotional level. The charismatic tutor creates an emotional response of enthusiasm in the learner. Engaging e-learning material has to create a similar response of enthusiasm. This might be with passive material.

Humour

Humour is used in learning material precisely because it generates an emotional response and is memorable. Video Arts set out to produce training films that were fun and exciting. This was a radical departure from the many films produced at that time. Viewers are shown the unfortunate consequences of inappropriate actions. These were presented in a humorous way. Learning did not have to be hard work. Humour has impact. Every good comic says that the key to humour is timing. The punch line has to be delivered at just the right time so that it carries maximum impact. The implication for e-learning is that humour may need to be restricted to the passive elements, as the user will control the timing of the interactive elements. Humour does not lend itself to repetition and the ability to repeat material is one of the advantages of e-learning. Where humour is used, it is best placed in a sequence that people do not have to revisit if they want to revise points in the course.

Games

If you watch anyone playing a computer game, the engagement and involvement is apparent. Encouraging interaction through games or simulations creates involvement and this involvement may generate excitement. There is a balancing act needed in the creation of games and simulations. Both are unreal situations and are used to train for real situations. The engagement comes from a competitive attribute that most of us have to some extent. There is a risk that the learner will focus completely on the game and concentrate on beating the game. An early interactive video produced in the 1980s was based on an appraisal interview (*Appraising Anita*). The product consisted of a series of responses Anita would make to questions asked of her or statements made. The product simulated the appraisal interview. At each point in the interview the user was given options of questions to ask. Anita would make an appropriate response and then another list of questions or statements would be presented and so on. The simulation had three outcomes, Anita burst into tears, she stormed out of the meeting in anger or she agreed with the points made in the interview and was willing to find ways to change. The simulation had many paths through it. Users might easily concentrate on beating the game rather than concentrating on the types of questions or statements that create a positive outcome in the appraisal interview, which was the purpose of the training product. Concentrating on beating the game reduced the transfer of the learning points to the real appraisal interviewee. Games have to be sufficiently engaging to be exciting but not all-absorbing.

Sensory impact

In the real world, all our senses operate to stimulate our thinking and feeling. By comparison e-learning is a very thin experience. Even media-rich e-learning only stimulates two senses and the visual stimulus is within a very narrow field. Human beings evolved as hunting and browsing animals. You might say that we are designed to live in jungles and pick up stimuli from all around us. Nevertheless, good e-learning can use some very simple ideas to be more memorable than a page full of text. Distinctive colours, clear diagrams and some pictures will have a visual impact. However, impact lies in the eye of the beholder and one person's impact may be another's irritation. Impact comes from an amalgamation of sensory input. Real-life events include smells, physical feeling, emotional feeling, sounds, sights and maybe taste. Any screen-based event will only contain sight and sound and in both cases these are attenuated. Wall-to-wall surround sound is possible and headphones will immerse the listener in a sensory experience and yet we know the sound is, in some sense, artificial.

The visual input is even more limited with just a narrow field-of-view. Providing truly memorable experiences via this medium is very difficult. The very size of the screen makes it difficult to impress and convey impact. I can give an example of the way the real world can convey more impact than a computer screen. Those of you with a physical science background may know that the rotation of the earth can be observed and measured from a pendulum. (Described as a Foucault pendulum named after the Frenchman who first used it to measure the rotation of the earth.) If a pendulum is set swinging, the plane of the swing appears to rotate. The rate of rotation varies from 15 degrees per hour to zero depending on the latitude. In fact, the earth rotates under the pendulum. This observation is normally taught in school labs with a short pendulum (a bob weight on a piece of string) perhaps 20 centimetres long. I can vividly remember this experiment conducted in a large hall with a pendulum thirty metres long. This was a university lecture hall with an audience of about 200 science students. The impact this had on me could not be conveyed through a computer screen. The Science Museum still has a long pendulum hanging down five floors, difficult to convey the impact of this through a computer screen, although comprehending what it displays (that the earth rotates) may be conveyed much more easily through a graphical computer display. For learning purposes, the impact must be positive.

Shock clearly carries impact and may, in the right circumstances, aid learning. Generally speaking, it is to be avoided. An individual's reaction to shock depends a great deal on circumstances and personality. However, the initial reaction is denial and rejection of the facts. Many people never get beyond this phase. If that is the case, the shock, even though potentially memorable, will achieve little learning. Therefore, impact in e-learning has to create a positive feeling, ideally one that can be anticipated and remembered

Incongruity

There are other ways a computer screen can convey impact, noticeably with visual images. A computer does have the unique capability of displaying an unreal but life-like event. Incongruity is another powerful memory link. A memory tip to remember people's names is to associate an image with a name, for example, an ant for Anthony, a robot for Robert, a native American saying 'How' for Howard. When you are introduced to a person with that name, superimpose the image onto the person. The incongruous nature of the image helps you remember the name. An image that still returns to me is three computers made to look like cars, one fast, one normal and one slow. The point is that there are three types of documentary collection and the main difference between them is speed of collection. (documentary collection is associated with getting payment from other countries for exported goods). The capability to use incongruity is readily achieved in e-learning and one that should be exploited by designers.

Trepidation

I mentioned in the introduction to this chapter, the need for excitement in creating a positive attitude to learning and 'trying something new'. The corollary of excitement is trepidation. The good tutor is able to reduce this feeling in a learner by boosting confidence and self-esteem. All of us will have some uncertainty, both about anything new and any learning task. If we intend to learn from written material, the sheer size of a book or manual may cause a sinking feeling in the pit of the stomach. Such trepidation has an emotional and an intellectual basis. It can be overcome, both by a positive anticipation that this learning task will be exciting and by the fear of the negative consequences of not learning. 'Learning helps to create and sustain our culture. It helps all of us to improve our chances of getting a job and getting on' (The Learning Age Consultation Paper presented to UK parliament February 1998).

While these benefits of learning are absolutely self-evident they are not immediate. Reflecting on the skiing analogy – myself on the edge of a dangerous-looking steep ski-slope

– what are the negative consequences of my not engaging in the learning that I can achieve by launching myself down the slope? The answer lies in my feelings about other people. Am I prepared to suffer the public humiliation of either walking down or riding in the chair? An essential pointer for e-learning is that the immediate negative consequences are mainly based on our perception of other people's view of us. On the other hand, the positive expectation that learning will be enjoyable and fun is something e-learning can influence. Human intervention will significantly influence excitement in learning. A good tutor with charisma and enthusiasm will generate that. She or he can do that through video and audio techniques. Other techniques can use stories from past learners (like us) who have enjoyed the e-learning experience. Ensuring that the e-learning is collaborative, brings in other people and maybe a tutor. At the start of this section I mentioned the role of the tutor in alleviating trepidation. This is also something that another learner may do, particularly one who has previously been successful.

What others bring to the learning activity

In the preceding section I have listed those activities and functions that are an important social element in learning. These are brought together in Figure 3.1. This shows a total of seven roles adopted by other individuals who are around the learner.

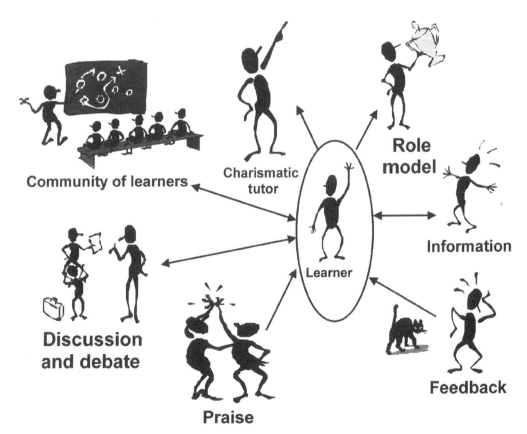

Figure 3.1 Social aspects of learning

Two of these roles are those that learners look up to, that of the role model and the tutor. E-learning can excite and enthuse in ways similar to a charismatic tutor but the impact this has on each personality types is very different. This will become more apparent in Chapter 6 where I discuss individual personality and its effect on learning preferences. Role models can be shown in e-learning material relatively easily and there are many examples, for example training videos and children's TV are full of role models demonstrating skills from numeracy to management skills.

Other roles are based more on an equal exchange. Learners gain a sense of solidarity and togetherness by being part of a community of learners. This boosts morale as a learner feels that they are not the only one who is struggling with quantum mechanics or how to use a computer mouse. Such a community can go further, by developing a learning culture that praises success and celebrates mistakes. These communities may be virtual ones exchanging ideas, debate and discussion via e-mail. Learners gain the capability of feeling part of a community without having to travel to join it. The nature of the debate and 'community spirit' will be different, and perhaps more muted, than that of face-to-face meetings. For some learners the benefit of reflective debate and interaction will outweigh the disadvantages of text- or audio-only interaction. A related role to the community of learners is that of the local expert; the colleague who answers questions. In e-learning this is replicated by the FAQ, or a help file or knowledge management website. All these electronic forms of questioning require the learner to work a little bit harder than when they ask a colleague.

The final area where other people contribute to learning is that of giving feedback and praise. E-learning can test (and thereby give feedback) for all the cognitive skills with the exception of synthesis. If this feedback is part of a case study scenario or simulation than it is very close to being fully work-place based. However computers cannot give feedback for interpersonal or most physical skills. (Given the context of e-learning using PCs and communication technologies, this is true, although larger computers and advanced sensors could do just that, for example analysing the perfect golf swing and monitoring a learner's performance) People observe learners and tell them how well they did against some criteria describing the desired behaviour. This feedback must then be given in a sensitive and appropriate style and responded to. Computers are not renowned for a sensitive style although, given good design, e-learning can deliver appropriate feedback. The impartial nature of computer feedback means that it will not be influenced by interpersonal differences, but it may feel trivial to the receiver. Feedback on learning is emotional as well as intellectual, hence, the need to deal with it sensitively. All this is possible, but what is rarely possible is the capability of listening to the learner's response in a way that makes the learner attribute importance and value to the relationship. The learner's cat, if they have one, will be more important to the learner than the computer.

Interpersonal differences

A recognized source of conflict between co-workers is the personality clash. Two people seem unable to work together. This is particularly damaging in the learning situation and may be an area in which e-learning demonstrates clear superiority. There is a risk that some individuals may not relate well to a particular tutor. Personal characteristics may grate and inhibit the impact of excitement and enthusiasm. This clash may be due to a difference in personality that is not understood. Not only is a clash between a tutor and the learner possible, it is just as likely a clash in the way they relate to topics that need to be learned. Although, I argue that Honey and Mumford's (1986) learning styles are best applied to a cycle of learning that learners progress through (Hills, 2001), let me for the moment characterize them as 'learning types'. A pragmatist likes to do something immediately as a result of learning. A tutor who prefers theorizing or reflecting is certain to irritate a pragmatist. The activist likes variety and action and again may be irritated by a tutor who prefers a more measured and (in their view) better-structured approach to learning.

We can also expect clashes between a pragmatic tutor and learners who prefer reflecting or theorizing. One of the hallmarks of a really excellent tutor is that he or she is able to accommodate different preferences at the same time. A good e-learning design should be able to do the same. In Chapter 5 I will present a model that will do exactly that. One advantage that e-learning has over a face-to-face tutor is that self-study material is used by only one person at a time, whereas the classroom tutor has to accommodate personal preferences for a classroom full of learners. There are already examples of learning sites which give learners options, from doing a task in a simulated environment, reading an explanation of a theoretical concept or completing a test. A consistent feature of good e-learning material is that the user has control and can do things in their own way.

But is that sufficient? I have described one definition of learning styles, there are others and there are other sources of differences. Preferences for auditory, kinesthetic or visual learning are of great significance for e-learning. Most of us have a preference for a particular sense. Rose and Nicholl (1997, pp. 90–105) describe the various strategies that are used by those whose preference is visual, auditory or kinesthetic. Visual learners need pictures, visual signposts, sketches and mind maps (see Buzan, 1989). Auditory learners need to read aloud, to sing and to speak. Kinesthetic learners need to write, annotate notes (helpful for the visual learner as well), use post-it notes and cards, tick lists and to walk about when learning. As will be shown in Chapter 4, versatility improves learning and those that use activities appropriate to all these three senses will be much more effective than those who rely on just one. These preferences have a major impact on the learning strategies adopted by children and young people. The nursery rhyme 'Ring-a-ring of roses' exercises the aural and kinesthetic sense. Learners dance, hold hands, sing and fall down. This is a powerful learning approach. Can e-learning do as well? It is worth reflecting that classroom tutors in business courses probably pay insufficient heed to visual or kinesthetic learning. In setting challenges for the future of e-learning, we should not forget that neither work-place learning nor classroom learning has risen successfully to the same challenges.

Interaction between learners

The communication aspect of e-learning can be used to engage learners with the material by engaging them with each other. This might be through the chatroom and by interacting with other learners and with the tutor, through a discussion forum or a synchronous event. In a classroom situation peer-to-peer interaction may occur as part of a 'class' debate facilitated by the tutor, it may occur within the class situation as asides between learners or it may occur outside the whole group either as a one-to-one between individuals or small groups of three or four learners. These situations have certain features and some of those features are replicated in on-line learning.

- Whole group interaction occurs in the presence of the tutor who may initiate it and will certainly facilitate the discussion, even to the extent of curtailing input from some people and drawing others out. Participants will vary in their activity in these sessions, based on their personality and their degree of confidence (or strength of feeling) about the topic. The on-line learning equivalent is the tutor-facilitated virtual classroom or the bulletin board. In the synchronous virtual classroom, the tutor must exercise a high degree of control. Only one person speaks at a time and interruptions cannot be allowed. Just to explain that last point, if the virtual classroom uses video conferencing technology then the quality of audio and video is high with good synchronization between sound and picture. There is still a delay between the speaker speaking and the listener hearing. When listeners interrupt they do so a fraction of second behind the point at which the speaker would have expected an interruption. The visual clue a speaker normally gets when someone wants to interrupt is also delayed. This confuses the speaker into thinking that what they said was accepted and then not accepted. One conference system I used, switched the picture on the basis of the audio input (when someone spoke a fraction of a second later their image replaced that of the previous speaker). This was something that you had to get used to otherwise it was a distraction. Internet-transmitted conferences aggravate the disconnection between speaker and listener. Not only is a listener's response delayed, their speech is not always synchronized with their picture. This dissonancy requires the tutor to control who speaks and when. Participants must do the equivalent of raising their hands to speak. Some Internet-capable virtual classrooms use exactly that metaphor to manage the way that the opportunity to contribute is passed around the group. Telephone conferences are a similar environment. Bulletin boards are an asynchronous equivalent. The tutor must manage the threads of discussion, creating new threads where more than one topic stems from one comment. Learners may all talk at once which is a cause of confusion. It is common for one comment to create multiple replies, each of which is done independently of the others. The tutor must hold the discussion together perhaps by summarizing key points every so often. Everybody's input is seen by everyone else.
- Asides between learners occur to a greater or lesser degree depending on how engaged learners are by the topic, their disparity in understanding and their freedom to do so. Many of us may remember a time in school when a teacher 'martinet' told someone off for talking in class, even when the discussion had a learning benefit. E-learning asides are actually very difficult to create. The most frequent technical solution is the chatroom, but even here you do not know if the tutor is involved or who else is listening. You might be in the chatroom interacting with a co-learner and have the whole of the rest of the class 'lurking' in there with you. (Lurking is the term used to describe someone who enters a chatroom but makes no input.) For those contributing to the chat, it is a bit like kissing your best friend in a greenhouse at night with the lights on – you just cannot see who is watching. Some virtual classrooms have the capability to send e-mails to other participants and to enter text chatrooms while the tutor is presenting. In practice, I see this used only rarely. The key to understanding why is to understand why asides happen. Asides happen because it is a way for two learners to build a relationship, show off to another learner, ask for help from someone they trust or relieve their feelings. Such asides have little to do with the tutor and occur where the tutor cannot participate. Possibilities are restricted to an exchange of e-mails or telephone numbers (assuming learners are separated by some distance). Some learning spaces provide an e-mail address that private

e-mails can be sent to. In most virtual learning spaces each party to an aside has to agree to future conversations taking place when neither understands the future benefit of such an interchange. Learners studying at home may be reluctant to share home numbers and may not have phone contact regularly at work. This remains a weak feature of on-line learning.

• Sub-group or one-to-one interactions occur during the social intervals required for refreshments that occur in every face-to-face course. Many learners will tell you that they find this the most valuable part of any residential course. Learners will relax in bars, coffee shops and restaurants because they are not focused on learning. Therefore they are more receptive to learning. They also engage in conversation with people like them in similar roles. People talk about their jobs and allow others to question them. Learners get answers that they need from people they can recognize as doing the same job that they do: no wonder they find these sessions helpful. Unlike e-mail help (which can be similar in content) these discussion sessions have no record or audit trail. The best alternative for on-line learning is for the tutor to create some virtual learning sets that have real problems to solve. This will encourage learners to swap contact details and engage in some sort of on-line discussion. From this beginning it should be possible to grow regular interactions between tutor–student and student–student.

Computer interaction has some advantages over classroom interaction (as well as many disadvantages). One advantage with the asynchronous debate is that every user who participates, is doing so at the time that is right for them. In a face-to-face situation there are many reasons why a person is not involved at the time, they may be reflecting, distracted by internal or external events, thinking about a future comment or be fearful or angry.

There are other reasons why someone may not interact in a bulletin board (discussion forum) or chatroom. I regard myself as disadvantaged with respect to keyboard fluency. I see many people around me who are clearly much more competent than myself. I also know of others who are less competent that I am. As a child I was expected to be articulate and numerate but not keyboard fluent. Perhaps for that reason I also find typing tiring. A chatroom exposes my lack of capability in that area, even though others might regard me as fluent; that is not how I feel about myself. Other reasons for lack of involvement might be associated with screen reading speed. These are both in addition to reasons associated with learning styles and personality. The use of a bulletin board gets round a lack of computer fluency but still leaves other reasons for a lack of involvement.

TUTOR TO STUDENT INTERACTION

It is apparent from the previous debate that a tutor has to take more control over virtual interactions than over real ones. It may be that as learners become more adept at using the Internet as a communication tool then this control will become enshrined in good manners and common sense behaviour. People may naturally discipline themselves to talk one at time and to notify the fact that they are lurking. Of course there are degrees of lurking. Lurkers may be actively writing notes, asleep, or observing closely what is going on. If as a tutor, we enter into a debate, we should not be so naive as to think we are interacting with everyone logged on. In the classroom situation, it is obvious when an individual becomes disengaged from the discussion. Even so, not all tutors have the perception to realize it. Consider how much more difficult it will be when the interaction is via a computer. Lack of input does not mean lack of engagement. If a tutor becomes worried that a learner is not engaging in debate then the best course of action is for the tutor to send a private e-mail or to make a phone call. The learner is protected in anonymity but given a prompt, if they are having technical problems then technical support can be made available (discreetly)! The tutor may gain some insight into how the learner is reacting and can tailor their response accordingly. Even with this type of one-to-one discussion this aspect of the learning interaction remains less in-depth than on a face-to-course. Not only does the tutor not appreciate the feelings and thoughts of the learner quite as well as when face-to-face, but the learner is not so well motivated by the personality of the tutor. Not observing the reactions of learners makes motivating them much more difficult. A good teacher's personal style will excite and enthuse and that will have an impact on the learner. Is the charisma of an excellent teacher and their enthusiasm for their topic diluted by electronic delivery?

CULTURAL BIAS

Another source of differences in the classroom is those which are culturally-based. For those readers living in Europe, cultural diversity will be apparent. Our view of other nationalities is based on stereotypes but quite real for all that. It is impossible to discuss culture differences without being accused of stereotyping. Americans are up-front and pushy, Germans are overly didactic, the Spanish are always found in groups and socialize at work a lot, the English keep themselves to themselves; these are just some of the stereotypes we hold on other nationalities. A previous chapter mentioned the history of the Internet and compared the different extent of take up. This indicated a North/South European divide and that may have some basis in cultural differences. It may mean that Northern Europe is colder and people spend more time indoors and consequently spend more time on the Internet. Any assessment of culture and its impact on learning requires some care but diversity of culture in the broadest sense will alter people's attitudes to learning and the methods of learning. It is a mistake to assume that cultural diversity is only based on ethnic or national differences. Within any one country, there will be regional differences, differences of upbringing and differences of age. We can think about stereotypes as a means of understanding those differences. The phrase 'laddish culture' is used to describe the attitudes of the young male to learning and other aspect of behaviour. The classroom may contain some who behave 'as lads' and some who take learning seriously and want to apply themselves. The skill of a good tutor is to manage these differences. The tools available to the tutor are non-discriminatory language, neutral body language, avoidance of actions or words that may cause an adverse reaction and a responsiveness to the feelings demonstrated by those in front of them. Can e-learning do as well and if so how?

INCIDENTAL LEARNING

Another feature of face-to-face group learning is the interaction outside the classroom. Ask people why they attend face-to-face courses. At least one response will include 'to meet other participants'. Evaluation forms will almost always include the phrase 'I learnt as much from the other participants as I did from the tutor.' What is learned will not have been laid down in the objectives for the course: it will be incidental to the content of the course.

Incidental learning may be described as a by-product of some other activity. It may occur during formal learning activities or from some non-learning activity (Marsick and Watkins, 1990, p. 12). By definition incidental learning is unplanned and outside the objectives that the learner and tutor/designer started with. Of itself, incidental learning is not likely to arise out of e-learning. That would require the e-learning material to react in some unexpected way and trigger unplanned responses in learners. However, from the learner's perspective they may gain skills that are incidental to their main purpose. This is likely to happen when the e-learning is part of a wider knowledge management structure, perhaps achieved by the simple expedient of adding many links to the World Wide Web to the learning material.

Incidental learning may well prove of greater benefit than the formal content. Conversations with other learners will lead in unexpected directions. One learner's question or comment will prompt the thinking of others and dredge otherwise unconnected snippets of knowledge. The e-learning enthusiast (by the way, I am one) talks about byte-sized learning elements, meta-tagged objects and chunking material. Yet imagine learners in a conversation with other learners. Remember these are the conversations valued by many who attend face-to-face training events. Learning will be picked up in small snatches of conversation. This is bite-sized learning over the doughnuts at coffee time. A single sentence or two in response to a question or comment and the listener gains a nugget of information directly relevant to issues he or she faces at the time. We are all accustomed to learning in this way and, it would seem, most of us value this type of learning.

Perhaps the greatest irony is that most of us fail to realize that we have learnt when we do so incidentally. Perhaps that is not surprising, as incidental learning is likely to be greatest when there is a high degree of interpersonal interaction with other learners. By definition, incidental learning is outside the scope of the planned objectives that we set ourselves as learners, unless the objectives are very broad. Incidental learning is a surprise, something that happens and therefore something we discover for ourselves. The action of discovery means that we own that bit of our learning more than if someone else 'tells' us the information. Discovery learning is a technique used in designing workplace assignments. The opportunity for discovery is contrived by the tasks that the learner completes as part of an assignment. An example of such an assignment was an induction training pack that required learners to carry out various tasks and to go and talk to various key individuals in their workplace. Some tasks were computer-orientated or required reading manuals. The conversations with work colleagues were felt to be the most useful part of the training pack. The irony of this feedback is that the designers constructed it so that these conversations took place but that the learners felt that they were suggesting an improvement because they did not learn as much from the reading material. This feedback mirrors the comments learners make on face-to-face courses about their co-learners and the conversations with them. Talking to someone else seems to help a learner place what is learned in context. This makes it more real. This reality lends emphasis and probably increases the motivation to learn or to put ideas into practice. So there is a pattern of incidental learning that is triggered largely by conversation with others and is outside the planned objectives of the learner.

I think it is unclear whether this learning is purely cognitive. On the surface these types of conversation between learners transfer intellectual knowledge, perhaps with some application of that knowledge in the cut-and-thrust of the debate. But if you listen to what learners say in this situation it includes phrases such as 'I met someone who is struggling with the same problems I face', 'It was good to know other people face the same challenges'; 'I feel I am not alone'. These are phrases associated with emotional needs and not intellectual ones. The theme associated with these comments is solidarity. The learner is not alone. Others are experiencing concern or achievement as they acquire new skills. There may also be a competitive element that is reinforced when others are struggling with topics. So peer support in learning arises out of conversations that may stimulate incidental learning and probably meets a learner's emotional needs. The challenge for e-learning is to provide peer support electronically in such a way as to stimulate learning outside the main objectives that have to be learned and also to ensure that support operates at an emotional as well as intellectual level.

Why do so many of us value incidental learning and what are the implications for e-learning particularly? Because incidental learning is unplanned we may choose to either accept or reject it. This means we have a choice and may feel more in control. Our decision to follow-up on an incidental item will be driven, perhaps by our curiosity, perhaps by an immediate recognition that we can apply the learning, perhaps to alleviate boredom with the main tasks or perhaps it has some immediate relevance to a previous problem. In the face-to-face classroom situation, this incidental learning arises either from discussion with others or because a stray thought enters our minds. I have already described the impact of conversation on learning. What I describe as stray thoughts are triggered by association. Perhaps a participant arrives on a course with an unrelated business problem worrying her or him. Halfway through the course a topic is being presented. This topic provides a parallel link to the business problem. Rather akin to the process of creativity I call the submerged log method (Hills, 2001, p. 114) this problem has been floating around in their minds, perhaps with solutions building. Suddenly a comment is made in the course or by a co-learner that brings that idea to the surface because the comment presents a solution to the unrelated business problem. The learner has translated an idea from one domain to another to solve a problem. Percy Shaw saw the reflection in the eyes of a cat and translated that into the design of Catseyes that are used to mark out lanes in today's modern roads. Incidental learning is creative, takes learners in unknown directions and solves problems. Learners make links and transfer learning from one topic area to another.

How may e-learning replicate the nature of conversation and the transfer of learning from one topic area to another? Software programs have been written so that a person exchanges sentences with a computer and firmly believes that he or she is 'talking' to a human being. The computer returns conversational phrases such as 'tell me more about that'. It will respond to certain trigger words such as family or parents and respond with 'so what was your relationship with your parents like?' This research was perhaps started by the thoughts of Alan Turing as to whether machines could think (Turing, 1950). This type of research is aimed at understanding the nature of artificial intelligence. This method of thinking has advanced ideas on what we can do with machines, or more strictly, what we can get them to do. The computer has to do more than respond to a key word or phrase with bland questions for incidental learning to happen. If conversations are to trigger incidental learning, then they must be free flowing and this happens with conversations with other people. What e-learning may contribute is an offer to a learner along the lines of: 'There is more information about topic X, would you like to see it?'. This is akin to using a search engine that offers more web pages like those it has already found in response to a search query. This is not the same as another learner saying: 'By the way did you know about Y?', or 'When I tried to do A at work then C happened'. Both of these are typical of what happens in incidental learning during casual conversations between learners. The ways in which co-learners may communicate like this are chatrooms, discussion boards and virtual classrooms. Of these virtual classrooms hold out the most promise, perhaps because they include audio. However, even these are stilted and conversation is not free-flowing. The options for true incidental learning are limited.

E-learning has one unique contribution to make to incidental learning that no other form of learning has. In the bibliography of this book, you will find reference to other books and articles. These references address topics that are incidental to the main theme of this book. However, if you choose to use these references, the action could hardly be described as spontaneous. At least one of my references was out-of-print at the time, so it might take a month or so to track down a copy. With e-learning hundreds of billions of documents are just one click away. How much more spontaneous do you want than that! When I use a search engine, two things are happening. First, I am trying to refine my choice of search words so that I find the item I am seeking. I have no way of knowing whether that item exists or not. Many similar items may exist, some of which are of dubious quality. So the first activity is one of searching, a predominantly right brain activity. I analyse and sort what I come across, as quickly as possible. This is predominantly left-brain activity. One way of distinguishing between left- and right-brain processing is to regard the right brain as a parallel processor and the left brain as a serial processor (see Russell, 1979, p. 54). While I am browsing, as well as analysing and sorting information relevant to my objectives, I also see some interesting snippets of information that may excite my curiosity or perhaps something that might be useful elsewhere. This is a typical right brain activity, recognizing patterns and building relationships between topics. This is a process of synthesis rather than analysis. This incidental learning requires more personal effort and drive than the crumbs of learning we may pick up over coffee by chatting to other people in similar jobs or with similar interests. In that sense incidental learning through e-learning requires direction and effort that is not required when it occurs in the classroom.

Summary

One of the many merits of e-learning is that it can be studied any time in any place. Learners do not have to go far from their place of work, they do not have to join with other learners in classrooms. Yet this social interaction with other learners brings many benefits. Learning is not just an intellectual activity, it is also an emotional activity, both in terms of the motivation of individuals and also what is learned. Many interpersonal skills require emotions to be managed and controlled. Being and interacting with other people generates much of the emotional energy that people have. The benefits that other people bring to the learning situation can be identified in seven areas.

(1) Another individual may act as a role model by demonstrating the required behaviour. We all have a natural tendency to mimic or follow people whom we perceive as knowing more than we do. The truth of this can be seen by watching people in a strange city, who will, for example, cross the road when others do. Role models do not have to be humans. There are many examples of puppets used to help children learn verbal and numeracy skills. It might be said that young children's television is dominated by cartoons and puppet characters.

(2) Other humans are used as information sources. This is akin to the role model but is usually much more a straightforward request for help. Most of us still find person-to-person dialogue to be more constructive in helping us learn than a person-to-computer

dialogue. Both parties benefit, since the individual providing the information gains an improved feeling of self-esteem by providing help and receiving the gratitude. It is easier for the learner because they have the information delivered to them exactly as they want it by continuing with the question and answer session to refine the relevance of the information that they receive.

(3) Other individuals provide a vital source of feedback to the learner. Learners get feedback from many sources, by observing the facial expressions and body language of people they are talking to and for physical skills from the environment around them, be that from hitting the ground when learning to cycle or from the computer when you are learning to type. The value that we give to feedback depends upon our respect for the intellect of the person giving the feedback and also on our emotional ties to them. By its very nature, computer feedback carries less impact than that from another individual. This may be of benefit in the learning situation.

(4) A specialized form of feedback is praise. The value we place on praise is based upon our intellectual assessment of the importance of the individual or system giving praise and on our emotional links to them. For example, praise from a senior work colleague is always valued, unless it is delivered in a patronizing or demeaning fashion. It is particularly difficult for a computer system to deliver praise because of a complete absence of any emotional tie. The reward of getting things right is usually sufficient for most e-learners. If they do seek praise it would need to be from another person.

(5) Another useful role performed by other people within the learning process is that of discussion and debate. Here it is important for the learner to be able to express their views and their thinking on the basis of their learning. This helps them to reformulate and embed the concepts being learned so that they can be understood in a number of different ways. The benefit is as much in talking to others and having them listen, as it is in listening to them responding both to the learner's arguments and views, as well as expressing their own arguments and views about the topics being learned. An important element in this discussion is the emotional recognition that other people feel the same way about what is being learned. To put it another way, a learner can get a major morale boost when they know somebody else also fails to understand a particular concept that they are struggling with. This morale boost reduces their anxiety thereby making it easier for them to focus on the learning. Ideally this discussion and debate is within a community of learners.

(6) Ideally any discussion sessions with fellow learners will progress the learner towards the point at which they feel they are part of a community of learners. We can gain solidarity from recognizing that we are not on our own. This brings with it a sense of team solidarity. Each individual will gain a sense of being part of a larger effort if they are sharing their learning with a number of others.

(7) Finally, we come to the role that the tutor fulfils in the relationship with the learner. This is much more than just someone who imparts knowledge. If that were all it took then every university lecturer would be an equally good teacher. A moment's reflection about your own education will make you realize that who taught a topic was as important as what the topic was. Many of us have been lucky to be exposed to a charismatic teacher who provided us with the motivation to study a particular subject. charismatic tutors do two things: they are enthusiastic about their subjects, making it lively and entertaining; they also demonstrate that they care about individual learners as individuals. Clearly no computer system can make a learner feel cherished and wanted. However, a computer learning application can bring about a feeling of

excitement and can generate enthusiasm in the learner. The main design features that will do this include the judicious use of humour, games and role-playing scenarios and a high degree of sensory impact using visual images, audio and movement. An e-learning program should generate excitement without tipping the learner into anxiety. This is something a face-to-face trainer would monitor naturally. They would get feedback in terms of body language from the learner and would know at what point the learner's excitement position became a concern. Computerized programs do not have this luxury but the simple expediency of ensuring that all learners have a get out option from any simulation or game or sequence of frames has to be a basic design feature for all e-learning. Another factor that makes it easier for learners to remember material is the use of incongruity. The placing or using of unusual or inappropriate screen objects is a simple and effective way of aiding the learner's memory. We remember things that are unusual.

Computers do not have a personality and therefore it is not possible for there to be a personality clash between a learner and e-learning material, or that, at least, is how it appears. In fact, a learner who prefers to reflect or theorize may be irritated by the need to complete a practical exercise or some activity before they have had the time, or perhaps are allowed to, absorb information and concepts. The really excellent tutor will make allowances for these preferences. It is necessary for e-learning material to be capable of making similar allowances. This should be perfectly possible since e-learning material only has to deal with one learner at a time. It is complicated by the fact that hundreds, possibly thousands, of different learners will use the same material. The material needs to be designed in such a way that different personality types can access the material in different ways.

The real contribution that e-learning makes over and above previous examples of technology-based learning is that of the communication aspect. Communication between learners occurs in face-to-face training and we can find ways in which this is replicated in e-learning. In a classroom situation we have interaction in the learning group as a whole. This is invariably controlled and managed by the tutor and similar interactions can be replicated in e-learning. First, we have a number of synchronous style events, which include video conferencing, telephone conferencing, Internet-based virtual classrooms and text-only chatrooms. The quality and richness of the interaction clearly matches the level of sophistication of the technology that is used. All are considerably more stilted than interaction in the classroom. The tutor has to take a much more pro-active role in managing interruptions and interventions. The style of a Victorian classroom is much more appropriate for the twenty-first century virtual classroom than the interactions we might find in any modern syndicate room. The tutor must control who talks and when. The situation is somewhat different in a chatroom, although unmanaged chat will produce a very confusing blur of text. The tutor will remember the contributions made to learning by others; role models, feedback, answering questions, praise, debate and a feeling of solidarity. All may be replicated in e-learning although all are 'less rich' in emotional content.

In the classroom, we may frequently see casual conversations between individual learners. Whereas in a classroom it may be perfectly natural to turn to your neighbour and exchange a few words, in any one of the electronic synchronous or asynchronous whole group discussions this is much more difficult. The two possibilities are that individual learners exchange private e-mails or pick up the telephone and talk to each other. Having done that, who knows, perhaps if they live not too far apart they will end up meeting somewhere. This has happened in the past with learning cohorts, where particular individuals have chosen to make the effort to meet each other. In many cases this happens after the cohort has completed any studying they are doing and the 'class' has dispersed.

A much more difficult interaction to replicate is the sub-group discussion that occurs in the social intervals required for refreshments. This is one of the situations in which most incidental learning takes place. People invariably talk about their jobs and in the process trigger questions from other people and somewhere in the interaction someone receives a little piece of knowledge that they find useful that they had not expected to receive. A particular issue with interaction between learners in virtual sets is that the members of such learning communities may be from anywhere in the world. There may be significant cultural differences between attendees that are completely hidden from each other. This can also occur with a learning community which is from one country. For example, age differences are not apparent in a virtual learning set, unless they are specifically stated and yet such age differences will have a significant impact on people's attitudes to e-learning and perhaps their competencies in using systems.

The final benefit of traditional learning that I mention which may be lacking in e-learning is that which is described as incidental learning. For many learners the most valuable part of a face-to-face course will be what they learn from others. Finding someone else who is struggling with the same problem as you carries significant benefit, both emotionally and intellectually. The closest parallel in e-learning is the ability for the learner to roam freely or with direction in the World Wide Web. For the incidental learning to be valuable this roaming must be directed towards task and job areas that are of concern to the learner.

4 *Observing Learners*

Visual presentation aspects of e-learning

The e-learning industry is a relatively new phenomenon. Chapter 2 with references to the history of training shows that the use of various mechanical systems and technology tools to support the learning process has a long history, in fact since the 1930s. During this period, there has been some research into the use of computers as a learning aid. There is also a body of observation and practical experience. The purpose of this book is to draw on past research and experience and apply that to the future of e-learning design. We therefore need to draw on the historical perspective and ensure that we can learn from the past.

Some universal truths have emerged from experience; for example the often-quoted benefit of a more media-rich experience. It has been said that we remember 20 per cent of what we read, 30 per cent of what we hear, 40 per cent of what we see, 50 per cent of what we say, 60 per cent of what we do and 90 per cent of what we see, hear, say and do (Rose and Nicholl, 1997, p. 142). The actual percentages vary with different sources. The principle seems to be universally accepted. Research on visual memory produces some very sound evidence that most of us have an exceptionally accurate visual memory. Russell (1979, p. 114) reports on research conducted by Haber (1970) where individuals were shown a series of photographic slides. 2,560 slides were used and one hour later the subjects were shown 280 pairs of slides, one of which was taken from the original series of 2,560. Individuals were asked which member of each pair was from the original series. On average they recognized between 85 per cent and 95 per cent of the original slides. This represents an astonishing capacity of visual memory to recognize previous images. The human capacity to recognize an individual's face, perhaps someone you have not seen for a number of years, is the most obvious example of our ability to remember images.

This is even more powerful where the images actually do something. Again based on research from 1972 (Russell, 1979, p. 112) subjects were given two sets of 24 words to remember. They were asked to remember these words in pairs using two different techniques. For the first half they were simply asked to remember the words. For the second half they were asked to create images in their minds of the two words in such a way that the images interacted. For example, if the nouns had been book and nail the image might have been a nail being driven through a book or a nail being used as a pointer along the lines of text in a book. The important element was that the images had to interact and do something.

Immediate tests of what was remembered showed that 80 per cent of the imagined pairs that interacted were remembered against only 33 per cent of the other pairs. This highlights the importance of movement and meaning in memory. The benefit of a richer learning experience with more visual images and more action is interpreted within technology-delivered learning as a need for video presentations. Video is relatively easy to design and produce. The design process is essentially linear and therefore has greater similarity with a face-to-face training event than computer programmed material. The majority of classroom tutors can convert their classroom sessions into video elements relatively easily. The techniques for creating both drama and comedy within linear video sequences are also well understood.

There are many talented people in the television and video industry who have turned their skills to creating video films and sequences that help people learn. Why is video not more prevalent in e-learning? At the moment we have a technology barrier that makes it difficult for e-learning to be media-rich. Undoubtedly video will be used in e-learning in the future. The ease with which behaviour can be demonstrated and cause and effect shown make it an attractive learning medium. The introduction of DVD and PCs able to play DVD discs make it much easier for this format to be delivered via computer. As with current videotapes, DVD sessions will be essentially passive in nature. They will be much shorter sequences interrupted by interactions in much the same way that interactive discs were. It is important that learners can do something and take action as part of the learning process. A report completed by the National Physical Laboratory (Rengger and Turner, 1988) recommended that as much time should be spent in active sessions as in reading and observing and learners must interact with the technology. Video material is essentially non-interactive and therefore needs to be interspersed with tasks, such as answering questions or selecting routes through the material.

Video is not essential for exploiting the capacity of the brain in remembering visual images. Although video may be conceptually easy to create, it is still awkward to deliver. The end-user technology platform has to be capable of playing either a DVD, CD-ROM or have a broadband connection. The user has to wear headphones or to sit in a location where the audio will not annoy other people. There may be few problems about delivering this in the home environment but there are problems associated with the work environment, be it office, factory, shop, warehouse or outdoors. The electronic delivery of video through local area networks requires a technology investment that few companies will be willing to do for learning purposes. The increased occurrence of broadband connection to the home and to schools will make this type of resource much more numerous in the future.

However, early examples of e-learning are much less media-rich, being predominantly text. There is no need for them to lack visual imagery. Designers do not have to wait for the wider availability of video material in order to present learners with visual images that they can see, interact with and remember more easily. Simple but meaningful graphics can be included with text material but the most common example of a visual image used to convey information is that of the mind map. For a full explanation of a mind map see Buzan (1989), although Figure 3.1 on page 59 is a rudimentary example. E-learning gives us the opportunity to create images that we can interact with. Past research shows that both the presentation of a visual image and the ability to interact with that image makes it easier for people to remember. Both design techniques are capable of being created within current browser technology and the average bandwidth limitation that both home users and many companies are constrained by.

The learner's need for control

An essential truth which has emerged from past experience is that the learner should be in control of that which they are learning. One drawback of both video material and many face-to-face presentations is that the learner may cease to feel that the material is relevant, or indeed interesting. It is all too easy for the learner to disengage mentally while remaining there physically. The power of e-learning is that at these moments the learner can interact and direct themselves to other material that they are more interested in. The technology in web browsers and the whole ethos of the Internet means that it is much easier for learners to control what they see and read on the screen. The ability to search, enquire, control and direct is a major step forward. Web technology encourages us to design in this way and this is something that designers should exploit. It is in this area that e-learning tends to blur into knowledge management. There is a significant growth in learning resource websites that make it easier for the learner to search and enquire. It is useful to know how learners might have behaved in the past when presented with a computer system that they have a degree of control over in terms of accessing material to learn from. There are two areas of previous research that I believe are both significant and relevant, although neither directly translates to current e-learning systems. The e-learning concept is too new to have a significant body of research for designers to draw on. We must therefore look back further and interpret previous research. The research I intend to review and interpret for its relevance to e-learning goes back in one case to 1990 and in the other to 1980.

Minimalist research

The research published in 1990 is by John Carroll and led to his developing the minimalist instructional theories for practical computer skills. Carroll made an in-depth study based on observation into how people learn to use computer systems. I believe that the research observations present a double relevance to the modern world of e-learning. People were observed using computer systems and were observed learning. E-learning is delivered through computer systems. The caveat is that the research was conducted at a time when computer systems were new. People had much less familiarity with them. Apple had only just developed the graphical user interface. It was therefore a new concept that few people were familiar with. Most computer systems were text-based with line-by-line entry. Therefore, there were many hurdles to people using computer systems that do not exist now. There is much greater familiarity with computers in the general population than when Carroll did his research.

I remember a sublime moment recently, which demonstrates this very clearly. While I was shopping, I overhead two elderly ladies who were animatedly discussing some point of mutual interest. Initially I thought they were talking about mutual acquaintances or the next social occasion they were looking forward to. The snippet that I overheard was one lady saying to the other 'and you put the little pointy thing on the button in the corner'. Clearly one was explaining to the other how to use a mouse and click on a button, the last thing I might have expected two elderly ladies to be discussing in the supermarket.

In the late 1980s, one could never imagine two such people discussing the operation of computer systems as a social activity. Notwithstanding the fact that Carroll's research is quite historical, it is based on observations about what people actually do when presented with a computer. I believe it still has important lessons for present day design.

I believe the second area of relevance is that Carroll studied people who were focused on practical tasks. They wanted to learn to use a computer system so that they could carry out tasks. There was clear evidence from all the subjects studied by Carroll that they were not interested in the computer system *per se*. They wanted to do something with it. This desire typifies adult learners who bring their own agendas to the learning situation. We are finally seeing learning products emerging into the user IT-skills market that reflect this desire. Far too many IT-skills training packages and courses are aimed at the ability to use a particular computer package. There is a plethora of training packages in basic spreadsheets, advanced spreadsheets and more advanced spreadsheets! What we see much less of is training packages and courses which might be labelled 'Using spreadsheets to prepare accounts for a small business', 'Using a word processor to prepare a report'. These practical skill learning packages and courses are beginning to appear on the market. They reflect what Carroll found, that computers are tools that enable people to do something other than use computers.

The learners that Carroll studied used instructional manuals and computer tutorials in a self-study environment. Many e-learning systems replicate the function of an instructional manual. They have the advantage of being interactive which a manual is not. They consist of words and pictures which is true of an instructional manual. A designer of e-learning material is encouraged to provide links to other parts of the manual, which the writer of the instructional manual is not encouraged to do. I use the word encouraged in the sense that best practice in web design means that links are in-built as a natural part of the design process and it is relatively easy to do so. Providing cross-references and page numbers in an instructional manual is awkward as these books are frequently updated by means of inserting new pages into a loose leaf format and it is of course for this reason that most manuals use a chapter and section breakdown of page numbers.

A limiting factor of Carroll's observations was that he focused on people who were learning to use computer systems. They were learning the skill of using applications that were novel and strange. There is much relevant material in his observations that apply to the design and creation of e-learning. Certainly, most e-learning at the moment is focused on PC training. It is reported that about 70 per cent of current e-learning is aimed at PC skills. Carroll's work has direct relevance to that area of skills and some relevance to the use of e-learning in general.

Holist and serialist research

The second area of research that I would like to draw on is the work by Gordon Pask. This research was conducted through the 1960s and 1970s before desktop computers actually existed. He used an electro-mechanical system to research the way learners interacted with frame-based material. His work led to the development of the concept of the two learning strategies of 'holist' and 'serialist'. His observations showed that learners had a tendency to prefer one or other of these learning strategies. (See Hills, 2001, p. 87.) Pask was working with very primitive systems and his learners were much more limited in what they could do compared to a learner with current e-learning material in front of them. I believe the research is useful for modern day designers mainly because Pask was specifically interested in the future of interactions between learners and computer systems. Pask is perhaps better known as a cybernetician, as such, his work has a very specific computer-focus. I believe that an examination of the research work of both Pask and Carroll, their observations particularly and the conclusions they came to, are important background for modern e-learning design.

Minimalist instructional theory

John Carroll observed learners of computer systems. They were aiming to complete practical real tasks with computer systems that were new to them. One group of about 30 had instructional manuals which were written for the purposes of self-instruction. Their learning was based entirely on these manuals. Carroll was primarily concerned with the way in which people learned to do real tasks. His view was that 'training, to the greatest extent possible, should involve real tasks.' (Carroll, 1990, p. 8). Carroll was interested in the way in which people would go about those real tasks as they were learning them. The manuals were lengthy and detailed covering every eventuality, this may not be true of existing e-learning material. The current level of technology makes it easy to produce a large quantity of text. The production of text tends to lead designers towards theoretical explanations rather than practical. The two examples that an e-learning designer might look towards, text and the web, both present significant quantities of text to users. The tendency for e-learning designers is to replicate that approach and produce yet more information perhaps structured in a more instructional style. There is clear evidence from Carroll's research that that is not what most learners want, at least in situations where they are presented with practical tasks. One of the subjects that he observed, commented on the self-study instructional manual; 'this is just information'. (Carroll, 1990, p. 8). A number of e-learning systems tend to display quantities of screen-based information that might be regarded in the same light by learners. Of course there is a place for such material. The Chartered Institute of Personnel and Development survey (2001, available from the author) reported that the majority of professionals use the Internet as a knowledge resource. While it may be true that certain professional and academic groups see value in acquiring additional knowledge, most learners learn because they want to do something new. Their focus is not the acquisition of knowledge but the novel task they are carrying out. The learning is not the end in itself, it is the means to an end. Most individuals, and I can speak for myself here as well, want to get the best return from the least effort and this is exactly what Carroll's research demonstrated.

His research was conducted at a time when computing was moving from the province of IT and computing specialists to becoming a widespread office tool and consumer item. He brought subjects into a laboratory and set them to the task of learning to use the software on the computer systems. As I have already pointed out this gives the research a very narrow focus. E-learning is used for more than the task of learning to use computer systems. However, e-learning is delivered through the desktop and how people use computers is very relevant to designing e-learning.

The subjects Carroll used were people whose normal jobs would require them to use the new office systems. Carroll collected information both by observing what people did and asked the users to think aloud and explain what they were thinking and perhaps what they were feeling. This is a frequently-used experimental method. Users are brought into a usability lab and observed. They are given real tasks to do in front of real computer applications and observed in the process. Each user would get the same sequence of exercises. My own experience includes using these experimental methods of observation and 'thinking aloud'. My job at the time was to develop training for the introduction of new computer systems into a banking network. The best test for the training material is to take a user from a bank branch and to ask them to work through the training material in the usability lab. After the training session, users are asked to complete tasks they had been trained in, on mock-ups of the software being developed. This provides a good objective test as to the effectiveness of the training. The combination of close observation and users thinking aloud provides evidence as to its effectiveness and ease of use. It also demonstrates the way in which people like to learn.

Both from my own observations and those of Carroll there are clearly learning problems associated with material that is written like an instructional manual. The tendency of the writer of a system manual is to ensure every eventuality is covered. There is a desire to provide a comprehensive guide. The result: too much material and not necessarily organized in a manner that is relevant to the learner. Hypertext does make it easier for the learner to find the single item that is relevant to the problem they are struggling with. Converting text to hypertext does not solve the problem that learners do not do well when following instructions in self-study material. Why not?

Carroll's initial study worked with six subjects; no one was able to complete the required tasks without serious difficulty. This and further studies revealed a general pattern to some of the difficulties early users faced when presented with the learning task.

EXPECTATIONS

The majority of Carroll's users were unrealistically optimistic about how easy they would find the various computing tasks that they were presented with. At the time we can lay some of the blame for these unrealistic expectations on the advertising and hype that was associated with new desktop systems. E-learning suffers from exactly the same problem. Advertising and promotional hype raises users' expectations way beyond the levels at which e-learning systems can actually deliver. There is a mismatch between expectation and delivery that results in one of two responses.

Most of Carroll's subjects, who were office workers, responded by blaming themselves and allowing their feelings of failure and frustration to make them feel stupid. The other group of subjects who were members of various professions blamed the training material rather than their own misunderstandings. They were willing to discard the training material as 'faulty'. These opposite views represent the two ways in which people view the world around them. Those who are self-confident and sure of themselves will strengthen that self-confidence and assume errors in the learning system. Those people, who are perhaps more accustomed to allowing others to make their decisions, are more likely to turn the blame on themselves even when the training material is less than helpful. The expectations that we all have of e-learning are set very high by the current hype and promotional activity of suppliers. Even within organizations the need to market e-learning aggressively is driven by the need to promote its use. Every organization that implements e-learning internally will include a marketing and promotional activity as part of the implementation process. As I indicate this is a double-edged sword. The message must be enthusiastic to encourage people to use e-learning. This makes it more likely that users will be disappointed with the actual experience.

INTERPTETATION BY USERS

Carroll found that new users would often lose all sense of place and structure in the applications they were using and in the training material supporting those applications. Nowadays every good quality website has a site map and the majority of good quality e-learning packages have a menu system and display on the screen a visual sign of where the user is within that menu system. Both approaches assume that the user will make the same sense of the site map and from the visual indications as the designer intended. The only way to find out whether that is so is to ask users what their interpretations are of either the site map or the visual display of one's menu position. The opportunities for misunderstanding are many and varied in the communication process. This is rife in personal face-to-face communication and there we have the advantage of body language and gesture enhancing the communication. The scope for misunderstanding must be much greater in computer-to-individual communication.

In team-based learning eight potential qualities of misunderstanding in communication were outlined. Five of these are emotional in context and 3 are intellectual. (Hills, 2001, chapter 7). Since some of the emotional causes of misunderstanding are based on the choice of language used, we can expect both emotional and intellectual causes for misunderstanding. Carroll reports a number of examples of where users completely misinterpret the vocabulary that is used. This would be particularly prevalent in early applications of computer systems where computer specialists had created the jargon. Much of this jargon has now entered common use. For example, ten years ago few of us would have known what a cursor was. I have referred earlier to an example of where I overheard a reference to 'the little pointy thing'. However, there are still opportunities for designers to create a vocabulary that leads directly to misunderstanding. An example relates to the introduction of a relational database for bank customer information. The system designers used the phrase 'sole customer' to refer to a relationship within the customer database. This was extremely confusing to branch staff since to them 'sole customer' was an individual, not a relationship within a computer database. Carroll quotes the concern learners had over the use of the word 'default'. Prior to the frequent use by everybody of computer systems, the term default would have meant to renege on a legal agreement. Nowadays many of us would accept it as the original settings of a computer system. As might be expected, Carroll found that this confusion about terminology created great difficulties for learners and diverted them from the main learning task. Even now, users may become unnecessarily alarmed about messages that say: 'an illegal operation' or 'fatal error'.

LEARNERS' RESPONSE TO DIRECTIONS

Carroll found that in the self-study mode, learners did not follow instructions either willingly or well. In the face-to-face tutor situation, common decency and reasonable manners will encourage the learner to do what the tutor asks of them. At least we might expect that in classrooms and groups of adults. There is no such constraining factor within a piece of e-learning. There is no tutor who gets upset when the learner does something completely different. Learners have greater freedom to follow their own styles of learning in the self-study situation, be it print or e-learning.

Presenting learners with a sequence of logical and well ordered steps in a learning process is ineffective because learners jump around material, skip bits and generally behave in ways that respond to their own goals and concerns. From a designer's perspective we may well expect learners to behave in an erratic fashion. Usually this is triggered by boredom as many learners do not like lengthy introductions or overviews. They jump ahead to an exercise well before they understand the requirements of that exercise. There is a need to do something, to have something to show for the learning activity. In other cases learners are distracted by an item that looks interesting and are easily diverted from the main task. In general it appears that learners do not like explanatory material. It is clear from the results of Carroll's observations that no e-learning designer can expect learners to follow a didactic approach. The designer may have very good intentions about leading the learner through a learning exercise, but the evidence suggests that learners are unlikely to adhere to the designer's intentions. The designer must allow the learner to practice lots of activities but also choose activities that they feel are relevant.

LEARNERS' INTERPRETATIONS

Carroll observed that learners may become quite determined and fixed in the concepts that they establish as they learn. Where this concept differs from the real world learners will be quite persistent in trying to change their view of what is around them to match ideas that they have developed. For example, Carroll quotes one learner who repeated a mistake 44 times. The error was caused because a learner was trying to access a word processing document using the same method by which it had been created. The learner failed to appreciate the distinction between 'revise' and 'create'. This particular class of error may not be relevant to modern computer or e-learning systems. The example illustrates the tenacity with which learners will cling to that which they consider familiar. We may expect learners to use tried and familiar routes through e-learning websites, much as they do any website, even though the designer may incorporate short-cuts. It is also unlikely that a designer will pre-guess the misconceptions that individual learners may have. The essential point to notice is that any group of learners will have many varied pre- and misconceptions. This will affect the way they interact with the material. Learners deduce and reason as they work through study material. As well as different misconceptions they will also establish a personal agenda of questions and queries. Every classroom trainer will tell you that different students have different questions. Furthermore it is very likely that in any learning group there will be some learners who will, with confidence, answer questions from other individuals within their group irrespective of whether the answers are valid or not. Learners also develop personal goals that are shaped by their understanding and the deductions they make while learning. It has to be accepted as a given that no e-learning designer can predict the way in which learners will interact with their material. Agenda and question and answer choices may be limited, but the designer cannot limit the thought processes that go on in the head of a learner.

ERRORS

It is no surprise that Carroll observed his users making many errors. Current day computing systems have simpler graphical interfaces. Imagine the situation when Carroll was conducting his research, where one tiny error can be missed by the learner and only reveal itself several steps later. In the particular case of training people to use computer applications Carroll found that the instructional manuals at the time were less than helpful. The self-study guides consisted of explanations where one step followed another. An early error would not necessarily be detected until the student had got to a point where the instructional manual became meaningless. Users were unable to backtrack to their original error, however, solving the problem became the learning goal.

Many modern training simulations prevent this situation by allowing learners to take only the correct route through the simulation. Any time they try to carry out an inappropriate activity they are blocked, with an appropriate message. This may apply to any training simulation, not just those of systems. Imagine, for example, a simulation of an interview sequence. Although a learner can be asked with great frequency through the simulation what their response is to a certain action, they may be constrained to only choose the correct response. If they select an incorrect response they receive a feedback message explaining why it is incorrect. Preventing learners from making errors or seeing the consequences of those errors impoverishes learning.

A simulated meeting sequence was used to train bank employees in managing meetings. This particular simulation displayed the results of many of the inappropriate responses of the user who was playing the role of chairperson. There were multiple routes through the meeting sequence. There was a sub-set of learners who deliberately selected incorrect responses. They may well have worked through the simulation, initially making what they believed to be the correct responses. They then went back and repeated the exercise exploring what would happen if they selected inappropriate actions. This technique is also used, frequently to humorous effect, in many training videos. Management and interpersonal scenarios are shown where participants in the 'drama' behave inappropriately with inevitable results of poor or humorous performance. The popularity of this type of training reveals how useful making errors is, especially in a safe and blame free environment.

Observation of learners demonstrate that they find errors helpful providing they know they make them or they result in only trivial consequences. Errors are a natural part of the learning process and although prompt feedback should be given, there are situations where a learner should be allowed to explore the consequences of those errors. We might describe this as the experimental method. Carroll specifically describes one learner who ignored much of the systematic instructional material and conducted a series of experiments with the system interface to help their understanding of the computer software. For example, to understand the wastebasket the learner threw away files and then opened the wastebasket to check whether he would find those objects in the wastebasket. The learner was confused by the dimming of display objects. He observed its connection to the position of the mouse by experimentation. This particular learner carried out a number of similar experimental tasks and as a result succeeded in creating an understanding of the system for himself.

The weakness of didactic instruction

The system's approach to training has a long pedigree. It starts with the introduction of classroom training, in some cases replacing the apprenticeship approach, required to meet the mass training needs of the Industrial Revolution. Factory schools were created to train employees in the particular skills of running various production lines. Both World Wars created a need to train large numbers of new workers in a wide variety of skills. This created a need for a systematic approach that was built upon later by the work of Gagne (1965) and Skinner (1968). The well-understood training cycle works from an understanding of business goals, through performance gap analysis, to identifying training needs and setting objectives.

Objectives are clearly expressed in behavioural terms. It is considered axiomatic that objectives are stated in terms by which their achievement can be recognized. The system's approach then makes an assumption that objectives can be broken down into a series of sub-skills. A simple example would be driving a car with a manual gearbox, there are a set of actions and procedures which must be followed in order to move the car from A to B. These have to be mastered before we move to the next skill of moving the car safely, taking due account of all traffic conditions. The underlying actions include being able to select the right gear, press the accelerator and clutch together so that a smooth start can be achieved and subsequently the driver can change gear smoothly. One then has to add the skill of using the brake pedal and clutch together to bring the car to a smooth halt. On top of that there is the requirement to turn the car from left to right by use of the steering wheel. The system's approach to training would encourage us to train someone in the use of the gear lever, clutch and accelerator, until they had achieved mastery of this task. When mastery is achieved learners may then move on to mastery of the steering wheel, then dealing in traffic conditions.

This is not done for two reasons. In most cases it is impractical. Agreed, given a disused airfield and a long runway it would be quite possible for a new driver to spend a couple of hours practicing the specific skill of gear and clutch without being able to steer. Someone else would have to turn the car round at the beginning and end of each trip down the runway. Commonsense tells us that most novice drivers would find this intensely boring and demotivating. What happens in practice is that the complete skill of moving the car from A to B is practiced in safe conditions where the instructor can take control of both the clutch and the brake. In fact, the underlying physical skill of clutch control is underpinned by the instructor, so the student can practice other skills associated with manoeuvring the car, such as turning the steering wheel, indicating and keeping a look out for hazards. The concept that an objective will be decomposed into sub-skills that are then used to derive a curriculum sequence is not practised in this simple case. Furthermore, the underlying skills are not practiced and mastered before the learner moves on to the more complex skills in order to achieve the main objective. The system's approach 'addresses itself to the logical and hierarchical decomposition of overall instructional objectives into target objectives and the decomposition of those into enabling objectives' (Carroll, 1990, p. 79, quoting Gagne and Briggs, 1979, pp. 23–39). If this method is followed in instructional design then all the learner has to do is to follow the steps. If they get each step right they will progress through the learning. This is very much the concept embodied in programmed learning where very small steps are taught and tested. The learner has to get each one right before they move on to the next step.

The observations that Carroll made very clearly proved that people do not follow steps in this way. From the very start adults have their own agenda, they want to take their own actions, frequently short-circuiting training material, jumping about within it and simply failing to behave in ways that the designer expects. It is significant that one area in which the system's approach has been successful is within a military environment. One only has to observe a squad practising drill to see that they are trained in the simple procedures of marching in step, halting on command and marching on command. This is then followed by straightforward left and right turns. It is only when these basic skills are mastered that the squad will move on to more complex drill manoeuvres such as forming squad and left or right flank. The military have, of course, a very disciplined approach and therefore learners are expected to do what they are told. The didactic approach that assumes an obedient learner also transfers the responsibility for learning from the learner to the designer. This may have certain validity in a face-to-face situation, where the tutor and learner can engage in a dialogue, but it has little relevance for any form of distance learning and self-study material.

How might we expect adults to behave in a situation where someone else has taken responsibility for their learning? When one individual takes responsibility for another this is a parental action. An understanding of a transactional analysis (see Hills, 2001, pp. 110–112) indicates that the likely response to a parental statement or action is a childish response. This is very clearly demonstrated by one of the observations from Carroll 'one learner, when instructed to read a passage but not do anything, exclaimed, "I'm tempted to do it anyway and then see if I can get out"'. This was a middle-aged professional who had become irritated and constrained by being asked to perform 'trivial steps taken out of the meaningful context' (Carroll, 1990, p. 76). This, of course, is not just a childish response, although we may see features of childish behaviour in it. It is evidence of a learner seeking to establish meaning in what they are being asked to learn. Adult learners come to learning situations with their own agendas, they have tasks to perform. In a face-to-face situation they can challenge and discuss with their tutor to seek the relevance of the learning topic to the objectives they have set themselves. If they fail in that process they are likely to disengage from the learning situation in the classroom. Self-study material does not have the opportunity for this challenge and debate between the learner and tutor. E-learning of course does have the facility for this tutor/student dialogue to take place, provided e-learning is supported in some means by a tutor.

What learners might say

In Figure 4.1, I paraphrase what learners might say in relation to the various situations that Carroll observed. Each one of us will have different preferences for taking control, for acting rather than reading through instructions or for not listening. Like any new initiative,

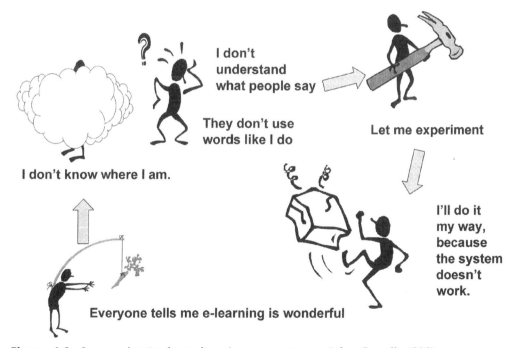

Figure 4.1   Learners' attitudes to learning computer use (after Carroll, 1990)

e-learning has been oversold. In that sense it is like every computer application, so Carroll's observation that learner's expectations are unrealistically high is true and that most learners blame the application rather than themselves. Every screen based application has the potential for the user to get lost in something they cannot see, even when each screen is labelled. Finally learners experiment, perhaps immediately perhaps after a time to establish theories about what will happen, perhaps plunging straight in, perhaps getting someone else to accompany them!

Minimalist design

Carroll was particularly concerned with the task of training individuals to use computer systems. IT application and systems training is a major part of e-learning content. I believe his observations may be applied in the wider context of all e-learning material. I will briefly summarize the ideas that Carroll applied to the IT application learning task and relate it to a wider context. Carroll experimented with the concept of guided exploration. This has some similarity with the concept of discovery learning in that learners are given goals and encouraged to explore for themselves how they achieve those goals. Carroll designed a series of cards that gave people tasks that were relevant to the job that they wished to do, as opposed to the working of the computer system they were going to use to achieve that task. In all, there were 25 guided exploration cards and users were able to select the order in which they would do them. All the tasks were related to each other and a learning designer placed them in a hierarchy and priority order. Carroll left it to the learners to select the order in which they would work on the tasks. This meant they assumed responsibility for their own learning. It is, of course, straightforward to replicate this approach in e-learning since each card would equate to an e-learning frame. Using the cards could be even simpler since links can be provided between associated cards. The approach he used showed significant advantages in speed of learning and effectiveness over the didactic instructional manual.

What started as an experiment led to the creation of material that was of considerable instructional value. We can see the guided exploration technique working in other areas where individuals are given assignments to complete in the workplace. The assignments are associated with real tasks that the learners know they have to perform. They use what resources are around them, such as colleagues and perhaps reference manuals. It seems the significant difference is that they take control and assume responsibility for the order in which they learn and the way in which they learn.

Following the success of the cards, Carroll moved on to designing the minimal manual. This only contained task-orientated material, with no additional explanations and was as brief as possible. Another concept that he explored was software that he described as 'training wheels'. Portions of an applications function were blocked off and disabled so learners were able to practise within a confined environment. The result was that learners were able to carry out basic operations, still with the probability of causing errors and thereby learning from them. However, the consequences of those errors were constrained to be as minimal as possible. In the previous car analogy this equates to driving the car on quiet roads with little or no traffic and with straight roads so that a sequence of gear changing could be practised. This is, of course, the natural territory in which you might find learner drivers practising. Carroll went on to investigate concepts such as smart help and the application of artificial intelligence to help people learn how to use computer applications. I would recommend that any reader who is responsible for designing e-learning that trains people to use computer systems should read Carroll in more depth. What I would like to do is to pick up some of the lessons from these observations that can be applied more widely to e-learning design.

APPLYING LESSONS LEARNED FROM OBSERVING USERS OF COMPUTER TRAINING MANUALS

The majority of instructional designers assume that learners will follow their training design completely and correctly. This patronizing approach assumes that the designer knows the best way in which a sequence of actions can be learned. Not only does this assume responsibility for the learner, it assumes that every learner is the same, potentially even more damaging than patronizing a learner. The rest of this chapter and Chapters 5 and 6 will show ways in which learners are different. All of us are unique but it does not necessarily help the e-learning designer to say that everyone is unique. What I will do in the following chapters is to apply a structure to differences. This structure is based on research. From this structure it is possible to establish principles for design that go some way towards treating people as individuals.

However, let me return to the assumption that learners do as they are told and follow training exercises. People fail to do this for a number of good reasons, none of which is wilful. I have already mentioned that a didactic approach tends to be patronizing and that we would all tend to respond to such an approach with irritation and potentially a childish response. Carroll gives a good example of the impact of patronizing feedback. It is common practice to provide feedback to the learner during a question and answer session. In the early days of computer-based training design work much of this feedback was trivial in the extreme. Carroll quotes examples of a tutorial providing feedback such as: 'Excellent!' 'Right!' 'On we go'. Carroll reports 'The learners did not like this. One noted that it was insulting to be commended for following an instruction that was not very difficult. Another called these messages "fatuous": "it's silly to say excellent when they just told you that you did it wrong!".' (Carroll, 1990, p. 58). One may forgive any learner for wanting to do their own thing when an e-learning system generates these sorts of feelings.

Learners also search for meaning that is relevant to them. Given that this is the situation, the best thing that the designer can do is to give the learner some freedom. Learners should be able to embroider learning material with their own patterns. If you watch any reader who is making a serious study of a textbook this is precisely what they will do. The embroidery will take the form of pencilled annotations, highlighting and underlining. The sophisticated learner may well use small diagrams in the margin and develop a personal colour-code for highlighting. The learner becomes involved with the material and alters its appearance. This self-elaboration improves memory retention and encourages understanding. In the e-learning context it may be encouraged by providing the learner with incomplete material. Carroll reports on earlier research work in the 1920s which indicates that 'tasks are better remembered ... if they are incomplete on first encounter' (Carroll, 1990, p. 83). Self-elaboration and involvement with the learning material will occur naturally in a discussion board attached to e-learning self-study material. Involvement in creating material on the bulletin board moves the student from a passive learning role into an active one. The e-learning designer can assume that every learner will reason for themselves and this is an opportunity for the designer to give space to the learner to apply this reasoning. This is one of the strengths of a simulation that encourages a trial and error approach. It is more challenging to develop ways in which knowledge-related material can allow space for learners to reason and deduce than it is to present that material in a didactic style.

START WITH MEANINGFUL TASKS EARLY

The majority of adults come to learning because they need to achieve something within the workplace. They may have to run a meeting, fix an equipment fault, conduct a disciplinary interview, take on a new role, analyse statistics, prepare a budget or analyse a balance sheet. This need remains at the forefront of their mind, particularly at an early stage within the learning experience. Later on, they may become interested in the material itself, but initially the real task will be nagging at their minds. Given that situation, e-learning material should allow learners to practise the task they want to complete. The requirement is to create a task that is sufficiently simple that learners can complete it with minimal learning and yet to be sufficiently realistic and relevant to carry meaning for the learner. With certain tasks it is relatively easy to see how that might be done. For example, a fault-finding exercise on a simple piece of equipment that is likely to have few faults. The thinking processes and methodology can be taught and the learner can apply them immediately. Other examples include financial management. Simple budgets can be prepared and straightforward balance sheets analysed. The whole task is completed but within a limited and constrained environment. The important thing from the learners' perspective is that they have carried out a task that is relevant to them when they are still thinking about their initial reason for studying.

DESIGNING FOR RANDOM USE

Much of the preceding discussion and examples drawn from real experience show that users of e-learning material behave in ways that designers cannot necessarily predict. The e-learning designer must assume that learners will behave in a random fashion. Once the designer accepts this behaviour then e-learning material begins to look more like knowledge management websites. Assuming the learner will behave in ways that cannot be predicted encourages the use of very small self-contained units of material to study. This is frequently described as byte-sized learning. The principle is straightforward, the practicality less so. The designer has to create very small chunks of material, each one of which is relatively self-contained. It should not be assumed that this 'byte' of learning will be the only component that the user might access at one time. It is more likely that they will arrive at this material from a number of different directions.

Programmed learning uses the same concept of very small chunks of material. The difference is that programmed learning controls the direction from which a learner arrives, they were fully tested before being allowed to leave and would leave that chunk of learning in a pre-defined direction. This constraint is not natural for learners, particularly adult learners. The adult learner will access small chunks of material in unpredictable order. Carroll described this as designing material that could be read in any order. There are two consequences to this approach. If e-learning frames are designed to be accessed in any order then they cannot be accessed in the wrong order. Some learners will arrive at an e-learning frame without the prerequisite knowledge that a designer might wish to assume when designing and constructing the frame. The implication for the designer is that the frame must be designed in such à way that the prerequisite knowledge is not essential. The frame must allow for the learner to be motivated and guidance from material that may stretch them. It should also point them, but not direct them, 'back' to knowledge or skill areas that would normally be regarded as a prerequisite for the frame they chose to tackle.

MAKING USE OF PRECONCEPTIONS

Adults come to any learning experience with a past history of knowledge and skills. They have prior knowledge and pre-assumed goals. The designer of e-learning material can make use of this prior knowledge in two ways. Perhaps most straightforwardly, learners can be tested for their prior knowledge and advised which part of the course or material they seem to have mastered. This has been a commonly practised technique in all good quality technology-based training and we can expect to find it in good quality e-learning material. The other way in which prior knowledge is exploited by the designer is in the use of metaphors and analogies. The creation of a business game, for example, assumes as prior knowledge that the learner will understand the concept of gaming. Not only does the user need to understand the concept of gaming but they need to be motivated to be part of such a game. The use of analogies is also a frequently exploited training technique. I opened this book using the analogy of a series of interconnected rooms to equate to the Internet and demonstrated two different ways that people use the Internet by comparing the actions of a mouse and a hamster. Related to the use of analogies is that of storytelling, a technique for learning that has been used down the ages. Storytelling and songs were the way in which history was imparted for each generation before the widespread availability of the printed word. Anthropologists who study pre-industrial cultures will tell you that storytelling is the most powerful form of communication. Almost every learner will appreciate a case study. Case studies are actually contemporary stories. They may be turned into exercises where the learner plays a part. They then become games.

There are many technology-delivered training products which make use of a task simulation exercise. Here is one example that is used to train bank employees to make decisions about lending using the bank's computer system. The case study starts with a screen based on a photograph of a branch, with an in-tray, a telephone and a computer screen. They are required to respond to letters and telephone calls from customers. They may also be presented with customers who 'walk through the door'. These customers wish to borrow money. The bank employee then uses the information in the computer system and is able to ask further questions of customers and, as a result of all that information, make a decision on whether to authorize the loan or not. This is a contemporary story, in which the learner interacts. Stories can also be memorable by being bizarre and unlike reality. All these techniques are effective because the adult learner has prior experience and knowledge that they bring to the learning material. Stories and metaphors are one way in which a designer can make use of this prior experience.

Applying these lessons in the future

I have discussed research and observations that have been around for some time. Many of the ideas resulting from this research have been put into practice. You might expect that matters have improved to such an extent that the observations recorded by Carroll lack any significance for e-learning designers of the future. It is true that a lot of the detailed findings have become common practice in the design of both computer system interfaces and also learning material. I still believe the broad sweep of Carroll's research to be absolutely valid in the design of future technology-delivered learning material. The capability of computer systems and the application software are increasing all the time and will continue to do so. The impact of usability research means that in general, systems are easier to use. We understand where people look when they first see a screen frame, where the eye goes to next. Incidentally, in the majority of cases, they look at the centre of the screen and then their eye moves to the left.

Even with our increased understanding, there is no guarantee that computer systems and applications will become easier to use. Their complexity is increasing and modern applications have far more functions and facilities than those they have replaced. This is true of applications and we must expect it to be true of e-learning material. This means that the learner has greater freedom in which to be unpredictable. The move from didactic material to electronic performance support systems goes some way towards addressing these issues, but increases the complexity of the support material itself. The research indicates that the problems users have would apply to a knowledge management or performance support site just as much as a linear didactic training site, 'most of the problems discussed apply at least as much to help systems as to training material' (Carroll, 1990, p. 45). The main lessons from Carroll's research have been simplified into four statements in Figure 4.2.

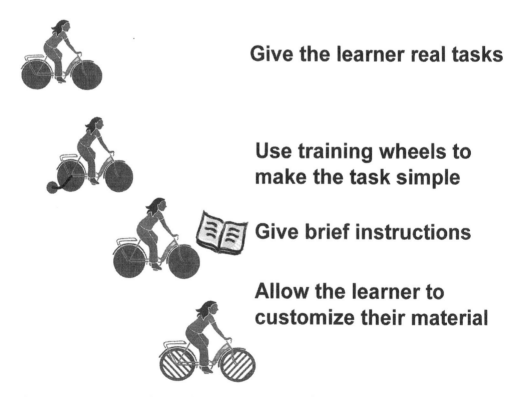

Give the learner real tasks

Use training wheels to make the task simple

Give brief instructions

Allow the learner to customize their material

Figure 4.2 Recommendations for designing learning for computer use (after Carroll, 1990)

The nature of individual preferences

The preceding discussion will not have been of much use unless we can apply the ideas to future design of e-learning material. I hope I have provided compelling evidence that the unpredictable behaviour of learners is a consequence of human behaviour. That unpredictability may be constrained in the face-to-face situation by the nature of the interpersonal interaction between the tutor and learner. Such a face-to-face interaction does not apply to e-learning, although e-mail interaction may do so. This book has to go beyond a statement that everyone is different and unpredictable. The e-learning designer needs a framework that helps them understand learners as well as learning. It is at this point that we reach a watershed in this book. All the discussions and observations I have recorded so far, discuss the general nature of the Internet and also the past developments in technology-delivered learning. I now want to look at the individual within that context. Particularly, I want to draw on previous research that helps to classify learners. By this means I hope to show that some learners are more like each other and in this way derive categories of learners. Perhaps the best known way in which learners can be classified is the learning styles of Kolb (1984). I will deal with Kolb's learning styles and learning modes in more detail in Chapter 5.

Holist and serialist strategies for learning

A STUDY OF HOLIST AND SERIALIST LEARNERS

An understanding of these strategies was developed by Gordon Pask (1976b) during the 1960s. Pask conducted a series of observations and experiments throughout the 1960s and 1970s investigating the strategies adopted by learners and the relationship of those learning strategies to the way the subject-matter was presented and taught. The learners that he observed came from the upper-age range in schools and also colleges. Some of his observations and experiments were conducted in laboratories, some in schools and colleges. The later studies in schools lasted over a period of six years and involved some 250 students. Prior to that he studied about 30 polytechnic students in the laboratory, who learned a fictitious animal classification structure for the benefit of his research. A second group of 30 studied real scientific and mathematical topics. Within the sessions conducted in schools and colleges the topics were non-trivial real learning tasks. They included the theory of heat engines, reaction kinetics, probability theory and statistics. However, in terms of Bloom's taxonomy, all the learning objectives are cognitive objectives.

Learners were not observed in the same sense in which Carroll observed learners. The way they interacted with the material was recorded and compared to what might be expected based on their pre-assessed learning style as either holist or serialist. The research demonstrated that individuals may be grouped according to their preferred strategy, either holist or serialist. The learning material was not presented on a computer, remember this research was conducted in the 1960s when computer systems were large and expensive, but was presented in a computer-like way. Learners were given the freedom to study material as they choose. The material was presented either as written material in pamphlets, tape slide presentations or as laboratory demonstrations. Each pamphlet or demonstration addressed a single concept. This equates to the learning objects approach favoured by current e-learning designers. It also replicates the frame-based approach, which has been a feature of technology-delivered learning since its inception.

Learners chose to adopt a strategy that was consistent for them. That is: holist learners stuck to that strategy and serialist learners stuck to theirs. There is a third group of versatile learners who are comfortable moving between the strategies.

STRUCTURING TOPICS (A MESH OR A HIERARCHY)

Before the material could be used in a self-study mode it had to be prepared and included within a structure or mesh. Pask postulated that learning is a conversation or communication between two participants. We may consider these participants to be the learner and teacher (Pask, 1976a, p. 12). Pask extended the idea of a conversation to include communication between the learner and material or equipment. Learning takes place as the nature of that conversation changes. In the 1960s, Pask used laboratory demonstrations to help people learn scientific and mathematical concepts. Nowadays we would have a screen-based simulation delivered by a computer. In both cases the learner is able to interact with that material and use it as a means to develop an understanding of a particular concept.

The relevant tutor within a learning conversation may take two forms. That of imparting knowledge and that of directing attention to what the learner needs to do in order to gain a greater understanding of the topic. In a true self-study mode the learner assumes the role of tutor; that is directing their own attention to what needs to be done. The former role, that of delivering learning information is taken up by the study material itself. By using demonstrations as well as written and pictorial material, Pask was able to make the self-study material interactive. This, of course, is a basic requirement of any modern on-line learning system. In structuring the learning material Pask stated an overall learning goal for the learners. To achieve this learning goal requires various concepts to be applied and understood. The learning goal can be broken down into a number of concepts and sub-concepts. At this point the approach sounds rather like the system's approach to training. The system's approach implies a hierarchy in that sub-concepts need to be understood before concepts, which in turn need to be understood before the overall learning goal can be achieved.

In Pask's experiments, this hierarchical structure is removed and becomes one of relationships. The idea behind this is that the order in which sub-concepts go to form concepts is not an immutable structure. For example, let us consider the three concepts of camera, lens and focused image. In what order do we need to understand these concepts before we can explain how a camera or a lens works, or how a focused image is created. We can start with the concept of camera, a pinhole camera. We can observe the focused image falling onto a sheet of greaseproof paper. We can observe the distance between the pinhole and the image and between the pinhole and the object. We can change one or other or both and see the difference in the image. (We can do all this in reality or with a screen-based simulation.) Having understood the concept of camera and image, we can then explain the functioning of a lens. Alternatively we can experiment with a lens, focus a beam of light onto a spot, for example. Having observed the function of the lens and grasped what it does to rays of light, we can then explain the functioning of a camera and the creation of a focused image. Which do we have to do first? If the hierarchy of concept genuinely does not matter then the order in which they are studied does not matter. This represents the significant divergence from the system's approach to training.

Learners in Pask's experiment studied subject matter broken down into a number of very small topics. The subject specialist was required to explain the derivation of each topic from each other. The derivation had to be cited in both directions. For example, if the three concepts were image, light ray and lens, then image and light ray can explain lens. Conversely lens and image can be used to explain light ray. This is fundamentally different to the system's approach, which builds knowledge in only one direction. The knowledge network that Pask constructed (he used the term 'entailment mesh') makes no assumption about an individual's prior knowledge. A hierarchical breakdown of objectives does make assumptions about an individual's prior knowledge, indeed it assumes they know nothing about the topic and have to learn each item in order. The hierarchal order builds up to the overall learning goal. However in the structure used by Pask there was no implicit hierarchy. Individual learners were able to have a 'conversation' about each topic either with a tutor, a tape-slide presentation, a pamphlet or a laboratory demonstration. When they claimed they had understood the particular topic they would explain that topic to a tutor. The tutor would satisfy him or herself that the explanation given by the learner was genuine and not simply a 'replica, parrot-wise, of a demonstration already seen'. In modern on-line learning we may interpret this as a frame-based interaction followed by testing. Once an understanding of the topic was proven this would be recorded in the computer system and the learner was able to move to another topic that had a relationship with the topic that was understood. This movement might be in any direction. Some of the topics would have analogical relationships with other topics. The movement the student would make from one topic to another was also recorded by the computer's system. The execution of this learning mechanism, with tape slide, paper and verbal testing with a tutor is archaic in the extreme. current desktop computers enable us to do all this simply and cheaply. Even though the implementation of the research may be regarded as archaic the intent of the research is not. Pask observed learners studying small items of material with which they interacted, and as a result of their deliberations selected another step to take in learning. The intent and findings from the research are valid for current generation e-learning systems. The topics are also non-trivial and perhaps their only limitation is that much of the research was conducted with scientific and mathematical subjects.

The learning strategies

Individuals adopt two main different learning strategies. The term strategies is used to define the sequence that learners use for their learning, this might be described as the plans they use. This differentiates it from the learning styles or learning modes, as described by Kolb (1984, p. 68) which describe activities that individuals prefer. In Chapter 5 the reader may wish to draw comparisons between the learning strategies as discussed by Pask and the impact of personality in terms of the preferences particular personality types show for particular learning approaches.

HOLIST STRATEGY

A comprehension learner applies the holist strategy. Such a learner prefers to pick up an overall picture of the subject matter. They will easily identify analogies and underlying

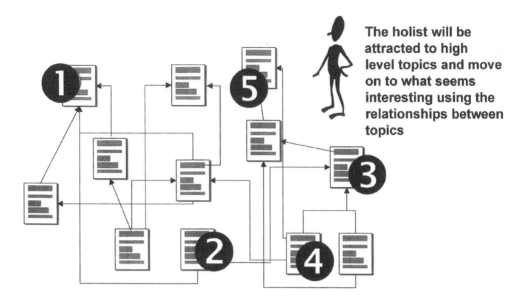

The holist will be attracted to high level topics and move on to what seems interesting using the relationships between topics

Topics exist in a mesh
Topics are related to each other
The mesh has a hierarchy in that topics build on each other

Figure 4.3 The pattern for holistic study (after Pask, 1976b, p. 131)

common principles between topics. They may be able to comprehend the subject matter relatively easily, but find it more difficult to apply or operate with the knowledge. Comprehension learners prefer global statements and understanding principles, rather than grasping detail. There are classes of comprehension learners. There are those who are irredundant comprehension learners who are selective about the material they use and avoid information that seems to replicate previous learning. They learn quickly with accurate recall of material learned. The redundant comprehension learner on the other hand uses redundant data and analogies that appear to repeat previous topics. They will be able to recall what they have learnt more quickly than other learners, but less accurately.

The holist strategy for a learner studying a few topics may look like Figure 4.3. Each topic is linked by a line that indicates a conceptual relationship. The arrow indicates that one topic may be considered to build on another. The holist starts at a point that she or he finds interesting, in this case a high level topic. They then dive to a low level topic and then to another one unrelated to the first topic. The result is that the holist samples bits of topics, never taking the time to grasp any one topic in detail, although gaining a rapid grasp of the overall nature of the subject.

SERIALIST STRATEGY

Learners who apply a serialist strategy are termed operation learners. They prefer to pick up on rules and methods used and the details of the topic. In concentrating on the detail they find it more difficult to see how topics fit together and to understand the relationships between them. The operation learner prefers to learn step-by-step. Again, two classes of operation learner exist. One class is described by Pask as the 'local rule learner' (Pask, 1988,

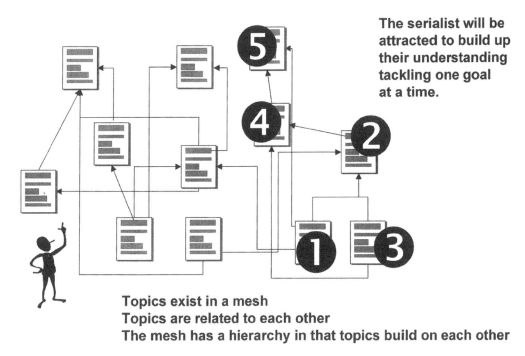

The serialist will be attracted to build up their understanding tackling one goal at a time.

Topics exist in a mesh
Topics are related to each other
The mesh has a hierarchy in that topics build on each other

Figure 4.4   The pattern for serialist study

p. 92). This class of learner progresses logically step-by-step. They ensure that they thoroughly understand a topic or sub-section before moving on. They frequently ask for guidance on the next topic. The other class of operation learner is the 'rote learner' who follows a single prescribed and narrow path. Rote learners are unlikely to be able to make use of the knowledge acquired. They will perform well in examinations where memory is of greater importance than understanding. The serialist strategy for a learner studying a few topics may look like Figure 4.4. In this case the serialist starts with a low level topic, advances to a higher level, goes back to fill in a gap and then advances to a higher level topic ensuring that each topic, and any related topics on which that one is dependent is grasped before moving on.

VERSATILE STRATEGY

If a topic is to be thoroughly understood or a skill developed and acquired, then both comprehension and operation learning are required. The effective learner, whether their natural tendency is to adopt a holist or serialist strategy, will have developed the ability to apply comprehension and operation learning. Pask described such learners as applying a versatile strategy. One observation was that if learners who applied a versatile strategy were left to themselves to use self-study material, they would migrate towards either a holist or serialist strategy. It would thus appear that there is a natural tendency to apply one or other of the strategies. This natural tendency may well have roots in personality differences, which are explored in Chapter 5.

Typical errors of comprehension and operation learning

We can gain a further insight into the effectiveness or otherwise of these two strategies by understanding the errors that are likely to occur from unsuccessful comprehension learning and operation learning. Comprehension learning makes use of valid analogies. An example might be the analogy between electrical potential and water pressure. The analogy is complete in that the flow of water is analogous to an electric current and the diameter of the pipe is analogous to the electrical resistance in a wire. There are also analogies, which are vacuous or spurious. Such analogies have some credence but break down very quickly. For example, the flow of cars along a motorway might be regarded as analogous with the flow of an electric current. However, applying greater pressure to that flow, by implication trying to move more cars along the motorway faster, causes a slower flow. The analogy is spurious. It would appear that holist learners are more likely to create spurious analogies. They have a preference for establishing relationships between topics and do so perhaps on the flimsiest of evidence.

Alternatively, students who apply a serialist strategy will fail to use valid analogies or apply common principles. A learner who applies a serialist strategy will ignore the water current analogy when understanding electrical current. They will not build links between water pressure, pipe diameter and volume of water flow and voltage, resistance and electric current. They will understand electrical current flow from scratch. This might be described as a failure to transfer learning from one domain to another. It does reduce the risk of a misconception but it increases the workload on the learner. It may also reduce their ability to understand as opposed to use their learning.

Teaching strategies

Learning strategies can be converted to teaching strategies, and as such they can be incorporated into learning material. We can, therefore, present learners with a choice of material. Pask developed programmed learning texts and structured his topics so that they could be used according to either holist or serialist teaching strategies. In his later studies in schools he matched learners preferences for learning strategies to the teaching strategies of the material they were studying. The learners, Pask observed, were categorized into those who preferred a serialist strategy and those who preferred a holist strategy. This was done by asking the learners to complete a learning task that was subsequently tested by discussion with a tutor. The topics in the exercise were artificially constructed, but included common principles between topics, a considerable amount of detail and also topics which had analogous relationships. Learners who demonstrated comprehension of the 'big picture' and understood common principles and made analogous relationships but who lacked the detail were classified as preferring a holist strategy of learning. Learners, who grasped operational detail but did not make relationships between topics or establish common principles, were categorized as those who preferred a serialist strategy. The topics were learnt through self-study and learners were able to apply either strategy to the topics depending on their personal preference. The groups of learners were otherwise matched for various intellectual skills.

Most of the topics that were included in the research were cognitive in nature. This is a valid domain for e-learning. Indeed, many learning theorists would argue that it is the only topic domain that is appropriate for e-learning, other than keyboard psychomotor skills. The learning tasks that were set and observed, related both to acquiring knowledge and applying that knowledge. Those students who achieved success in acquiring and applying a knowledge topic went through a phase of building a description of a topic, followed by a phase in which the description was realized or applied. He concluded that this process 'appears to be the dominant mode of human learning' (Pask, 1976b, p. 143). The description-building phase is comprehension learning and the application-phase is operation learning. If it is true, as postulated by Pask, that the dominant mode of human learning is to comprehend and then apply a topic, then learning requires the application of a holist strategy followed by a serialist strategy. Indeed, the versatile learner who shows an ability to apply both strategies shows more success in learning than one who applies only one of the other strategies.

Evidence of effective learning

Learners who allow only one strategy to dominate their approach exhibit the errors that are inherent in those strategies. Holist learners use analogies and because of their preference for establishing relationships between topics, a high proportion of these analogies are spurious. This is not to say the analogies are of no value in learning. Drawing a metaphor between cars on a motorway and electrons in a copper wire may be useful in remembering and understanding the concept of current flow. It is an example of applying prior experience to learning. A point made by Carroll is that everyone brings different prior experience to a learning situation and will make different interpretations, depending on that experience. Learners preferring holist strategy relate more of their prior experiences to the topics they are learning, in the process creating more analogies. They create misconceptions by applying analogies in an invalid manner.

Learners who prefer a serialist strategy on the other hand, prefer not to create analogies between topics. The operation learner concentrates on applying the topic in a practical procedural sense. They prefer not to create links with other topics, concentrating on the job in hand. When asked to explain a topic they rarely make reference to analogous topics or relationships.

In trials in schools, in the mid-1970s, Pask structured the teaching material to follow either a serialist or a holist strategy. The holist approach presented the big picture, emphasized relationships and drew links between topics. The serialist approach was methodical and concentrated on an individual topic. There was a significant difference in a learner's retention of the topic matter when they were either using structured material so that it matched their preference as a strategy, as against using material that applied a strategy that they did not prefer. 'A mismatch of learning and teaching strategies leads to no relevant learning' (Pask, 1988, p. 91). Furthermore, matched learning, (when the presentation of material aligns itself to the strategic preference of the individual) proves to be more effective than the learner finding their own way through material. An earlier experiment reported in Pask (1976b) provides firm evidence of a significant difference in the retention ability. Learners whose preference for a strategy is matched with the presentation of that topic achieved average scores above 90 per cent. Learners who were presented with material that did not match their strategic preferences had average scores between 35 and 45 per cent. Pask concluded 'matched instruction favours learning and mismatched instruction completely disrupts it (specifically, for explanation eliciting questions) and leads to specific types of misconception' (Pask, 1976b, p. 138).

Applying these findings to e-learning design

The implications for the e-learning designer are quite significant. Forcing an inappropriate strategy on an individual means that their learning is disrupted. It is probably impractical to determine a student's preference for a learning strategy prior to an e-learning session. However, users can be given choices. They can be allowed to exercise those choices in relation to terms that they will understand. It may be that the simplest approach is to present material in accordance with a serialist strategy but throughout maintain options for the holist. The holist might prefer a Menu selection that says 'would you like to know more about a topic like this one'. The serialist, on the other hand, may prefer a button that says 'would you like to see an example?'

Although learners may have a preference for a strategy, preference does not imply competence. 'Competence in using a strategy does not always go alongside disposition to adopt it' (Pask, 1976b, p. 132). This particularly seems to apply to holist learners who find themselves adopting a serialist strategy. In many cases their apparent preference for the serialist approach is imposed upon them by a previous institutional bias. Schools frequently present material in a methodical manner and many, if not most, school examinations favour serial recall. Holist learners frequently feel an obligation to 'behave themselves' and study material topic by topic. The converse is occasionally observed but occurs much less frequently. Perhaps this is because learners are rarely encouraged to take a global view. Pask's research work was based in polytechnics and schools and is quite dated. It may be that the modern academic and educational system is much less inclined to deliver material in a serialist manner than it was 40 years ago. I leave it to the reader to draw on their personal reflections of the presentation of school material, as to how often they were encouraged to relate one topic to another and to go off at a tangent.

As previously mentioned, learning seems to move from a comprehension to an operational phase. It therefore requires some part of a holist strategy and some part of a serialist strategy. Pask observed that the most effective learners, versatile learners, were those who could apply both strategies. The benefit of being versatile must be designed into e-learning without making it prescriptive. Not only is material presented so that the learner has a choice of strategy, it also means that they should be encouraged to adopt holist strategy early on in a topic and serialist strategy at a later stage. Pask explored the concept of learning-to-learn skills specifically in the area of versatility in learning strategy. As individuals progressed through material they were given feedback on their particular preference for approach. The requirement for comprehension and then operational learning is explained and learners are encouraged to analyse their own strategies and discuss these with tutors. Discussion is both one-to-one and group-based. The group will contain those who adopt different strategies. Their movements through the topic material are recorded and presented as feedback to them. This enabled learners to discuss their preferences with others who share their preference and with those who do not. These discussions provide a learning-to-learn dialogue.

Holists understand the attraction and worth of a serial approach and serialists understand the attraction and worth of a holist approach. While it may be impractical or too costly for many e-learning applications, the concept of giving individual feedback on their learning strategy must be valid. The evidence from Pask's research work is that this learning-to-learn feedback to individuals had an improvement in performance. Once learners began to understand what they did and why, they were able to develop versatility: holist learners would apply an operation-style approach once they became comfortable with a big picture. Serialist learners would try to hold themselves back from a methodical or rote approach at the detailed level in order to gain some impression of where that topic fitted in to the overall scheme of things. Versatility can be developed and will improve the effectiveness of learning. This versatile approach may be designed into on-line material without constraining a learner to adopt an approach that they do not prefer.

Summary

A huge amount of academic research has been directed at understanding the skill of learning. Some of this has direct relevance to the use of e-learning. There is clear and rigorous evidence that we remember images better than we remember words. That in itself is not sufficient to improve learning, the images themselves must convey information about the topics being learned. Another improvement in learning comes when learners interact with the content. This interaction not only gives people something to do, it also gives them a feeling of being in control. Learners are able to search, enquire, control and direct their learning. Two pieces of research are particularly significant in the e-learning field, the first is that of John Carroll who observed people using computer systems and the other is that of Gordon Pask who used an electro-mechanical system to research the way learners used frame-based material. A number of conclusions can be drawn from Carroll's research.

(1) Learners have unrealistically high expectations of the capability of e-learning material. This is mainly driven by the hype that is used to justify the expenditure on the development of the system and the promotion that is used to encourage the learners to access it.

(2) Learners will interrupt information in an e-learning system in ways that the designer had not intended. This might be information that helps them navigate in the system and retain a sense of where they are within it. It might be information used within the system, perhaps because learners bring preconceptions and prior knowledge to their learning. The designer uses words in a particular context that may mean something different to the learner.

(3) Learners will not follow instructions. This may be wilful because they expect to exercise control over what they do rather than be told to do something. It may be because they misinterpret what the designer has asked them to do or they have become bored or confused.

(4) Learners acquire concepts at an early stage of using material and cling on to these concepts, even if they are erroneous, as they work through the material. Not only do users acquire these misconceptions at an early stage of the course, but they may also bring them to the material particularly when they have a little bit of knowledge about the subject. Users of computer systems and e-learning make mistakes. The learner rarely recognizes these mistakes when they are made. Mistakes are, of course, a powerful learning mechanism when they happen in a safe and blame-free environment.

(5) Learners want to get on with doing the whole job as soon as possible. Learning routine steps bit by bit before the whole task can be tackled is boring and restrictive for many people. The didactic approach used by many e-learning designers encourages the designer to try and control the route the learner takes through the material. From previous observations it can be seen that this is self-defeating.

In the specific area of training people to use computer systems, Carroll recommended:

- start the learner with meaningful tasks
- use task-orientated guides with little explanation (as brief as possible)
- never patronize
- develop application software with some functionality blocked off so that learners can complete real but simple tasks
- allow learners the opportunity to annotate and personalize their learning material
- design all material so that users may use it in any order, and
- build on a variety of preconceptions that learners bring to the learning task.

Pask observed students aged between 17 and 19 studying in schools and colleges. He structured all the learning material into a 'mesh', the sequence of which was captured in an electro-mechanical system. Some of the items in the mesh were practical laboratory demonstrations, some of them were reading a textbook or being part of a discussion with a tutor on a specific topic. Learners were able to tackle the items in this mesh in whatever order they felt was appropriate. This research maps to modern e-learning very closely. Pask discovered that some students worked through the material methodically tackling one topic at a time. Pask used the term operation learners to describe those who preferred this serialist strategy. The 'operation learner' likes detail and prefers to learn in a step-by-step process. Others moved around the topics much more freely while endeavouring to gain an early indication of the complete nature of the topic. Pask used the term 'comprehension learners' for those who preferred this holist strategy. These learners preferred to get an overall picture, understanding theory and relationships, rather than working in detail.

Pask found that some learners were able to switch between a holist and serialist strategy. However, even those who started with a versatile strategy would, if left to themselves, migrate towards either a holist or serialist approach. This tendency has roots in personality differences. This preference for learning strategies can be readily converted to teaching strategies, as recommended by Pask and also to design strategies for e-learning. The simplest way of using these findings would be to provide learners with a choice between understanding detail, or relationships with other topics and understanding concepts. E-learning is ideally suited to providing learners with this choice and rules can be included in the software that recommend that learner's switch between strategies.

5 *Personality and Learning*

In Chapters 1–3, I set the scene for the factors in e-learning that impact on the individual and in Chapter 4, I reported on research that demonstrates individual differences in the way that people use technology systems for learning. I will review research into individual differences in approaches to learning and study based on personality differences. The research is not directly related to the use of technology in learning but what I will do is to interpret the research to the e-learning situation.

We are all of us unique with our own approaches and preferences for learning. This is a glib statement and can only be turned to good use if we can place our individual uniqueness into a structure and then draw inferences from that structure. I could pick almost any type classification; team types, learning styles, personality types, cultural norms, IQ or EQ groupings. Although I will touch on several of these through this chapter, I want to concentrate on the Myer-Briggs Type Indicator (MBTI)™ personality types and the research associated with them. The MBTI types have been researched and understood for a number of years. The result is a substantial body of knowledge demonstrating differences in learning methods and career interests based on personality differences. Whereas in the classroom a good tutor will perceive how different personalities respond, the e-learning designer cannot perceive that response and the on-line tutor will find it much more difficult to do so. Both the designer and on-line tutor will be aided by a capability to systemize their understanding of the possible different responses individuals might make to their material. My aim is to develop a structure and learning model so that e-learning design takes account of individual differences and the on-line tutor is better equipped to understand why learners respond as they do.

Bias due to personality: the effect on e-learning

It is likely that our preferences for learning approaches are driven by personality more than any other factor. Clearly, successful learning strategies used by each of us in the past are more likely to be repeated, than those we found unsuccessful. The foundation of this chapter rests on the work of David Kolb, Gordon Pask and the research associated with the MBTI. An understanding of an individual's preferences for learning can be used to understand how individuals might approach e-learning and the features that are needed by those with different preferences. There is some strong evidence (Myers *et al.*, 1998, p. 294) that different personality types are found in greater-than-average proportion in different jobs. There is a logical sequence that may lead us to expect that e-learning only appeals to a limited range of personality types.

(1) Personality type preferences affect the preferred work environment (Meyers *et al.*, 1998, p. 292)
(2) The IT industry environment appeals to a limited range of personality types (Meyers *et al.*, 1998, p. 294)
(3) E-learning is largely driven and used by the IT industry. Over 70 per cent of the courses available in 2001 were IT related.
(4) E-learning has greatest appeal to those in the IT industry.
(5) E-learning has appeal to a limited range of personality types.

While such a logical sequence may or may not have any substance in reality, it does open up the intriguing possibility that, if we can classify learning preferences by type we can structure e-learning to appeal to all. The aim of this chapter and the next is to:

* understand a relationship between personality type and learning strategies
* link a range of strategies to e-learning design issues.

I would like to start with personality types and their impact on learning. The first step is to establish some understanding of personality type.

Example of type personality inventory – MBTI

Much of this chapter analyses current research into learning that is related to MBTI profiles. As such you will need an understanding of the MBTI classification. A brief explanation is provided here. Katherine Briggs and Isabel Briggs Myers based their development of a type classification and a questionnaire on the thinking of Carl Jung (1875–1961). The Myers-Briggs Type Indicator (MBTI) provides a report based on an individual's answer to a questionnaire. Isabel Briggs Myers, who started work on the inventory in 1941, felt that individuals would benefit from being able to understand the make-up of their personality. There are a number of books on MBTI and the one that is probably easiest to understand is *Understanding your Personality* by Patricia Hedges (1993).

The MBTI defines 16 personality types. These are derived from four dimensions, each of which is a dichotomy, that is an either-or choice. For each dimension any one individual will have a preference for one end or other of the dimension. The question-naire gives an either-or-result for each dimension. The mathematically-minded will see that this is four squared giving 16 combinations. This, in turn, produces 16 personality types. A basic tenet of the MBTI is that each of us has a best fit with one of the 16 types. This may take time to emerge as we grow and mature and get to know ourselves better. So the results of the questionnaire may change over time, but our underlying best fit with a personality type does not. The results of the questionnaire will help each one of us to find a best fit but the questionnaire is not, in itself, a categorization tool. In other words, do not believe the results of the questionnaire unless you personally feel that it is right for you.

MBTI personality dimensions

There are four dimensions to the MBTI. The first dimension is described as extrovert/introvert. The extrovert is interested in the external environment, that is people and objects that are outside the individual. The introvert is interested in the world of concepts and ideas, sometimes referred to as the inner world. (This dimension should not be confused with the commonly understood definition of extroversion or introversion that tends to be related to sociability.) The initials E or I are used to indicate the opposite sides of this dimension.

The second dimension is described as Sensing/iNtuition and relates to the way people gather information. An individual strong on Sensing will rely on their senses to gather information from the outside world. They are likely to be observant and able to pick up details from the world around them. People who are strong on iNtuition rely on hunches and their own thought processes to gather information. They are likely to be good at making connections between ideas, and will construct theories readily. They are also able to look beneath the surface and grasp the big picture of what is going on around them. The initials S or N (for iNtuition) are used to indicate the opposite sides of this dimension.

The third dimension is described as Thinking/Feeling. This relates to the way people make judgments and decisions. An individual who is strong on Thinking analyses facts objectively and makes decisions based on cause and effect. People who are strong on Feeling draw conclusions based on empathy with the views of others and may describe themselves as allowing their heart to rule their head. Their decisions are subjective. Those who score highly on the Feeling dimension are likely to make decisions that other people will support. The initials T or F are used to indicate the opposite sides of this dimension.

The final dimension is described as Judging/Perceiving. This describes the way people like to live their lives, either preferring to gather information or to draw conclusions. People who score highly on Judging prefer to live in a structured and well-planned way. They are likely to be systemic and well organized. People who score highly on Perceiving prefer to gather information and will always be easily side-tracked by something that looks more interesting than the task in hand. The initials J or P are used to indicate the opposite sides of this dimension.

Thus, any one individual will have a personality characterized by a group of four letters, one from each dimension. Understanding the MBTI properly, requires a book in itself and I would recommend further reading. However, the way in which different personalities prefer to learn is of profound importance in e-learning. To help you understand these personality differences I will describe some interactions between different personality types. The examples are drawn from a number of different working environments, but based on personal experience.

THE MBTI EXTROVERT/INTROVERT DICHOTOMY

I was part of a creative team working on a research project. One day there is a very long intense discussion with lots of ideas flowing about. There was a real buzz in the team. One introvert in the team was very creative with lots of ideas but always tended to sit a little apart. His chair would be just outside the circle, part of the team but a little bit separate. Suddenly, in the middle of this intense debate the introvert gets up and walks out. The extroverts get worried and concerned, after all they were having a really creative buzz and feeling full of beans. Another team member who knows him better says, 'not to worry as he sometimes did that'. The introvert went and bounced a ball against a wall just to give himself space to think and re-energize his thoughts. He could not think with everyone round him and it was more tiring being with people than being on his own.

THE MBTI SENSING/INTUITION DICHOTOMY

Again, two colleagues are working closely together, this time on budgets. One scores highly as a Sensing individual, the other as an intuitive. The N creates complex spreadsheets to allow the budget figures to be put together, but then forgets to put the detailed figures in. The S enters an entire detailed breakdown, line by line, into a relatively simple spreadsheet that reports totals. The S never feels that the N gives him enough information and the N feels burdened by detail when he would like to experiment with different ways of putting the budget together. The N learns to pass the S much more information, although without absorbing or processing it. The S learns that the N will not be worried by detail and will not be able to answer any questions about detail. Also, the S learns that the N may well come along with a new idea and that the financial data needs to be in a flexible format to accommodate new ways of presenting information. In this case, a very productive working relationship emerges with each individual playing to the strengths of the other.

THE MBTI THINKING/FEELING DICHOTOMY

Consider a project management environment in which relationships are short-term as project teams are formed and dissolved. For most of the people in the working group this is acceptable. However, two are finding difficulties with the working pattern. They both have high scores on the Feeling dimension. This means that they value relationships with others and like to make decisions based on their appreciation of the views of others. A short-term project culture makes this difficult. The solution in this case was to give both these individuals large-scale projects involving significant numbers of people with whom they would work over a long-term time scale. This allowed these individuals to build productive and effective relationships with clients and co-workers on the project. An individual with a high Thinking score will prefer relationships in which logic and rationality are of greater importance. One important point to bear in mind is that the MBTI is about preferences; it is not about abilities. A high-scoring Thinking dimension individual may be just as effective at building long-term relationships as a high-scoring Feeling individual. However, the high-scoring Feeling individual will find it easier to make decisions if there are people around them. The high-scoring Thinking person may find it easier to make decisions in the absence of people. Either method may be equally effective, although decisions that require others to implement them need to take account of people, and someone who scores highly on the Feeling dimension will do this more naturally, as they prefer to take account of the views and feelings of others.

THE MBTI PERCEIVING/JUDGING DICHOTOMY

Two people are working together on a project, one scores highly as a perceiving individual; the other scores highly in judging. The work is a computerized accounting system. The individual with a high P score has come up with the idea and gained sanction to proceed with the development. He briefs the individual with the high J score. However, his brief is very general and broad based. It emphasizes the possibilities rather than the solution. The individual with a high J score wants to get to work immediately but is not getting enough planning detail from his colleague. The situation can be improved by good system design that works through a series of specifications in a pre-planned and orderly fashion. Those with high P scores need the creation of many deadlines, stepping stones along the way to the finished product. Those with high J scores need to be held back from rushing into the final solution until possibilities have been explored and clear specifications for the end result worked out. In the case described, in which I was personally involved, none of these things happened and the J had created massive amounts of finished code before the solution had been clearly enough identified. Regrettably, a lot of this work was wasted.

MBTI functions as learning activities

This brief summary of each dichotomy fails to bring out the richness that comes from understanding the behaviour of others in terms of the MBTI model. I have mentioned differences I have observed in the way people interact just on the basis of differences in one dimension. In fact there are 16 different types and a multiplicity of ways in which people interact. If e-learning is to provide individuals with an individual experience instead of a sheep dip then it must make allowance for all these differences. The MBTI provides one means of providing a structure that enables e-learning to take full account of individual preferences.

Considerable research on learning preferences for the 16 types has been completed (Meyers *et al.*, 1998, pp. 254–264). One of the results of this research is that we can sensibly use eight groupings when we consider the relationship between learning and personality. The reason for there being eight is firmly based in MBTI type theory and I would like to explain some features of this personality theory in more detail.

I have previously described the meaning of the four dimensions of the MBTI and the difference between the middle two that describe a function (you may prefer to think of a function as an activity) and first and last, both of which describe preferences; (for the E/I dimension a source of energy derived from company or solitude; for the J/P dimension a preference for order and closure or for new information and open opportunities). The interrelationship of the functions with the preferences leads to a dominant function that may be expressed internally (introvert) or externally (extrovert). Each of us has a secondary or auxiliary function that we may express either internally or externally. It is no surprise that we also have tertiary and inferior functions (there being four functions) that we prefer least. I suggest that you might like to think or view the functions as activities. The activities form a sequence of action.

In *Team-based Learning* I relate the action of the four functions to a business process (Hills, 2001, p. 48). However, a movement through these four functions can also be considered as a learning activity and this will be discussed later. Using these functions to describe learning activities is the key to making e-learning an individual experience. The work of Honey and Mumford (1986) demonstrates that each of us has a preference for a learning style. They also argue that learning works best when a learner works their way through all the styles in a cycle of learning. Before I introduce the functional model of learning I would like to review some research from David Kolb. Type theory says that each of us will prefer one of the activities (or sets of behaviour) over the other three in descending order of preference.

Kolb's learning modes

David Kolb established the principle that each of us has preferences for learning approaches. His research work describes four basic learning modes, concrete experience, reflective observation, abstract conceptualization and active experimentation. In turn these styles have been described by Honey and Mumford as action, reflection, theorizing and practical application (programmatic behaviour). Kolb states 'most people develop learning styles that emphasize some learning abilities over others' (Kolb, 1984, p. 68). He further went on to show that everyone tends to use only two of the basic learning modes. From this he described four learning styles (Kolb, 1984, pp. 77, 78). One word of caution about terminology, Kolb uses a learning styles inventory to analyse an individual's self-reported preferences for the four basic learning modes. Honey and Mumford describe these modes as styles. Kolb goes on to describe individual learning styles that result from the pattern of preferences we have for his basic learning modes. The learning modes may be described briefly as:

- concrete experience which is external to the learner based in real events
- reflective observation which is internalizing what happened and is internal as the learner's mind explores inferences and relationships
- abstract conceptualization which is internal as new ideas are constructed into theories and concepts, and
- active experimentation which is external as ideas are tried out in the real world to see what happens.

These are shown in Figure 5.1 and with relationship to the learning styles that Kolb observed. There are four learning styles.

- *Convergent learning style* relies on theorizing and practical application. The converger moves from theory to practice and back again.
- *Divergent learning style* relies on action and reflection. The diverger uses imagination and adapts what they experience in different ways in their minds.
- *Assimilative learning style* relies on theorizing and reflection. The assimilator uses logic and reason to convert observations and reflections into concepts, ordered structure of knowledge and theories.
- *Accommodation learning style* relies on pragmatism and action. The accommodator is one who carries out plans, puts things into practice and relishes the new experiences that result.

Kolb also discovered that a preference for certain styles was overrepresented in specific employment groups. How an individual who preferred each style might describe themselves is shown in Figure 5.2 together with the employment groups in which they are over represented. Kolb's proposition is that each of us will relate to one of these styles. Perhaps you, the reader, might like to consider which of these styles relates to you or to someone you know. If you work in business you may be surrounded by accommodators and convergers. I

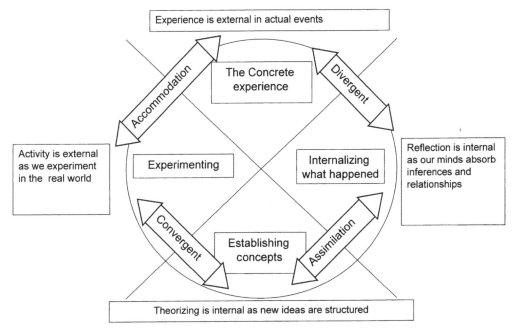

Figure 5.1 Learning modes

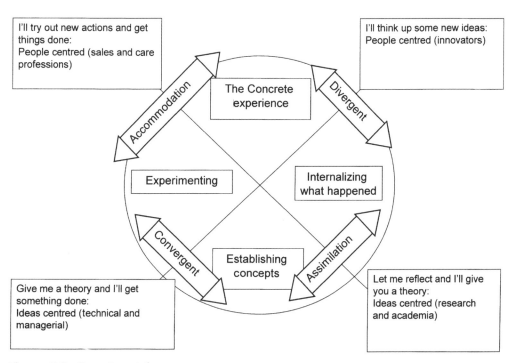

Figure 5.2 Learning styles

believe I can draw on my own experience and describe behaviours that we may associate with each style.

People I have worked with whom I believe are assimilators would be described as observers and thinkers. They find large group discussions tiring and would need to leave groups or teams and find some solitude. They would come back with a set of well-ordered thoughts. Certainly a common behaviour that I remember from others is the need for some simple physical activity as part of the logical reasoning process. Kolb found that people with these preferences tend to gravitate towards research and academia. This would be true of some of the people I remember.

The convergers I have worked with, on the other hand, gravitate towards technical and managerial roles. I have known people who like nothing better than to put an idea into practice. Usually self starters, they are less concerned about what actually happens but much more interested in the planning and organizing. Many of them are great project managers. Give them a framework to work in and a goal to aim for and they pitch in organizing and getting things done. I have worked with lots of people who I might describe as convergers. Of course, evaluating and learning from experience are not necessarily things that convergers like to do.

Accommodators seem much more rooted in 'what is actually happening'. Those I have worked with are gregarious and interested in people. They are flexible and responsive to changing situations, quite happy to change plans and goals as a result of what actually happens. I have heard others describe them as happy-go-lucky and they do seem able to live for the moment. I have known many instances where convergers and accommodators have made great working partners. They seem to be comfortable in the customer service and sales type roles. Kolb found that they were also well represented in the caring professions.

I find it more difficult to recognize divergers I have worked with. These are people with a tendency to come out with startling ideas in meetings. A feature of this learning style is a preference for generating new ideas and implications. One individual I remember would suddenly lean back in his chair and each time you knew that he would say something off the wall and knock everyone's thinking for six. Not all these ideas were practical but at least he could be relied on to generate alternatives. The thought processes were very sudden and spontaneous unlike the assimilators who would take the time to sort their ideas out.

I started this chapter with the MBTI, but spent some time describing the ideas of Kolb. My purpose is to establish the principle that each of us has preferences for the way we learn. These preferences are likely to be rooted in our personality. This has fundamental implications for e-learning. E-learning has to accommodate all learning preferences and, if these are rooted in personality, then all personalities. Kolb used a great deal of data and research and this gives a very solid foundation to his findings. The four learning styles he defined are universal across the population of learners and each of us will relate to one of them. Kolb also discussed the relation between styles and personality (Kolb, 1984, p. 80). He based his discussion on Jung's psychological types which is also the foundation for the MBTI.

MBTI functions as a learning cycle

Earlier I mentioned that the four MBTI functions might be considered as steps along the learning path. I would like to return to this and discuss these four functions in more detail.

SENSING

The Sensing function(s) is about using the five senses to observe the real world. Sensing is about establishing what is real, what exists. The function is related to the immediate present and to actuality. Those who have a preference for this function are likely to be close observers of detail, have a good memory of past experiences and enjoy the moment. For all of us this is the first step along a learning path. Babies taste, touch and feel objects so that they may sense the world around them. Young children watch the behaviour of adults. Students listen to their teachers. All the information we receive comes to us through our senses. Accurate sensing of this information gives a good start to learning. Let us consider reading for a moment. Perhaps this is the most frequently used method of acquiring information. Accurate observation of what is written is a precursor to understanding what is written. Much of e-learning is text material frequently presented through a medium (the computer screen) that is not totally friendly to the eye and that does not allow us to use various techniques to help us observe the written word closely. On paper, we can underline keywords and highlight sentences. Of course by that action we have moved beyond the Sensing function. Sensing is also about experiencing the richness of the moment, what the chair we are sitting on feels like, the aromas, whether we are hot or cold. Holding a pen or pencil is part of that experience. Making comments and inferring what is important and what is not introduces our iNtuition.

INTUITION

The Intuition function concerns establishing meanings and relationships. This goes on inside us, perhaps independent of the real world. Sometimes the activity is partially subconscious and the result is that we have a hunch. We may perceive hidden meaning and future possibilities in what is around us. We may discover a pattern between two events or ideas. The Intuition function drives our imagination, our preference for constructing theories, for establishing concepts. It also drives our preference for creative thought and our willingness to consider the future. This is a step along a learning path. Our Intuition function enables us to take information from the real world and to organize it and establish links with other concepts. The act of underlining a word in a book is part of that organizing process, a flag that reminds us; 'that word is more important than the other words around it'. Intuition is the function that encourages us to bring what we have previously learnt and use it to help us to learn now. The hyperlink feature in e-learning prompts us to do this. The web-like nature of the Internet makes it easy to follow links through, to move from one idea to another and then back again.

THE DESIGN CONTRAST BETWEEN SENSING AND INTUITION

MBTI theory tells us that a preference for Sensing (S) or Intuition (N) is a dichotomy. All of us will prefer one or the other although some of us may have difficulty choosing, because we may not yet have fully developed our natural type characteristics. A brief aside to explain that throw-away comment. Suppose I prefer Intuition to Sensing. As a result I like drawing inferences, making associations and establishing relationships. I do this in my head. Imagine (easy for me to do) I am a young child in the back of my parents' car and I see a sign warning of a school. I say to my parents 'that looks like an older brother and sister. Are they going to school or going home?'. My parents (who prefer Sensing) say 'don't be silly! That is a red triangle on a pole warning drivers there is a school nearby.' That teaches me that being intuitive is a silly thing to be so I submerge my preference in the 'correct' behaviour. It may take many years for me to realize that being very literal and accurate about my surroundings is not something I immediately enjoy. Over time I will develop more appreciation for iNtuition and explore relationships and associations as part of my perception. Although I have cultivated the ability to closely observe my surroundings this is not something I feel natural in doing. So my self-reporting of my preferences may change over time as the conditioning my parents imposed on me wears off. Each of us prefers either Sensing or iNtuition. What about you? Do you live for the moment? If so, have you developed the ability to think about the future and the opportunities and possibilities that it may present? On the other hand, do you prefer drawing logical inferences and making assumptions about what is happening and what might happen? If so, have you developed the ability to attend to the present moment and what is actually happening around you?

In a classroom situation one of two possibilities may emerge. The tutor or teacher may impose their preference for taking in information. The literal-minded Sensing tutor discourages flights of fancy and the introduction of new ideas. The figuratively-minded intuitive teacher discourages attention to detail and facts and avoids closure on a topic. Half the class is thus disadvantaged by being encouraged to exercise a preference for assimilating information that does not really fit their personality. If the teacher is perceptive she or he will vary their style and the way the topic is studied so that for some of the time attention is paid to facts and concrete examples and for some of the time the focus is on theory and the relationships between ideas. This way at least for some of the time learners can assimilate information in ways that suit their personality. The individual nature of on-line learning material means that is possible to ensure that all the time a learner can assimilate information in a way that suits their personality. The designer can design two programmes and allow the learner to chose, or even make the choice for them based on an MBTI questionnaire. Learners may prefer this but it may not be in their best interest.

SENSING AND INTUITION AS PART OF THE LEARNING CYCLE

The two functions I have just been describing relate to the way we take in information. Within the context of type theory, all of us will prefer one or the other. However, within the overall concept of learning, both activities are required. One follows on from the other. We observe and record the detail of what is happening around us. We concentrate on facts and actuality, recording the experience as it happens.

Let us consider an example. You are chairing a meeting, around you a group of familiar and unfamiliar faces. You see and hear what people do and say. Your Sensing function lets you concentrate on what is actually happening here and now. But you may also draw inferences and make assumptions. In your own mind, you may establish who agrees with whom before they say so. You may make an association with another topic or meeting. It is your intuitive function that lets you concentrate on making links and organizing information. Both these activities are those of perception, making sense of the world around you. Although your preference is for one or the other, both are part of absorbing information from all sources. Both are part of the learning process. If e-learning is to stimulate the Sensing function, it will use images, diagrams and words that describe the concrete present, the here-and-now. If e-learning is to stimulate the iNtuition function it will allow the user to establish links and to make associations.

Making judgments about what you learn

Taking in information, or perceiving, is only half the learning story. Each of us will make decisions and exercise judgment based on the information we perceive. The Thinking function works on the basis of ideas, concepts and logical connections. We use the Thinking function to work out cause and effect. Thinking judgments are usually objective and impersonal. If people are considered in the decision-making process, it is as functioning objects, not as real flesh and blood. People making judgments with this function try to be impartial and unbiased in relation to the way in which the judgment is reached. Personal values and wishes of those involved will not be taken into account (or at least the preference is not to do so). This will include the personal values and wishes of the individual making the judgment. Concern for fairness, impartiality, logic and objectivity will influence the Thinking process. Decisions will be based on information considered relevant.

Making judgments with the Feeling function is more subjective than with the Thinking function. Judgments rely on an understanding of the personal desires and wishes of those involved. A much broader view of the issues is taken. Decisions resulting from a Feeling judgment are likely to be more attuned to others' wishes. A Feeling decision is not an emotional decision, it is made rationally, but an individual's preference is to take account of others rather than relying on facts. Opinions are given equal weight to facts. Those with a Feeling preference try and understand others and what is important to them. They are more interested in the human dimension of a problem than in the technical aspects. They are likely to achieve a harmonious judgment. Decisions are made in a multi-dimensional manner, more like a web or net with any factor relating to any other.

A Thinking judgment is made in a more linear manner with each objective assessment following on one from another. It may be difficult for an individual with a preference for Feeling to explain how they have arrived at a decision. Imagine perhaps a landscape in which hills and valleys appear and vanish. Each rise or fall represents the views or wishes of the humans involved in a decision. As the values and desires of those involved are considered the view keeps changing.

Making decisions and judgments is about organizing and structuring thought. We know that theorizing and planning are essential parts of the learning process. We know from Type theory that our preferences for Thinking or Feeling will be a dichotomy. So some of us have a preference for reflecting and theorizing in relation to the wishes and values of others and the rest of us will do so on plain hard objective measures.

I would like to reflect on a situation in which I was explaining Darwinian evolution theory to a group of teenagers. Darwin's theory was founded on close observation of the natural world. He observed differences in species and related these differences to the environment in which he found them. I might hazard a guess that Darwin's preference for judgment was Thinking because he expounded a theory that took no account of the feelings and values of others. The result at the time was a storm of controversy and protest. To imagine that humankind arose from a primeval slime was startling to many and anathema to some.

For the group of young people in the 1960s, there was an interesting parallel, some were fascinated by the logical deductions made by Darwin and the chain of reasoning that he used. Others were more interested in the drawings and the details of the animals that he observed. Still others were interested in the voyage of the Beagle and the story of how Darwin brought his ideas back to England and struggled with the establishment. There were two who said that they could not believe any of this. They believed implicitly in the words of the Bible, their parents did and had taught them to do likewise. The values and beliefs of those closest to them were more important than the theories and observations of Darwin, supported as they are, by a range of other observations of the natural world and the fossil record.

COMPARING THE USE OF THE JUDGING FUNCTIONS

The two functions I have just described relate to the way we make decisions and judgments. In the learning context, this concerns the way we structure and organize our thoughts and ideas. As with the functions of perceiving it is useful for both functions to be used as part of the learning process. Learning is not just about facts and logical assessments – it is also about motivation, achievement, and what others tell us. Exercising objective judgment is a good follow-on from establishing associations and relationships. Categorizing and summarizing facts and ideas is the exercise of logic and helps us remember things. This is not so much making sense of the world around us, but establishing the impersonal cause and effect that demonstrates how our surroundings work, or at least our view of them. My choice of words implies physical surroundings. But this judgment process includes concepts and ideas, for example, the interpretation that each of us makes as to the meaning of aversion or avid.

Exercising judgment on the basis of human issues adds a further dimension to rational order as it overlays a subjective structure of harmony to the impersonal logic of cause and effect. Imagine chairing a meeting and the ways in which you gather information. On the basis of what you perceive you will decide what to do. Objective judgment indicates that each person should speak for the same length of time and that a previously planned timetable should be followed. Cause and effect logic indicates that the meeting should progress to a clear output. Not only should objective arguments be used but everyone should agree with obvious hard logic. On the other hand, making decisions about how the meeting is run based on Feelings indicates that active talkative people should be allowed more time to contribute, that quiet reflective people will be asked to contribute at a later stage, that people will be swayed by personal feelings and that allowing people to express concerns or air opinions is as important as reaching a conclusion. Similarly, imagine learning algebra, an apparent objective subject wholly dependent upon cause and effect and objective logic. But what is it used for, by whom, when? These subjective elements may help a learner to make more sense of the topic. Learners may find it helpful to anthropomorphize elements in the topic. For example imagining Xs and Ys as little people who swing across the 'equals' sign throwing away their plus or minus nature in the process.

AN EXAMPLE OF THE FUNCTIONS AS A LEARNING CYCLE

The four functions work together as part of a learning process although each of us has a dominant function so that we prefer one of the activities more than the others. To recap:

- Sensing (S) is based in the real world, the detail of the here and now with an emphasis on concrete examples

Drawing inferences, using metaphors and abstract relationships. iNtuiting ideas and concepts	Try out cause and effect, make objective assessments, complete tests. Thinking through organizing what has been learnt.
Observation of real events, practical examples, concrete experiences. Sensing the world around you	Try out conclusions on others, make subjective assessments. Feeling for a subjective result.

Figure 5.3   MBTI functions as learning activities

- Intuition (N) encourages the imagination of future possibilities, associations and relationships
- Thinking (T) brings order to thoughts and events by the application of logic and determining cause and effect, and
- Feeling (F) establishes rational order that rests on harmony between subjective values.

Imagine a learning process that follows through these four activities. Please refer to Figure 5.3 where brief descriptions of the activities from a learning perspective are shown. Imagine you are a manager or supervisor and one of your staff members is performing poorly and you need to formally interview them. You have never done this before. The first thing you do is to find out as much as possible of what is real and immediate about disciplinary interviews. You may want to read as much as possible (or as much as you prefer). You will talk to others: find someone who has conducted such an interview. You might want to see a real practical example by observing another manager. Along the way, you will make comparisons with other interpersonal situations. For example, you may discover that people do not always listen to what is said, that strong emotion prevents clear understanding. You remember a situation with an angry customer who did not clearly state how they felt and would not listen to the facts. You imagine yourself sitting in the meeting and you rehearse what you might say, repeating word patterns in your mind. You exercise logic by writing out a sequence for the interview, jotting down what you will say and the questions you will use. As you try the interview for real, the Feeling function becomes more important. You gain an appreciation of the other person's viewpoint and reasons. Maintaining an even balance between understanding the other and achieving your objectives achieves most from the interview.

Feedback on your own performance comes from Sensing what actually happened, iNtuition by drawing comparisons with what you were told or read. You then make a rational assessment of how well you did, both in terms of the logical flow of the interview and on the balance of the subjective values of both you and the interviewee. The exercise of this judgment gives you a personal sense of achievement. You have taken yourself through a learning cycle by exercising the four functions. The order in which you carry out these activities will be driven both by your personal preferences and the order in which they become available to you. You will prefer one of these functions more than the others and will probable be more practised at it than the other functions. You will spend more time in learning with this function, perhaps to be more accurate you will spend less time with the other functions because you are less comfortable with those types of activities.

How does e-learning contribute?

A consideration of on-line learning solutions indicates that e-learning can contribute to all these functional preferences. On-line material delivers facts and concrete examples and through e-mail you may converse with others who have completed a similar task. All the information you need will be at your fingertips. E-learning allows you to explore some concepts in more depth and relate some of the skills to other situations. For example, questioning skills are a vital part of any interview. It is, potentially, easy to jump from a module on 'the disciplinary interview' to one on questioning, or perhaps on the rights of employees. Intuitive associations lead to the desire to know more, a desire that e-learning can readily satisfy.

Once the information has been collected and associations made then e-learning exercises can explore rational judgments of cause and effect. For example, you might enter questions you will use and phrases you will use into a proforma that structures the interview. The e-learning module may allow you to move items round the screen to try out different sequences. A clever piece of software may well be able to assess your efforts. Simpler than that would be a quiz that asks you to sequence the interview. E-learning readily imparts concepts, practical examples and objective testing, but will e-learning be able to contribute to learning by use of the Feeling function; the preference for establishing rational order by creating an even balance between different subjective values? Computers are not renowned for making subjective judgments. Algorithms (or computer programs) may appear to do so, but they do so by the application of remorseless application of cause and effect. On the other hand, e-learning does put us in contact with other people who do judge subjectively. We can ask such questions as: 'how might an interviewee respond if I said to him or her, some of your colleagues say you have a personal hygiene problem'. Any answer to that has to be subjective. By talking to others, we get several different views on difficult interviews and we can learn and explore ways of maintaining harmony through the interview.

Personal preferences for learning activities

The first part of this chapter explored the impact personality type has on learning, concentrating on type preferences as described by MBTI theory with a brief description of some of Kolb's research and theories. The emphasis has been on the interplay between preferred behaviour and the part each behaviour may play in learning. The cyclic nature of learning is emphasized by Kolb, and Honey and Mumford. Kolb's research indicates that we will prefer two of Kolb's learning modes and use them in one of four combinations. Type theory indicates that each of us has a dominant, auxiliary, tertiary and inferior function. Our natural wish is to focus on one or two of these functions. Our personal preference means that only one of the MBTI activities will be well practised with a second function that we are comfortable with. The second preferred function will always be of a complementary nature to the dominant function. If the dominant function is a perceiving function then the secondary is a judging function. If the dominant function is a judging one then the secondary function is a perceiving one. These two will be the best practised and allow an individual to perceive and make decisions.

Earlier in this chapter it was argued that the four functions represent a learning sequence from reality or theory to logical or subjective organization of knowledge. The natural cycle would seem to be from perceiving detail and examples, through perceiving relationships and inferences, to making logical decisions on cause and effect to making subjective assessments of what learning means to the individual learner. This is shown as a cycle of events in Figure 5.4. This is an idealized model of learning activity and individuals will rarely move from activity to activity in the order shown. Neither should we expect them to, or constrain them to do so. All the observations that are referred to in early chapters show very clearly that learners do not behave in the way learning designers feel that they should. There is a progression from perceiving to judging but those with a preference for judging are likely to organize and structure information before they have absorbed all, or any, relevant information. Their starting point may well be: 'I will judge whether or not I will be interested in this material and what use it will be to me before I start'. Of course those who prefer perceiving are likely to keep looking for information to add to what they are learning long after they have absorbed all that is relevant.

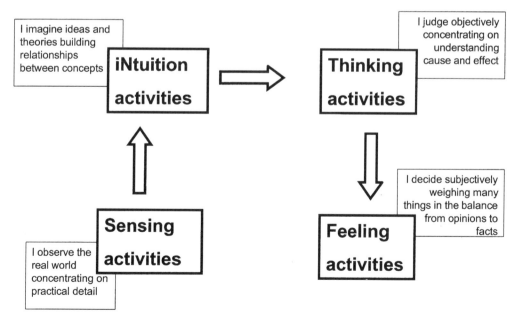

Figure 5.4   Idealized learning route through functions

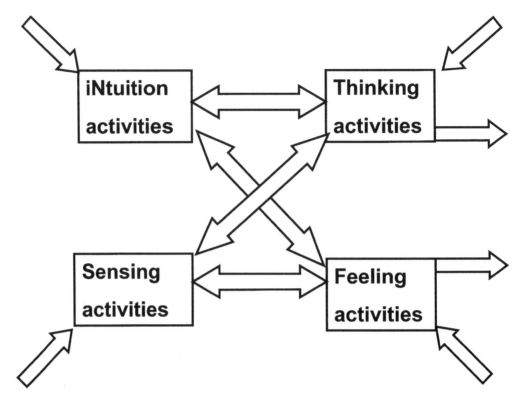

Figure 5.5   Preferred routes through functions

In practice learners are likely to follow a variety of routes dependent upon the dominance of their various functions. A learner might start with their dominant function; for example: why should I (subjective decision); what is the connection with what else I know (objective decision); that is an interesting idea (abstract); what is happening here (concrete example) (see Figure 5.5). Thus, we can see four entry points. Once engaged with the topic the learner may move to any of the other three functional activities. There will be two exit points, if only because a learner must make a decision to cease learning. If we can categorize approaches to e-learning in accordance with these activities then we will be able to relate these categories to personality types and begin to predict how different learners may prefer to learn from e-learning material and design accordingly.

I propose that we can place learning material into one of these three categories. The categorization I am proposing is based on content presentation and on interaction. Content may be presented in terms of detail, as examples, or from a practical aspect. It may be interrelated with other theories and topics and presented as a 'big picture'. We know from the work of Pask that learners prefer strategies that may be characterized as holist or serialist. A hypothesis is that holists have a dominant or secondary preference for iNtuition and that serialists have a dominant or secondary preference for Sensing. Not only can we present e-learning content of both types but we can allow learners to adopt a strategy of accessing the material in the manner that they prefer. Please remember that in discussing content presentation I mean the type of content (example or theory) rather than in how it displayed to the learners. All e-learning content must make full use of visual presentation as well as text, ideally this should include audio and some opportunity for kinesthetic learners to take action and move.

Learning is about making judgments about what you are learning as well as absorbing information. The judgments learners make about learning are required by the interactions the learning process provides for them. In the real world we may interact with those around us and we can chose who to interact with and the nature of that interaction. In the e-learning world our interactions are constrained to a greater degree than they are in the real world. We may categorize most e-learning interactions with the system, or computer, as those that allow learners to make judgments about cause and effect. For example, the typical simulation of a meeting where the learner can exercise a choice about what happens next and the computer plays the next appropriate scene. The nature of on-line material means that any interaction where the learner is involved in organizing their thoughts about what they have learnt is very logical and based on cause and effect. In relation to personality differences this type of decision-making is preferred by those who have a dominant or secondary preference for Thinking. Those who have a dominant or secondary preference for Feeling will prefer to make subjective decisions about their learning.

The nature of subjective decision-making is that many answers may be right. This is not something that can be easily programmed into e-learning material. However, e-mail tutors are able to support subjective decisions and hence work that has many correct answers. This is one way in which we may categorize e-learning:

- examples
- theories
- objective assessment
- subjective assessment.

Just with the use of these four concepts we may present e-learning solutions that make allowances for the preferences of individuals. We may present examples of a theory in practice, we may present the theory and related concepts, we may ask for objective decisions with interactions and we may ask for subjective decisions. What might these concepts mean for individual learners? How are these activities used by each individual who has a particular preference or personality?

An understanding of all the preferences enables us to gain some comprehension of the role that e-learning will play for that individual. From the preceding section, we can already see that those whose dominant function is Feeling may find that e-learning is rather too analytical and objective for them. However, the first step is to understand the way the four functions express themselves in learning preferences, the relationship with the preferences for energy and whether we prefer perceiving or judging. The four dichotomies act together to create the sixteen personality types, so we cannot consider the functions on their own. Chapter 6 describes how the different personality types prefer to learn. It is based on research with learners mostly in traditional educational environments. Before I embark on a description of each personality type and their learning preferences I will explain the relation between the preferences and the functions.

OUR SOURCE OF ENERGY

In establishing personality the four functions do not act in isolation. Each is influenced by preferences or orientation. The Extraverted attitude draws attention from the world outside us – the people around us. Extraverts need to interact with others frequently to maintain enthusiasm, to talk, to gain stimulation from the surroundings. Remember the four functions and that each of us has one function that we prefer most, the dominant function, for the Extravert this function is apparent and obvious, it is exercised in the external world so others see it. Assume the dominant function is iNtuition. If this is extraverted then the individual is obviously interested in new possibilities and the association of ideas: obvious in the sense of making it apparent and involving others. They love to challenge others and need to express their intuitive ideas 'on the outside' so to speak. Later on I shall describe each type in this context, for now remember each of us has a dominant function and for the Extravert this dominant activity (or function) is obvious to others.

The Introvert gets her or his energy from inside, from inner reflection and experience. Dreaming, imagining, linking concepts and ideas give the intuitative Introvert energy and stimulation. The Myers-Briggs definition of Extravert and Introvert is not the same as the normally accepted meaning of sociable and shy. Extraverts may well be outgoing and are likely to prefer the company of others. They will be comfortable in the company of others for longer periods of time than Introverts. For these reasons, Extraverts are more likely to be sociable than Introverts. Introverts may well be more interested in their inner thoughts than in the company of others. Therefore, in social situations they may appear withdrawn and disengaged from conversations occasionally, especially when their own thoughts become directed elsewhere as they follow links and associations in their own mind. It is also true that the Introvert becomes less comfortable in company the longer the time spent with others. Sometimes becoming so drained with the chit-chat around them that they need to break off and go away quietly for some time to recharge their batteries with internal thoughts.

What effect does this have on the dominant function, that is the activity the individual prefers. This is where life becomes a little complicated because the effect is to hide the dominant function from others. So intuitive Introverts prefer being quietly imaginative and enjoy academic achievement. They are likely to imagine further ahead in the future than other types. However, what others see is the auxiliary (what I have previously described as the secondary) function, that is the second most preferred activity. This will be either Feeling or Thinking so what others see is one of the judging functions. Others either see the exercise of logic and decisions based on cause and effect or they see a need and willingness to balance values and beliefs of others to gain a harmonious judgment. Underneath this outward show the most practiced function of associating ideas continues as the most preferred activity.

In Chapter 6, I will describe all personality types in this way but even with these two examples it is apparent that e-learning will mean two very different things to an Extravert intuitive and an Introvert intuitive. The first will want to use the Internet to make connections with other people, to exchange ideas, to explore concepts by discussion. The second will use e-learning on their own, happily exploring concepts and ideas in isolation. They will establish relationships between facts and information perhaps spending more time thinking than reading or looking at web material. They may find a course too constraining and want to explore beyond the arbitrary boundaries imposed by a designer. The communication aspect of e-learning will only become important when decisions are being made about what action to take. They may want to check their logic against others or indeed against a machine quiz. If their auxiliary function is Feeling they will want to know how others might respond to actions they are planning, perhaps participating in an on-line discussion board with questions such as 'how would others respond if I did so-and-so?'

OUR PREFERENCE FOR ORGANIZATION

Let me continue and establish the full picture of type attitudes and describe that of Judgment and Perception. A person with a judging attitude likes to make decisions early, organize plans well in advance and generally ensure that everything has a right place and everything is in that place. Of course these decisions may be either objective or value-based depending on whether the individual is Thinking or Feeling. A judging attitude drives a preference to decide as soon as possible. In the learning context there is a need to seek the correct answer quickly. The learner feels more comfortable having learnt. There may be a correlation with Serialists; that is those whose learning strategy is based on one step at a time. They like order and structure and may well respond to e-learning courses that are self-contained and neatly laid out. Their preference for order and structure means that they may well respond to drill and practice, especially if their judging function is Thinking with a consequential preference for making decisions based on cause and effect. The early designs of programmed learning, either text or machine-driven, support this preference for the correct answer was always only one step away.

Historically, computer-based training and the CD-ROMs that followed, were similar in design concept. The instructional systems design approach may encourage this view as well. The emphasis is on structured learning rather than providing a learning experience. There is an assumption that learners will organize their thoughts in much the same way as the designer. This is implicit in training provided by an employer for an employee to 'do a job'. The process and structure of 'the job' must be learned, by implication, in the order laid down by the designer. People with a preference for judging will be more comfortable with this than people with a perceiving attitude.

A person with a perceiving attitude is more comfortable absorbing new information rather than determining actions. This perception may be based in the immediate real world, on close observation, on internal mental patterns, relationships of ideas and future possibilities. A person with a perceiving attitude prefers gathering new information rather than making decisions, they like to react to what happens and remain open to new ideas and interesting relationships between concepts. A perceiving attitude influences against making decisions and organizing information.

In the learning context there is a need to keep thoughts open and concepts unstructured. The learner enjoys the gathering of information rather than making use of it. There may be some correlation with the holistic learner who likes the big picture and moves from one topic to another without always fully resolving and organizing that topic. In e-learning the learner will enjoy the availability of hyperlinks and the freedom to jump from one topic to another while still being able to return easily. An e-learning course that is well organized and self-contained may leave learners feeling restricted and boxed in. They will appreciate the constant availability of extra material, for example, pop-up boxes, providing extra snippets of detail about concepts or current facts.

DISTRIBUTION OF FUNCTIONAL PREFERENCES

I have now described the MBTI functions and attitudes leading towards two goals. First, a description of how the functions and attitudes react with each other and from that to a discussion of the impact on e-learning. Type theory predicts that each of us will have a dominant function, in that we prefer activities appropriate to that function. Further, the

Table 5.1   Combinations of functions in MBTI types

Dominant function	Auxiliary function	Tertiary function	Inferior function	Type
Sensing	Feeling	Thinking	iNtuition	ISFJ
				ESFP
Sensing	Thinking	Feeling	iNtuition	ISTJ
				ESTP
iNtuition	Feeling	Thinking	Sensing	INFJ
				ENFP
iNtuition	Thinking	Feeling	Sensing	INTJ
				ENTP
Thinking	Sensing	iNtuition	Feeling	ISTP
				ESTJ
Thinking	iNtuition	Sensing	Feeling	INTP
				ENTJ
Feeling	Sensing	iNtuition	Thinking	ESFJ
				ISFP
Feeling	iNtuition	Sensing	Thinking	INFP
				ENFJ

remaining three functions are preferred in a descending order, dominant, second (auxiliary), third (tertiary) and fourth (inferior). Furthermore, type theory also says that if our dominant (or most preferred) function is perceiving then our inferior (or least preferred) function is also perceiving, the auxiliary and tertiary functions being judging functions. The opposite also applies. Thus the four functions can be found in a limited range of combinations as shown in Table 5.1. This still makes eight. Just to help you relate this table to the earlier description of type: the first two functions will appear in your type description and the types are listed in the last column of the table. The preferred function will be the one that is most practiced and you are likely to be best at the activities and behaviours associated with that function.

Those who prefer Sensing are likely to be acute observers of the real environment. They are likely to be realistic, down to earth and practical. What they are least practiced at is thinking about the future, dealing with abstract concepts, with theories and imagining possible futures and opportunities. However, they still need to make decisions and take action so they will have developed one of the judging functions as the auxiliary supporting function. This will be the second most preferred activity. If this is Thinking they are likely to be logical, objective, impersonal and fair. What they are less practised at is in assessing the impact on others, weighing decisions in accordance with the values and beliefs of those around them and taking account of opinions. They will be better at both Sensing and Thinking functions than they are with the behaviours associated with the less preferred functions of iNtuition and Feeling. Another point to note about the table is that the inferior function is matched to the dominant function, thus everyone who prefers Sensing most prefers iNtuition least, everyone who prefers Thinking most prefers Feeling least.

The behaviours associated with our dominant functions are the ones we spend most of our time following. Those behaviours will be the ones we are naturally drawn to when learning. However, they are not necessarily the behaviour that others see most of. If the type

Table 5.2   Distribution of dominant functions

Dominant function	MBTI types	Percentage in the population
Sensing	ISTJ, ISFJ, ESTP, ESFP	39.1
Feeling	ESFJ, ENFJ, ISFP, INFP	26.7
iNtuition	INFJ, ENFP, INTJ, ENTP	13.9
Thinking	ISTP, ESTJ, INTP, ENTJ	20.2

is Introvert then the behaviour seen is that of the auxiliary function. Typically, a face-to-face tutor will make judgments about learners on the basis of behaviours that they observe. This means that they perceive that Introverts prefer their auxiliary, or secondary, function. An advantage of e-learning is that the learner is free to chose an activity that aligns to their preferred function even if that preferred function is hidden from those around the learner. For this reason, Introverts will value e-learning because it allows them to exercise their most preferred function in private. Of course the choice will only be there if the designer has included it within the design of the material.

In learning terms it is ideal if we provide material and activities that are appropriate to an individual's dominant function, irrespective of whether the function is hidden or seen. If we ignore whether the function is Introverted or Extroverted then the population may be considered in four groups. Table 5.2 lists those groups and shows the expected distribution of those preferences. By amalgamating types in this way it becomes possible to contemplate designing e-learning to match these four groups. We can predict, on the basis of type research, what percentage of the population may have a particular dominant function. The research is based on type classification from which we can determine the dominant function. Table 5.3 shows these percentages, based on UK and US research with representative samples of people. It must be within the bounds of possibilities that

Table 5.3   Distribution of dominant and secondary functions

All four functions (in order)	Type	Percentage in the population
Sensing Feeling Thinking iNtuition	ISFJ, ESFP	22.0
Sensing Thinking Feeling iNtuition	ISTJ, ESTP	17.1
Intuition Feeling Thinking Sensing	INFJ, ENFP	9.0
Intuition Thinking Feeling Sensing	INTJ, ENTP	4.9
Thinking Sensing iNtuition Feeling	ISTP, ESTJ	15.0
Thinking iNtuition Sensing Feeling	INTP, ENTJ	5.2
Feeling Sensing INtuition Thinking	ESFJ, ISFP	20.2
Feeling iNtuition Sensing Thinking	INFP, ENFJ	6.5

Notes:

A dominant perceiving function (S or N) is always associated with an auxiliary judging function (T or F) and in turn a tertiary judging function and an inferior perceiving function.

A dominant judging function (T or F) is always associated with a auxiliary perceiving function (S or N) and in turn a tertiary perceiving function and an inferior judging function.

The data is calculated from tables in Kendall (1998) containing an analysis of the UK population and Myers *et al.* (1998) containing an analysis of the US population. The distribution is based on MBTI scores from 4622 individuals.

Table 5.4   Distribution of dominant and auxiliary functions

Dominant or auxiliary function	Percentage in the population
Sensing (taking in information)	74.4
Feeling (making subjective decisions)	57.8
iNtuition (inferring and connecting ideas)	25.6
Thinking (making objective decisions)	42.2

e-learning can provide activities that will be appropriate for each function. In doing so, it must be recognized that activities for one function will not be preferred by those for whom this is not the dominant or auxiliary function.

It follows that these activities and behaviours also dominate the ways in which you, as an individual, prefer to learn. It may help to understand how many of us has a particular function as the dominant one. The last column of table 5.3 shows the percentage of the population whose functions are in the order indicated. I have derived these percentages from the MBTI Manual (Myers *et al.*, 1998) and the Manual Supplement (Kendall 1998). We can go one step further and find out what percentage of the population have each function as either their dominant or auxiliary function. Table 5.4 shows this breakdown. The percentages add up to 200 per cent as I have considered the two most preferred functions. The perceiving functions add up to 100 per cent as do the judging functions. If we consider e-learning as a means of providing information to learners we see that three quarters of the population prefer examples and practical detail, they are less interested in concepts and relationships. We could just show examples and role models and satisfy most learners. If we consider e-learning as a means of helping decide about learning and organize what they have learnt then almost 60 per cent of the population prefer making subjective decisions including the views of others in that process. If you refer back to table 5.3 you will observe that 42 per cent of the population have both Sensing and Feeling as their first two functions. Almost half of us prefer to learn the detail from examples and organize that in subjective ways based upon interactions with others.

E-learning can deal with what is real and immediate by describing practical examples and real stories. Remember we all have to take in information and make decisions and if our dominant function is about making decisions, then this must be supported by a function that is about taking in information. Almost three quarters of the population prefer to take in information that is real and immediate, based in the practical day-to-day world. The traditional manner of learning from a colleague while doing the job is the most frequently used manner of training in the UK. This is borne out by the Learning and Training at Work 2002 Survey (Spilsbury, 2002) that reports 82 per cent of employers provide informal on-the-job training and 62 per cent provide off-the-job training. This type of training is in the real world and it is immediate. No wonder most of us prefer this method of learning. For those of us close to a PC, e-learning can deliver learning that we can put into practice immediately, frequently referred to as byte-size learning. It may appear that Table 5.3 tells us what we need to know about the activities and behaviours that people prefer when learning. If we concentrate on the real and immediate we will provide 75 per cent of the population with the behaviours they most prefer to use when taking in information. We can meet the preference for taking in data for the majority of the population by concentrating on the real and immediate and describing practical examples rather than abstract theory.

Table 5.5 Dominant function related to our source of energy

	Dominant function	Auxiliary function	Seen in the classroom
ISTJ	Sensing	Thinking	Thinking
ISFJ	Sensing	Feeling	Feeling
INFJ	iNtuition	Feeling	Feeling
INTJ	iNtuition	Thinking	Thinking
ISTP	Thinking	Sensing	Sensing
ISFP	Feeling	Sensing	Sensing
INFP	Feeling	iNtuition	iNtuition
INTP	Thinking	iNtuition	iNtuition
ESTP	Sensing	Thinking	Sensing
ESFP	Sensing	Feeling	Sensing
ENFP	iNtuition	Feeling	iNtuition
ENTP	iNtuition	Thinking	iNtuition
ESTJ	Thinking	Sensing	Thinking
ESFJ	Feeling	Sensing	Feeling
ENFJ	Feeling	iNtuition	Feeling
ENTJ	Thinking	iNtuition	Thinking

I propose that we can, in fact design for all MBTI activities and give learners the choice for how to access the material. Every e-learning course will offer data that is real and immediate, data that is abstract and theoretical, a requirement for subjective decisions and a requirement for objective decisions. It may be tempting to consider that this could all be delivered via e-learning. This would fail to recognize what energizes us: do people and the outside environment stimulate us or are we energized by internal feelings and ideas? Table 5.5 provides a way of looking at our dominant function, its relation to our source of energy and which function we allow others to see. This relates our dominant function to being Introverted or Extroverted. In traditional classroom training this distinction is important because this helps us to understand whether an individual's best function is seen by others, as shown in Table 5.5. When interacting with others the Introvert will use their second preferred function, sitting alone at a PC terminal they are more likely to use their preferred function. Not only are they more likely to use a function others do not see but they are likely to be more active in a learning sense. The environment is more likely to stimulate their internal energy.

The reverse appears to be true. Based on research in brain electrical activity (see Myers *et al.*, 1998, p. 261) it seems, when external stimulus is low, Extraverts have lower brain activity than Introverts do. The implication is that Extraverts need involvement with other people to perform at their best. Further research shows Extraverts have a preference for active experimentation and concrete experience, two of Kolb's learning modes. Slightly over half the population are Extraverts and therefore prefer learning approaches that are collaborative. Of the remainder, a further 25 per cent have a primary function that is Sensing and so prefer to relate to that which is real and immediate. It would appear that a significant proportion of the population needs concrete practical experiences that involve other people and this is the type of environment that they need for learning.

Individual needs

I have set a scene for considering an individual's preference for learning behaviours dependent on their personality type as defined by MBTI theory. Given that understanding we can determine their preferences for e-learning activities. We must consider the four functions and their preference order for each individual, whether the dominant function is seen by others or internal in focus. Each dichotomy of function and attitude also has a range of preferred learning activities and these intertwine. For example, Sensing types are likely to prefer serialist learning, memorizing facts and methodical study. Feeling types require a supportive relationship, a concern for caring and holistic learning. It may appear that SFs have a dilemma between serialist and holistic learning. However, either the Sensing or Feeling function will dominate and the learner will therefore prefer a learning strategy that matches the behaviours of their dominant function.

Summary

The MBTI is a tool to measure personality type. There are four dimensions, each of which is a dichotomy. These four dimensions combine into 16 personality types. Two of the dimensions are based on functions; the function of taking in information (or perceiving) and the function of judging on the basis of that information. Some people prefer to take in information by close observation of the surrounding world, recognizing detail and reality and being concerned with practical issues. Others take in information by recognizing logical connections, making inferences and taking a broad view. They seek to understand patterns and different perspectives. This is the Sensing/iNtuition dimension concerned with how we see, or perceive, the world. The other dimension based on function is the Thinking/Feeling dimension. This is the judging function. Some people take decisions by understanding objective criteria and consequences of a course of action. They analyse cause and effect and seek to be highly objective. Others make decisions based upon subjective judgments: on what is important to them and to others. They empathize with others. Each one of these four activities, at opposite ends of each of the two dimensions, may be mapped to learning activities.

The other two dimensions are preferences. Firstly the preference for making decisions, the Judging/Perceiving dimension. Some people prefer a well-ordered and structured life with early decisions and plans and timetables in place. Others prefer to be more spontaneous, always being interested in new experiences and last-minute changes. This preference will be apparent to others, for example someone whose preference is for Judging will be seen by others as making decisions, either objective cause and effect-based decisions (the Thinking function) or subjective decisions based on many factors, including intangible ones (the Feeling function). The fourth dimension (and the other preference) is the Introvert/Extrovert dimension, concerned with where people direct their attention. Some are more interested in what is outside them and others are more interested in internal thoughts. The E or I preference defines where people get their energy from, the Extrovert being energized by company and the Introvert being energized by their internal thoughts.

The four dimensions combine to create 16 personality types. Each personality type will prefer a dominant function (iNtuition, Sensing, Thinking or Feeling); the activities associated with an individual's dominant function will be their most preferred style of learning activity. This might be a preference for taking information in or for making decisions. The dominant function will be balanced by an auxiliary function, which is in a different dimension to the dominant function. For example, if the dominant function is Sensing, the auxiliary function is either Feeling or Thinking. The four functions are in a descending order of preference for each one of us, and the order in which they occur is a factor of personality.

Different individual preferences for learning activity were reported by Kolb. He described four basic learning modes and his research reports that people exercised a preference for two of those learning modes. Kolb proposed that each of us will relate to one of those four styles, Converger, Diverger, Assimilator and Accomodator. Kolb recognized there may be a relationship between his styles and personality.

I propose that we can use the MBTI functions to establish a learning model that we may apply to e-learning implementation and design. E-learning has the capability of making allowances for individual preferences. Each item of e-learning activity can be mapped to one of the four MBTI functions. The way a course is structured can then be mapped against the preferences for organization, the decision-making preference and where learners get their energy from, the preference for the involvement of others. A course might be presented with little involvement with other people where Introverts may be comfortable, but with an option for interactive sessions with others, where an Extrovert might be more comfortable. E-learning material may be well organized, to suit the Judging preference but with an option for the learner to go anywhere at any time either outside or inside the course, which may suit the perceiving preference. MBTI research provides evidence of the distribution of these preferences. The research tells us what percentage of each personality type we may expect within the population and therefore how many people in a typical target group for e-learning might prefer a particular style of learning that matches their dominant function.

6 Using Personality in e-Learning Choices

Designing e-learning for individual preferences

The previous chapter presented conclusions from a significant amount of research based on type differences and the relationships with learning. I have extrapolated that research to draw some inferences about e-learning. I believe that a pattern is emerging that is useful to the e-learning designer. I will now consider each type and from that establish design patterns for e-learning that will create material that makes allowances for individual preferences. In the following section, I have listed each type and the order in which their functions are preferred, given a brief statement on their preferences and then explore in greater detail the learning activities that are likely to be preferred.

I have also given an approximate percentage for the population who are of this type. This is derived from Myers *et al.* (1998) and Kendall (1998) and combines UK and US data. The percentage data is summarized in Table 6.1. It gives an indication of the proportion of the population who will have the preferences for the learning activities that I have listed. I have also expressed this percentage for male and female populations. Some types show a

Table 6.1 Distribution of type typical for US and UK populations

Type	Males (%)	Females (%)
ISFJ	7.7	18.8
ISTJ	17.5	7.5
INFJ	1.4	1.7
INTJ	3.1	0.7
ISTP	9.3	2.4
ISFP	6.3	9.2
INFP	4.0	4.0
INTP	4.6	1.5
ESTP	6.5	3.3
ESFP	6.6	10.4
ENFP	6.0	8.9
ENTP	3.9	2.3
ESTJ	11.3	7.4
ESFJ	7.0	17.5
ENFJ	1.8	3.3
ENTJ	3.2	1.2

Note: This table represents both US and UK percentages as published in Myers *et al.* (1998, pp. 158, 159) and Kendall (1998, pp. 58, 59).

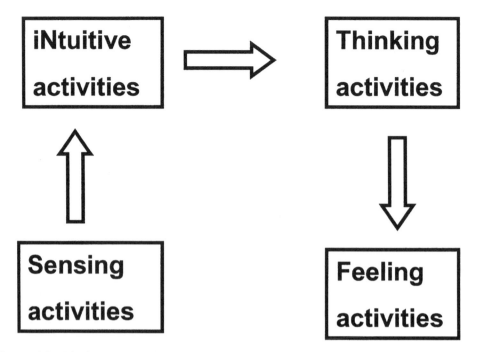

Figure 6.1 Idealized route through functions

marked difference in spread according to gender. Feeling types for example are represented in 72 per cent of the female population but only 38 per cent of the male population. The opposite balance occurs with a Thinking preference which is overrepresented in the male population. It is no wonder that a typical female trait is perceived as empathy with others and a typical male trait as applying logic to decisions that affect others. Still one quarter of females prefer to make decisions on objective criteria and one third of males prefer to make subjective decisions that are likely to include the opinions of others.

Before I launch into this list there is one very important caveat. Each of us prefers our dominant function and therefore practises this most often. The principle of personal development is to develop the other functions (auxiliary, tertiary and inferior) and practise the behaviours so that we become comfortable and familiar with those as well. The order of the functions does not imply competence, or lack of competence, in the activities and behaviours associated with these functions. Indeed in the previous chapter, I highlighted the importance of the four functions working together in a learning situation so that we naturally move from what is real and immediate (S) to associations between concepts and ideas (N) to objective decisions about course and effect (T) through to determining actions on the basis of comparative merits and values (F). This idealized view is shown in Figure 5.4 in the previous chapter (page 111). It is important for all of us to develop the full range of functions so that we can be competent in all behaviours, although we will always prefer some over others. The following sections describe each personality type and the preferences they have that are relevant to learning. One of these descriptions will match you and your preferences, so you should recognize one of the following descriptions as yourself. All these descriptions are founded in research fully reported in Myers *et al.* (1998). The inferences about individual's preferences for e-learning are largely my own.

Introvert types

ISFJ – MALES 7.5 PER CENT, FEMALES 18 PER CENT

This type gains stimulus and energy internally, focuses on the real and immediate, makes decisions on subjective human values and likes structure and order. Introverted Sensing dominates, supported by Feeling decision-making which is what others see. Thinking is a less preferred activity and iNtuition least preferred. There is a preference for carefully gathering and absorbing facts and information for later use. They appear academic and studious with a steady approach to learning, favouring serialist strategies. They will value concrete experience and although introverted will get value from working with others. Their data gathering activities are internal with no need to involve others. They do live in the real world as opposed to the world of concepts and ideas. Long sections of theoretical text will not be liked. Descriptions of practical examples or real world activity that they can observe will be preferred. The auxiliary function of deciding, based on relative merit and values will be seen by others. When they decide to take action on learning then wider issues relating to other people are brought into play, although only the immediate and real information will have been gathered. The Introvert preference means that they will be thinking internally and be irritated by external activity that distracts them. Their best answer rarely comes immediately. The Judging preference means they will want clear goals, structure and a well-ordered learning environment. They like plans and a well-mapped out future.

The ISFJ seems ideally suited to e-learning, being happy studying on their own in an ordered and self-contained world, but the Feeling preference means that action and decisions need to take others into account. An ISFJ will value a supported learning environment perhaps with a local counsellor or coach. Such a person must not be distracted, but on hand to help translate the learner's perceptions into rational order; perhaps making lists, selecting and noting key points or answering questions. Feeling judgments are based on group values and time spent in a discussion board may be more valuable. Indeed the focus of inward energy means that electronic communication with others may be less energy-draining than talking to a real person. ISFJs are likely to appreciate the self-containment of e-learning, the opportunity to quietly gather data at their own pace, without launching off into the wider Internet. The learning plans feature of LMS will be appreciated with clear time-dependent goals for progressing through learning. Discussion boards and tutors will be valued at a later stage of learning to test out decisions rather than gather more information. Chatrooms are more likely to be used for lurking rather than participation. The opportunity to manage their own learning may only be valued when they are given direct guidance and set goals by someone they respect. The asynchronous aspect of e-learning communication is a benefit giving them time to reflect before replying.

ISTJ – MALES 18 PER CENT, FEMALES 7.5 PER CENT

This category gains stimulus and energy internally, focuses on the real and immediate, makes objective decisions on cause and effect and likes structure and order. Introverted Sensing dominates supported by Thinking decision-making which is what others see. Feeling is a less preferred activity and iNtuition least preferred. There is a preference for carefully gathering and absorbing facts and information for later use. ISTJs appear academic and studious. Research studies show that this type is overrepresented among those who score well in academic exams. They favour order and method in study, being serialist learners. They value concrete experience and although introverted get value from working with others. Data gathering is internal with little need for involving others. Descriptive practical examples of real world events will be appreciated more than sections of theoretical explanations and ideas. The auxiliary function of deciding is based on the exercise of logic and determining cause and effect. It is this auxiliary function that will be seen by others. The ordering and structuring of facts will be a preferred learning activity as will determining cause and effect. Action will be determined by the immediate facts to hand and the exercise of objective logic. The Introvert preference means that they will be self-contained and distracted by external activity. Their best answer does not come immediately. The Judging preference means they will value clear goals and order and structure. Clear pre-set goals and objectives are liked especially when tied down with plans, a precisely defined future and study goals.

The ISTJ seems even more suited to e-learning than the ISFJ. Web-delivered learning provides a self-contained clear structure that the ISTJ can study on their own at their own pace. The importance of logic in making decisions is appropriate to a computer learning environment. They have less use for collaborative learning although the Sensing function does need to collect data from the real world. Video segments may provide this real world input (which may also be valued by other Sensing types). Their application of objective logic does not need to be tested against others so the ISTJ has less need of human contact than the ISFJ. Their focus on internal energy means that others drain this energy, so electronic communication will be preferred, both for its remoteness and the fact that replies can be considered and thought about before being made. Discussion boards, tutors and chatrooms are likely to be of less interest than with many other types. The LMS feature of learning plans and monitoring progress against plans will be appreciated, bringing order and structure to the learning challenges. The opportunity to manage their own learning will be appreciated although clear-cut logical goals set by others are also likely to be appreciated.

INFJ – MALES 1.5 PER CENT, FEMALES 1.5 PER CENT

INFJs gain stimulus and energy internally, focus on patterns and relationships, make decisions on subjective human values and like structure and order. Introverted iNtuition dominates supported by the auxiliary function of Feeling decision-making which is what others see. Thinking is a less preferred way of making decisions and Sensing is the least preferred activity, so this type does not prefer to pay attention to what is real and immediate. Research shows that INFJs make successful students in traditional education. They have a preference for patterns and relationships, liking ideas, theories and complex, but linked arrangements of concepts. Action taken in learning will be based on a very broad picture. Their preference for internal thoughts means that they will be self-contained in study but distracted by others. On the other hand decisions are based on subjective human values. The INFJ needs interaction with others to make judgments about their learning. For the INFJ learning must not be a lonely experience but it may be remote from others. The insights and complex thoughts that an INFJ prefers tend to be private and only shared with those close to them. The required closeness and trust is unlikely to be achieved with other e-learning students. Because people with INFJ preferences seem intuitively to understand issues of human relationships, they may well perceive difficulties and issues faced by other learners they interact with. Helping others in the learning process may well add to their sense of value and worth. This is offset by a liking for complex big picture explanations that gloss over fine detail. This may overcomplicate learning for others where a group works together over the Internet.

Research shows that this type is overrepresented in successful academic learners and their inward focus implies e-learning will not drain their natural energy. However, the value they place in close committed personal relationships implies that they will expect a lot from a tutor (or e-tutor) and that a tutor relationship needs some permanency, almost an active mentor more than a tutor.

INTJ – MALES 3 PER CENT, FEMALES 0.5 PER CENT

This type gains stimulus and energy internally, focuses on patterns and relationships, makes objective decisions based on cause and effect and likes structure and order. In educational terms the INTJ shows many similarities with the INFJ. Research shows that they are overrepresented in high academic achievers. Their introverted iNtuition dominates and this results in a liking for complex theoretical and abstract ideas. They value knowledge and this encourages an inward drive for more. Again they are big picture learners synthesizing rather than analysing. What others see is the auxiliary Thinking function expressing itself as logical decision-making. They appear private individuals, very self-reliant who apply high standards to themselves rather than others. They are long term thinkers (research shows that INTJs project thoughts about what they will do further into the future than other types).

They seem well suited to e-learning provided that they do not feel overburdened with detail. Their preference for planning far into the future makes it easier for them to contemplate quite large study programmes for e-learning. This is combined with little need for interaction with others and an expressed preference for learning (actually expressed in research results as being overrepresented in 'taking classes and going to school').

ISTP – MALES 9.5 PER CENT, FEMALES 2.5 PER CENT

This group gains stimulus and energy internally, focuses on the real and immediate, makes objective decisions on cause and effect and prefers variety and new ideas. In educational terms, the ISTP prefers solitude, willing to work on their own. However, research shows that they are one of three personality types most likely to be in trouble at school (with the INTP and the INFP). This may be caused by a need for independence that is characteristic of this type. Their Introvert Thinking dominates and this results in a desire to understand the structures and concepts that underpin facts. However, they also deal in the real and concrete disliking discussions of theoretical possibilities or associating ideas. What others see is a liking for picking up detailed information and a willingness to change direction as a result.

E-learning gives the opportunity for working on their own that ISTPs like and presentation by computer is more likely to appeal. Myers *et al.* (1998, p. 81) describe their minds as working 'almost like computers, organizing data, reasoning impersonally and objectively'. However, their need for the real and immediate must be met by e-learning, and in some detail. Descriptions of real examples will have much greater attraction than presentations of theory. Notwithstanding that statement their auxiliary Thinking function means they will show a liking for cause and effect demonstrations perhaps through simulations. Research shows that ISTPs tend to prefer maths and practical skills, liking hands-on analytical work.

ISFP – MALES 5.5 PER CENT, FEMALES 9 PER CENT

This category gains stimulus and energy internally, focuses on the real and immediate, makes decisions on subjective human values and prefers variety and new ideas. In educational terms, although willing to work on their own, they need encouragement and motivation from those around them. The dominant Introvert feeling means that they are quiet, reserved and private individuals. Privacy does not mean isolation and ISTPs value harmonious relations with those around them. They tend to concentrate on the present and the past (research shows that they project themselves the fewest number of years into the future when asked to talk about the future). Pure Internet communication is likely to be unsatisfactory because of the need for a personal relationship with an on-line tutor. A telephone call may well be needed to establish what is seen as a harmonious relationship between a remote tutor and the learner. Research reported in Myers *et al.* (1998, p. 258) mentions a study which showed INFPs to be least persistent in study in one college and most persistent in another. One possible explanation for this is that ISFPs are most dependent on the encouragement of others and the learning environment in their immediate vicinity. This encouragement will have to be that of real people close to them. If e-learning is to be a successful form of study for them it will require local coaches and mentors as well as remote tutors.

INFP – MALES 4 PER CENT, FEMALES 4 PER CENT

INFPs gain stimulus and energy from within, focus on patterns and relationships, make decisions based on subjective human values and like variety and new ideas. The INFP shows great similarity to the ISFP in educational terms being quiet and reserved. However, their Introvert iNtuition means they are much more interested in ideas and concepts. Research shows they enjoy writing, reading, art and music. None of these are activities in which e-learning has particular strengths. They need to see patterns and build up associations in the subject matter they learn. Theory is more important than practical examples. E-learning can cope with this need, indeed the nature of hypertext makes it easy to show associations and encourage learners to launch out of e-learning into the wider web world to investigate and probe. However, the auxiliary Feeling function means the INFP need to care and be concerned about people, indeed they readily show loyalty to people or perhaps a humanitarian cause.

The success of e-learning for them may well depend on the relationship established with a remote tutor or some other human aspect to the learning. Such relationships need to be authentic with genuine understanding between the two parties. Again telephone calls are likely to be more important in making e-learning successful than asynchronous e-mails or discussion boards. Because of their public and rather impersonal nature chatrooms are unlikely to establish in-depth relationships for the INFP.

INTP – MALES 4.5 PER CENT, FEMALES 1.5 PER CENT

The final type gains stimulus and energy from within, focuses on patterns and relationships, makes objective decisions based on cause and effect and prefers variety and new ideas. Like the ISTP, the INTP will work on their own for long periods of time quite happily. Their independence is likely to thrive in an e-learning situation since they are freed from the constraints of a classroom tutor dictating the pace and the content. The INTPs liking for association and relationships between ideas is met by the freedom to jump out and search on the web for related concepts. Of course, their independence and liking for new concepts will combine to ensure they never finish what they start.

The implementation of much of e-learning has an inherent lack of structure and order. The use of tutors, cohorts and collaborative tools (or virtual classrooms) brings some order. Assignments have to be completed on time, virtual events attended and fellow students helped. Such discipline is important to the INTP although they may resent it. Their strong liking for making associations and for novelty will mean that a serially-presented e-learning module will quickly became boring. The freedom to move around the material at will is valued by the INTP.

Common features of introvert learning preferences

I have concentrated on those who gain energy and stimulus from within themselves, the Introverts in MBTI type theory. The initial assumption might have been that Introverts would flourish in the remote and apparently impersonal environment of e-learning. Research and a study of type theory shows that Introverts do need people. They need people for two reasons, some need people as a sounding board, others to build their own confidence and to encourage them to learn. If we begin to consider the MBTI types in categories we can see that there are design options for e-learning that will reflect the individual's needs. If an analysis of MBTI and e-learning merely showed that 16 different types of e-learning solutions were needed then such an analysis is of little practical use to a designer. But a very simple look at the role people play for MBTI types shows that we can classify the role of other people as either:

- a sounding board for ideas and concepts, or
- a source of motivation and guidance.

There are also those Introverts who have little need for others in the learning process, their sounding board is the application of objective logic and motivation comes from within. The I-T type fits this profile.

Another obvious difference that emerges is the need for theory and concepts as opposed to practical examples of the real and immediate. MBTI types divide very obviously into those who focus on the real world (S) and those who focus on the world of ideas and concepts (N). It is a simple process for the e-learning designer to present information in two ways:

- theory and concepts
- examples of the application of those theories and concepts.

Most designers would do that naturally. The advantage of e-learning is that the order in which that information becomes available can be altered by the learner. A simple menu that allows the learner to choose whether to see a practical example or read the theoretical concept first enables those whose preference is for Sensing to focus initially on the real and immediate and those whose preference is for iNtuition to focus initially on theory and concept.

The different value learners place on freedom and order also present a simple opportunity for the designer to make an allowance for individual preferences. Those who prefer variety and new ideas like the freedom to roam at will through material. Those who prefer structure and order will like a clearly laid out course that they will study in the order intended. Hypertext makes it simple for the designer to create material that is laid out with a study plan in mind and yet allows some learners to jump around the material at will. The designer must also recognize that learners with a preference for variety will not prefer to finish what they started. In any study programme some discipline is needed. The very same learners who get into trouble at school because of their independence will avoid the tedious completion of topics. Such learners require milestones and targets that they willingly subscribe to or better yet, create themselves.

This introduces an important role for the learning log and learning plan. E-learning provides an ideal environment for a learner to set their own unique learning goals and then be monitored against the achievement of those goals. An individual's need for freedom and independence is balanced with the requirement for order and discipline that is needed for learning to have successful outcomes. Learners also need to express some freedom and independent thought. Those who prefer structure and order need to be sent out on web 'safaris' to search out and bring back nuggets of information. It would appear from research and a study of type that the majority of those who like structure and order also like to use others as a sounding board. Where e-learners are in a cohort, then it is simple to present the results of a web safari to others.

However, I am perhaps coming up with too many conclusions when I have only discussed half the number of MBTI types. I have presented these thoughts at this stage so that you can see where this discussion of types and educational research is leading. E-learning gives us options for presenting learning material in particular forms and with particular options. It will be possible to map individual's preferences against those options, in many, if not all, cases as one of two alternatives. A discussion of just the Introvert types so far shows that there is an obvious choice between presenting concepts or examples. Bearing this in mind let me continue this discussion of types working my way through the Extroverts.

Extrovert types

ESTP – MALES 7 PER CENT, FEMALES 3 PER CENT

This type gains energy and stimulus from the outside world, focuses on the real and immediate, makes objective decisions based on cause and effect and prefers variety and new ideas. ESTPs like the freedom to experience the world directly. Learning is about seeing, touching and smelling. Their dominant function seen by those around them is Sensing. Research shows that they value working with others and take what is presented to them at face value. One research study (reported in Myers *et al.*, 1998, p. 233) showed them to be one of two types (with ESFP) with the lowest overall grade in college. Another study showed that this type had some of the highest numbers staying at college. A combination of research and type study indicates that ESTPs are likely to be very much influenced by the world immediately around them. Therefore, they learn well when the environment encourages learning.

E-learning has a couple of inherent weaknesses for this type. However real and practical the examples presented, they cannot be as real and practical as what is happening out of the window or in the room. But this is little different to the classroom. The tutor presenting does not present material that is real and immediate. On the other hand, workplace learning is real and immediate, can be seen, touched and smelled. The ESTP learns better when plunged into a real world problem. The environment provided by others influences them. A tutor may motivate learning but others in the immediate environment must value learning as well. They represent a significant challenge for e-learning. Those in the immediate environment have more influence than remote tutors or co-learners. Even a close relationship with a mentor seems unlikely to counteract the wider environment. It might be said that the ESTP is a fairly typical 'party animal' living for the moment in the company of others (a role even more enthusiastically taken by the ESFP). E-learning does have one asset for the ESTP, they want the freedom to do their own thing their own way. At least e-learning frees them from the constraint of a tutor.

ESFP – MALES 6.5 PER CENT, FEMALES 10.5 PER CENT

This category gains energy and stimulus from the outside world, focuses on the real and immediate, makes decisions on subjective human values and prefers variety and new ideas. The ESFP has the same extroverted dominant function as the ESTP. Like them, they prefer to learn directly in the real world, hearing, touching, seeing, and smelling everything in detail. ESFPs are perhaps more dependent on others. Research shows that they 'look to others for guidelines' (Myers *et al.*, 1998, p. 255) and are very accepting of what is presented to them. ESFPs are good in teams and prefer to learn by doing. They will learn best in an environment where those around them focused on learning as a natural part of living and working. Their decision-making is strongly based in empathy for others. Co-learners will provide a sounding board but are also there to be helped. Co-learners are a very important part of their learning process, ideally being part of the workplace. Perhaps more than other types the ESFP needs someone to study with. An e-learning solution that is designed for self-study must allow at least one other to co-study preferably co-located. Where study is with a cohort then, ideally, some of the cohort will be close enough for personal contact. This may be quite a dilemma if an INTP is co-located with an ESFP. Other features that may make e-learning more attractive for the ESFP are workplace assignments, real world practical examples and the freedom inherent in hypertext, all things valued by the ESTP as well.

ENFP – MALES 6 PER CENT, FEMALES 8.5 PER CENT

ENFPs gain energy and stimulus from the outside world, focus on concepts and patterns, make decisions on subjective human values and prefer variety and new ideas. The dominant function of iNtuition means that ENFPs see links between ideas easily and make connections and associate ideas that others do not. Their external focus means that they are stimulated by new ideas, experiences, activity and people. For them, life is always full of exciting new possibilities. Research shows that this translates both into learning success and difficulties. ENFPs are reported as significantly overrepresented among those achieving academic success but also as one of three types most likely to have trouble at school. Type theory indicates that ENFPs need the encouragement and support of others. It may be that if they do not feel appreciated this translates into frustration resulting in troublesome behaviour.

The implication for e-learning is that tutors, and perhaps co-learners, must provide that appreciation and encouragement. E-learning can also present many new ideas and exciting possibilities gaining and retaining the attention of the ENFP in this. They will be attracted to the freedom inherent in e-learning but may resent the discipline of study. They will prefer concepts and theory to practical examples. ENFPs are highly gregarious and sociable and because they have a large circle of friends it is possible for those in a remote cohort to be included within this circle. However, they also need close and personal relationships and it is probable that at least one co-learner will need to fulfil that role within the learning context.

ENTP – MALES 4 PER CENT, FEMALES 2 PER CENT

This type gains energy and stimulus externally, focuses on concepts and patterns, makes decisions objectively on cause and effect and prefers variety and new ideas. ENTPs share the same dominant function as ENFPs. They are stimulated by the same things and for them life is also full of exciting new possibilities. Research shows that they are perhaps more likely to get into difficulty at school than ENFPs. This may be a reflection of the fact that they tend not to base their decisions in subjective human values. They may be less likely to behave in a manner that conforms, unless the logic for so doing is clear and apparent.

They will value e-learning that presents concepts and ideas and gives them the opportunity to explore both associated ideas and new ones. They are stimulated by problems but would rather dive directly into solving them than in planning a solution. They will value e-learning that gives them this opportunity. People are perhaps less important in the learning process and a flexible e-learning solution with or without co-learners is likely to suit them.

ESTJ – MALES 11 PER CENT, FEMALES 8 PER CENT

This group gains energy and stimulus from the outside world, focuses on the real and immediate, makes decisions objectively on cause and effect and prefers structure and order. The dominant function of Thinking means that this type is very comfortable with the logical layout of most e-learning material. The order and structure usually required when material is displayed by computer feels natural and appropriate to ESJTs. Their function of Thinking is seen by others and they will use it to organize and structure their learning. Goals, targets and learning plans will be attractive. Consistently laid out websites using tried and tested design standards will be preferred to a, perhaps, haphazard exploratory web safari. Their auxiliary function of Sensing means a preference for the real and immediate. Practical examples will be preferred to theoretical explanations. This type likes to be in control of the situation around them. Research shows that they are overrepresented among teachers, educators and educational administrators in the business and technical environment. ESTJs are one of four types who are most frequently found among those who achieve the highest grades in education. Research into expressed attitudes show ESTJs are more likely to regard achievement and accomplishment as important and more likely to enjoy playing sports. The need to gain energy and stimulus from the outside indicates a need for social interaction. The desire for control means that ESTJs frequently take leadership positions in social or business situations. This does not necessarily mean that people always have to be there to be sources of stimulus and energy. Other external stimuli may also energize and enthuse the ESTJ. Thought-provoking video segments may provide the needed external stimulus particularly if this is of a charismatic thought leader or well-respected industry figure. However, there is probably no substitute for people contact. ESTJs are naturally sociable and enjoy interacting with others. Some of this need can be fulfilled through e-mail contact and the telephone but personal contact will be important. This does not have to be with a tutor, indeed the ESTJ's need for control means that they may well prefer to be working with a learning set on some learning task or assignment. This brings them into contact with their co-learners in a situation within which they can naturally step forward to a leadership role.

ESFJ – MALES 7 PER CENT, FEMALES 18 PER CENT

This category gains energy and stimulus from the outside world, focuses on the real and immediate, makes decisions on subjective human values and prefers structure and order. The dominant function is one of Feeling and this is very much directed at others and external situations. ESFJs tend to love organizing others in social environments. They have a great need for harmony and tend to be well practised at defusing conflict and tension in others. E-learning may well feel very sterile to the ESFJ. Their ability to show warmth and encouragement to others will not come across in e-mail or virtual meetings of any type. Their auxiliary function is Sensing leading to a preference for practical and immediate information and facts. They will not like theoretical explanations and abstract ideas. Research shows that this type values harmony in their social, business and family life and they tend to prefer occupations concerned with care for others, one of which is education. One study showed that ESFJs were the most frequent type to qualify in education and in health occupations. It is likely that those around them have a very significant impact on their attitudes to learning and their motivation to persist with study. This type is likely to be very dependent on a good relationship with their tutor for them to learn successfully. It is almost as if their need for harmonious relationships will make them study because in that way they can please their teacher or tutor. It seems unlikely than an on-line tutor can have the same impact on an ESFJ as their colleague with whom they interact in person on a day-to-day basis. Energetic theoretical debate that make chatrooms and bulletin boards attractive for some people present two aspects that ESFJs dislike. An essential feature of any debate is conflict. Conflict is not harmonious and this makes an ESFJ uncomfortable. Debates are about theories rather than facts and practical issues which are preferred by this type.

E-learning material that describes real people in real situations will appeal, especially where these people demonstrate the ideal. ESFJs will learn by example. An e-learning example can never be as forceful or as clear as a colleague, but it is a way of demonstrating best practice. ESFJs are likely to respond well to people like them in circumstances like theirs. A video segment of an actor will have less impact than a video segment of a colleague doing much the same job as they do. This is reinforced when their colleague is pleased and proud of what they are doing. Interactions seem important to the ESFJ because they like those around them to be happy. The delivery of e-learning faces a significant challenge in trying to meet this need. A framework of local support provides one of the most straightforward ways of meeting this need.

Learning centres where people congregate for the purpose of learning gathers people around the ESFJ. If they can help others with their learning this becomes a reward in itself. Clearly this can be achieved with the learning set concept where groups of learners work together to solve a common learning problem. But it can also be achieved by bringing together groups of learners on different courses and topics who talk about their experience of studying, how they organize their lives, how they feel about studying at a computer. The dilemma is that some people (most notably the INT types) will feel this is a waste of time and highly intrusive. Why bother with all this people stuff? Since this is unlikely to lead to harmony this is not helpful to the ESFJ. So the framework of local support means bringing people together who have similar needs in interacting with others and in helping others.

ENFJ – MALES 2 PER CENT, FEMALES 3 PER CENT

ENFJs gain energy and stimulus from the outside world, focus on concepts and patterns, make decisions on human subjective values and prefer structure and order. The dominant function is one of Feeling and this is seen by others. This appears as a well-practised empathy that understands other people, their concerns, their wishes and what drives them. Like the previous type, the ENFJ prefers harmony and appreciates praise. ENFJs like to be supportive, sympathetic to others and like drawing out the best in others.

E-learning may seem sterile to them except that they are interested in new ideas and possibilities especially those that may contribute to greater harmony. Their auxiliary function of iNtuition creates this interest in ideas and connections, especially those related to people. Research shows that ENFJs are one of two types who are expected to have least trouble at school. This is shared with the ISFJ and may be based on their preference for order as well as the value they place on harmony. One might expect the other FJ types to similarly respond well to a school environment. The dominant function of Feeling means that this type requires encouragement and support to do well. The implication is that they will do well, or better, in a supportive environment. Correspondingly they will suffer the most in a non-supportive environment. Indeed one US research study showed that the ENFJ type was among the lowest for staying at college. This conflicts with their self-reported statement of what is important to them (see Myers *et al.* 1998, p. 259). The statement that education and learning is very important to them is overrepresented in responses from ENFJs.

Other activities valued by this type are appreciating art, writing, music and reading. The evidence and type theory suggest that ENFJs are very reliant on their environment for success, particularly for success in learning. The same support structures that were suggested for the ESFJ should also work for the ENFJ. However they will relate more closely with content that deals in theory, ideas and makes connections with other ideas. ENFJs would rather be imaginative than practical.

ENTJ – MALES 3.5 PER CENT, FEMALES 1 PER CENT

The final type gains energy and stimulus from the outside world, focuses on concepts and patterns, makes objective decisions based on cause and effect and prefers structure and order. The dominant function of Thinking which is seen by others makes ENTJs analytical, very objective and ruthlessly logical. To others they may appear very harsh and critical. They have a strong urge to sort out problems they see as illogical and inefficient. The auxiliary function of iNtuition means they are interested in concepts and ideas rather than practical detail. This combined with a preference for structure and order makes them great planners. Strategic forward planning combines their preference for big picture thinking and action.

Research shows that they tend to be academically successful with achievement and learning high on their scale of values. Certainly type theory and research indicates that

ENTJs have the self-reliance and independence to use e-learning on their own. ENTJs seem to be energetic, fluent and commanding personalities. This type is overrepresented among those who enjoy exercise which indicates a need to be energetic. This with their introverted iNtuition means that they may intimidate others with their self-confidence, energy, decisiveness and apparent speed of thought.

E-learning will be appreciated as it allows them to set the pace. It does lack the stimulating interactions with others that energize and motivate the ENTJ. The ENTJ thrives on challenge and debate and may well enjoy an active bulletin board. The ENTJ enjoys challenging others and expects to be challenged in return. Any bulletin board debate would have to be argumentative but leading through to a conclusion and something learned.

Common features of extrovert learning preferences

I am sure that it will be no surprise to the reader that a discussion of type theory and research for Extroverts introduces more external issues than the previous discussion on Introverts. Extroverts need people more than Introverts, but some of the reasons for this need are different. The preference for leading people begins to emerge among some Extrovert types. This may manifest itself as a preference for organizing people, frequently in the social context rather than the work context.

Other Extrovert types have a preference for helping others and the learning environment gives many opportunities for that. In the previous section on Introverts, I described two roles fulfilled by people (1) to give encouragement, (2) to act as a sounding board for ideas. To those we can add another (3) to be helped and organized. Another aspect of learning also emerges when we consider Extroverts. Both the ESTP and the ESFP like practical examples but they like to immerse themselves in the real world. They need to touch and feel as well as look and read. This need can best be met in the real world, in the work place. Those who advocate e-learning, as I do, should take some comfort from the fact that the classroom, as an alternative to e-learning is probably, also not real enough for these types as a learning environment. They learn best in the workplace, dealing with real and immediate issues.

Can we create 16 different courses?

I have listed the 16 personality types and described how they might relate to e-learning based on an understanding of type and on the research available. It would be bizarre in the extreme to suggest that e-learning was designed with 16 variations so that it would suit each personality type. One of the great commercial advantages of e-learning is that one product can serve the needs of hundreds, if not thousands, of individuals. Dividing the number of users by 16 quickly destroys the commercial argument for e-learning.

Perhaps we could concentrate on the preferences of the majority. After all 40 per cent of all females are represented by just three types (ISFJ, ENFP, ESFJ) and 39 per cent of males are represented by another three types (ISTJ, ISTP and ESTJ). If we concentrated on producing e-learning that works with these six types then that would meet the needs of most users. Even with this approach we have problems since the female personalities are fairly disparate. At least all the male types I mention are STs so they will prefer concrete examples and objective decision making. If we add in the ESTP males then almost half of all males are ST, a far more useful statistic to work with. STs prefer content that is practical and objective, not difficult for e-learning to present. This predominance of ST among males may also explain why computing seems to appeal to males more than females.

Computing is practical dealing with objective decisions and cause and effect. This environment appeals to the personalities of 46 per cent of males and about 21 per cent of females. It would be simpler for the designer to fix in his/her head a concept of the ideal learner and design with that one person in mind. Many designers work in that way spending time and effort understanding the so-called target group. That approach will not work if the designer uses a didactic controlling approach (the teacher teaching rather than the learner learning). This is demonstrated very strongly by the research work of Carroll. It is more productive for the designer to concentrate on the topic and the nature of the topic.

It is far more useful to consider the features of e-learning than which personalities would appreciate those features. What we do need to do is to make each feature relevant and valuable to one of the four activities that make up the functions, provide for interpersonal interaction for those that need that source of energy, test objectively and assess subjectively. On that basis it may be possible to use all features in such a way that individuals get to use their preferred learning environment. Although e-learning is the same for everyone, an element of choice can be built in. If this choice matches the dichotomies of the MBTI then e-learning can go a long way to matching the personalities of users. The first step along that particular road is to describe the features of e-learning in a way that relates to the preferences of particular MBTI personalities.

Features of e-learning related to personality preferences

CONTENT TYPE

One difference that is plain in all the previous descriptions is that some people are more interested in the specific and in detail than others. Generally speaking those whose dominant or auxiliary function is Sensing prefer to focus on practical real examples. They prefer the concrete to the abstract. Those whose dominant or auxiliary function is iNtuition prefer to focus on concepts, theories and ideas. They prefer the abstract and the overview feeling uncomfortable with detail and disinterested in the concrete. One way of describing this is to say an S (someone who has a preference for Sensing) will prefer to experience and an N needs to understand. E-learning gives us the option of presenting abstract theory supported by real life examples and for the user to view the material in the order they prefer. An S can study and immerse themselves in the detailed examples completing the learning exercise with a brief look at the underlying theory and concepts. An N is someone who has a preference for iNtuition and can study and puzzle over the theory and complete the learning exercise by a quick glance at one of the examples. The content of both needs to be developed to an equal depth, a challenge in itself for the designer who will have one of the two preferences. Not all types fit ideally into these two groupings. The ISTP likes to understand the logic and cause and effect that the real world examples demonstrate but they dislike abstract theory. This group is overrepresented among those who like mathematics.

Both Introverts and Extroverts are equally represented among those who prefer theory and those who prefer concrete practical examples. Examples that are closer to reality will be preferred by the Extroverts particularly the ESTP and ESFP as already mentioned. Examples that learners can relate to the world in their immediate vicinity will benefit the Extrovert who prefers Sensing (ESs). Perhaps even going so far as to give them assignments to do in the real world before coming back to the e-learning. Those who prefer iNtuition will prefer theoretical explanations and abstract concepts. So far, most of this chapter will appeal to Ns more than Ss. There is a difference among the Ns with some preferring to roam within the subject matter and others to deal with one subject at a time. The INFP, INTP, ENTP and ENFP all like being distracted by new ideas and concepts. The ability to step out of the e-learning and follow a thread of hypertext links will be a complete joy. Around each corner, or into each next screen, there is a new and exciting idea. All too frequently the N-P becomes so enthusiastic about the new possibilities that they completely forget where they started from; their original purpose. Also INTPs and ENFPs value their independence and freedom (along with ISTP and ESTP types). This makes it even more difficult to bring them back into e-learning after a period roaming on the web.

CONTENT PRESENTATION

Even with these differences it is relatively easy to set a pattern for content presentation. Content should present both abstract concepts and practical examples. Learners should be able to choose which they do first. Ideally, material presented second should be shorter than that presented first. It will be less appealing to the learner. I use the word 'ideally' because in the practical real world, designers and developers have to work within budgets and duplication costs money. The way around this is to build in short cuts to the material, then those learners who feel they have already mastered the topic with their preferred approach (concrete or abstract) may jump through material quickly.

The constraints of budgets impose some reality into the ideal world of the designer. These constraints mean that one product has to suit both sides of the S-N dichotomy. The same material will be used by both personality types. The designer may assume that the second part to be studied may well be skimmed over.

KINESTHETIC NEEDS

Among the personality types that prefer to focus on the real world and practical examples, there are those who have a need to touch and feel. Both ES-P types closely observe the world around them, are highly practical and realistic and very much focused on their immediate real experience. For them, learning comes from all their senses. The e-learning designer needs to go beyond the screen and look at ways of giving these types the opportunity to touch and feel. E-learning will include assignments that learners complete based on practical exercises that they complete. One of the advantages of learning IT skills through e-learning is that the learner is one click away from a practical exercise. Perhaps this is the real reason for the predominance of IT skills within e-learning portfolios. Practical exercises can be created in other topics in much the same way as they always have been in text-based workbooks.

An induction course produced by a major bank 15 years ago consisted of an organizer who listed tasks and activities that the learner completed during the first week at work. These tasks and activities included talking to members of different departments and completing many of the backroom routine tasks that were a feature of many job roles, for example, inquiring on account information. These tasks and activities were linked through the training pack with review periods, all still possible with e-learning. Designers may include opportunities for learners to complete short assignments in the workplace. Not every learner will place equal value on these types of exercises.

VISUAL AND AURAL NEEDS

I have already commented on the importance of visual presentation (see the beginning of Chapter 4 and also Chapter 1, pp. 14–16). Rose and Nicholl (1997, pp. 93–105) describe the importance of visual, aural and kinesthetic learning. Suffice it to say at this point, to remind the reader that each topic within any e-learning design must, wherever possible stimulate the sense of vision, feeling (activity) and sound. Pictures are straightforward to create, although difficult to design well but sound may be more problematic. Sound requires large bandwidth if speech or music is used. However a diagram that makes sounds when touched is one way to stimulate the aural learner. A lot will depend on the nature of the topic and there is a balance between patronizing and generating sounds that aid the learning. For example, I do not advocate the sound of cheering when a question is dealt with correctly, perhaps the sound of a button being pressed, useful in the drag and drop type of question interface.

CONCRETE AND ABSTRACT PRESENTATION

The designer seeks alternative ways of presenting content, one is concrete with examples, and the other is abstract with theory. There are additional opportunities for some learners to explore the world of concepts by exploring the web and for other learners to explore the real world by assignments away from the computer. The abstract concepts should have opportunities to explore web links that develop the ideas and concepts further or relate them to other familiar topics. This design approach makes allowance for the S-N dichotomy with additional allowance for ESs who prefer to get close to the real world and N-Ps who like exploring new ideas.

OBJECTIVE AND SUBJECTIVE DECISION-MAKING

By presenting options, the designer can find ways of providing choice in the judgments learners make as they structure and organize their learning. The designer seeks alternative ways of engaging the learner in decision-making. One way must be objective and based on cause and effect, the other must be subjective and take account of the views and opinions of others. Learning is about making sense of the world and part of making that sense requires a learner to organize and structure what they learn, make decisions about why they are doing it, what it is, when to apply it and so on. Whether these decisions are objective or subjective is a personality preference and learners need to be offered alternative ways of making the same decision.

It is a significant challenge to use the pure on-line content element of e-learning to make subjective decisions: such decisions may have multiple answers. This is where discussion groups and on-line tutors become important. The capability to reflect views and ideas to others is important for those whose dominant function is Feeling; ESFJ, ENFJ, ESFP and ENFP types about 27 per cent of the population. It is possible to present scenarios and case studies in which there is no preferred answer. The learner may perhaps read or listen to two or three solutions that provide a reasoned and balanced argument on subjective grounds. Making objective judgments, on the other hand, is something that e-learning is quite good at. All types of simulations, case studies and questions may be used as activities that appeal to the function of Thinking. About 20 per cent of the population have this as their dominant function.

INVOLVEMENT OF OTHERS

The preceding discussion brings a realization that subjective decision making requires interaction with others, either as sounding boards or as providers of feedback. Many e-learning designers do not see a need for others to be involved in the learning process. For many, learners can work successfully on their own at the screen. The need is to keep them there by making the environment more exciting and challenging. Frequently, designers with this approach ask for more audio, more video and more games, seeking to solve the dilemma of why some people are reluctant learners by turning e-learning into entertainment. This thinking creates focus on the design and functionality of the website itself.

For many designers, their focus is on the creation of the web environment. Their responsibility may be limited to the creation of web-based material. Even where a blended learning solution is being developed the web material may well be developed by different people to those creating text or face-to-face lesson material. There are very good economic reasons for this. Web developers are still in short supply. A broad range of skills is needed by a good e-learning designer and these skills take longer to acquire. Fewer people can develop e-learning than can develop other training material. The time of a good e-learning designer is rarely used to create text or classroom delivery material. It is to be expected that they focus on the self-study aspects of e-learning rather than on the communication aspects. There may be another factor that influences e-learning designers to focus on content presentation on the screen. People tend to do well at areas that suit their personality. People are also attracted to careers that suit their personality. It is possible the population of e-learning and web designers has more than its fair share of INT-types. Myers *et al.* (1998, p. 294) published research showing occupational trends of the 16 personality types. This is based on work from 1993 when there was much less need for computer and screen designers than there is today. NTs in general are attracted to work of a scientific and logical nature, INTs preferring to work independently on their own task with ENTs more attracted to managing within a scientific or technical environment. From this research evidence we may assume that NT types are overrepresented among e-learning designers. NT types prefer theory and logic. INT types may see little need for involving others in the learning process.

One of the underlying assumptions of this book is that e-learning designers view the world through their own eyes and expect others to learn like they do. The evidence from personality research is that no one view of the world makes allowance for the learning preferences of others. My aim is to create a theoretical model with practical examples that enable designers to create material that meets the needs of the complete range of personality types, irrespective of their own preferences, whatever they may be. One of the major differences between individuals is their need for others. We are fairly evenly divided into those who gain energy from the outside world and others and those who gain energy from inner reflection and thoughts. Fifty-four per cent of males and 46 per cent of females are

Introvert. The use we make of others in the learning context varies with our personality and many Introverts use other people as part of their learning support. The types who have least need for others in the learning context are NTs. These are the same personality types that are more likely to be attracted to careers with a theoretical basis such as science or computing. The implications of this are obvious. The INT seems to prefer self-study and has little need for other people to help them learn. ENTs need the involvement of others to keep them energized and motivated rather than to help them learn.

The virtual learning set

Given that Extroverts are energized by others the designer must seek ways of providing that energy. The simplest way is to expand the ideas of Reg Revens (Pedler, 1997). This concept translated to a virtual environment requires the use of telephone conferencing, virtual classrooms, chatrooms or bulletin boards.

Different personality types will behave differently in such sets. For example the ENT will organize others both to help themselves learn and to help others do likewise. Typically the ENT will 'take charge' of a learning set and plunge into a learning activity, particularly the ENTP who needs immediate action. This need to be able to organize others as part of their learning is shared by a number of other types. Both ES-J types thrive on the harmony of others. They draw their energy from the enjoyable and harmonious relationships that are experienced by others in their company. For these types learning sets need to be cheerful jolly places where everyone has fun.

Harmony is important to the ISFJ as well. Feeling types will in general be more empathetic to others than Thinking types. A Thinking type may well be oblivious to the feelings of others, so harmony is an irrelevant concept to them. Among the Feeling types the ISFJ and both INF types, have the greatest need for harmony. In the learning context INF types will want to help others develop. They feel that they understand others. The INFP has a personal need to be involved in work that leads to their development and to that of others. The ISFJ is fundamentally co-operative, sensitive to the needs of others and with a wish to be kind. Their need for harmony seems based in this need for kindness to all. You can only be kind to everyone when everyone is in harmony. One dissenting voice means that the ISFJ has to decide to disappoint somebody. The ISFJ also learns by observing others. It is almost as if, as an observer, they can remain a little detached thereby resolving the dilemma of pleasing everybody. The preference for learning by observing others is shared with the ISTJ. Both these types prefer reflection and for both types this is a powerful learning approach. The ISFJ also needs to test their ideas with others. It is almost as if their learning decisions have to be referenced against other people. This may be about how they organize their learning as much as what they have learnt. We may expect a wide range of behaviour in any virtual set. No pure content-based on-line package will be flexible enough to allow individuals this range of behaviour.

Praise and personality

Professionals within the education and learning arena have long argued that praise is a universal need. Praise must be valued by the recipient and this obvious statement encourages me to reflect that the giver of praise must be valued by the recipient as well as the praise itself. Type theory shows that some of us are more independent than others and are less likely to respond to praise unless it is backed up by logical assessment. Type theory indicates that we do not all need praise of the same type and some of us may need very little praise. Type theory suggests that most (but not all) Feeling types need and seek approval. Research indicates that both ESFJ and ENFJ types work best with praise, as both these types also seek harmony. It may be that their need for harmony and their responsiveness to praise are both driven by their need to please and be kind to others. To a greater or lesser extent INFJs, ISFPs, ESTPs, ESFPs and ENFPs respond and appreciate praise. If the remaining types need less praise, why is praise so widely regarded as vital to learning. In *Team Based Learning* (Hills, 2000), I put forward the proposition that all learners need a sense of achievement. This is the concept behind the acronym FAME (Feedback, Achievement, Motivation and a source of Expertise). These are the four ingredients that make for successful learning. Personality determines how we respond to feedback and where our sense of achievement and motivation comes from. Evidence from type theory indicates that for some of us, but not for all of us, achievement and motivation does come from praise. Type theory also suggests that those of us who make decisions based on subjective human values are more likely to respond positively to praise. Others are more likely to gain a sense of achievement based on other criteria, perhaps objective measures or some inner sense of value and worth. Most of the types who make decisions based on logic seem less responsive to praise. Perhaps for them scoring high marks in a test is more important than a manager saying 'well done'.

The contribution made by others to an individual's learning

I have now discussed a number of features of the impact other people have on our learning. These features include:

- praise from others
- harmonious relationships with others
- the opportunity to observe and reflect on the actions of others
- the need to get a response from others as help in formulating ideas
- the need to organize others or be involved in teams as part of the learning process
- the need to help others develop.

A pattern emerges as to which types need involvement with others and the pattern is most striking by considering the types who have least need for an involvement with others. These are the INTJ, ISTP and INTP. The ISTJ finds observation of others helpful, but requires little other involvement. One might assume that the ISTP would find observation of others helpful as well, if it were not for their determination to be free and independent.

HARMONY AND PRAISE

Another striking pattern emerges with the need for harmony. The ISFJ, ISFP, ESFP, ESFJ and ENFJ all thrive in harmonious relationships. For some types the need to create and maintain harmony seems an end in itself. Many people with these personality types learn because of the involvement of a teacher or tutor. A need for harmony seems linked to a responsiveness to praise. An exception perhaps is the ISFJ, whose decision-making seems based on internal values and past experience. Therefore current praise from an external source has less importance than a past experience.

DEVELOPING OTHERS

A pattern that emerges is the need to help and develop others. This is characteristic of the INFJ, INFP, ENFP, ENFJ and ISFP types. These types tend to derive personal satisfaction from drawing out the best in others.

ROLE MODELS

An important learning need is the opportunity to observe the work of an expert. This is particularly valued by the ISTJ and ISFJ. They share the dominant function of introverted Sensing and therefore are characterized as quiet observers and reflectors.

FORMULATING IDEAS

A less clearer pattern emerges if we consider the role of others in formulating ideas. The ISFJ will value a sounding board, an opportunity to use someone else almost as part of the reflection process. The ENTJ on the other hand will value debate and the cut and thrust of an intellectual argument. The ESTP favours energetic problem-solving and in challenging the accepted ways of others. Other types get value by discussing ideas with others at various points that move from a spectrum that goes from challenge (ENTJ) to support (ISFJ). The good classroom tutor is adept at detecting these different needs and meeting them in different ways at the same time. Can we do as well with e-learning?

TAKING CHARGE OF OTHERS

Finally, there is the need to organize others to a greater or lesser extent. All Extroverts gain energy just by being involved with people. In some cases this need for others is the pleasure gained from harmonious relationships, with other personality types it is the pleasure derived from drawing out the best in others, with other personality types, people present a source of situations and challenges that energize and excite them and others simply enjoy leading a team that achieves something collectively.

TYPES OF PERSONAL INTERVENTION IN LEARNING

My aim is to systematize as many of these needs as is appropriate for e-learning and to identify design guidelines that enable designers and implementers to meet the needs of different personality types. I would like to return to a discussion of the functions as a means of establishing systematic guidelines for the involvement of others in helping the learning process through the Internet. I also intend to make some generalizations. The reason for this is to limit the guidelines to three or four of the most important. First, let me remind you of the types of people interaction that can be achieved through e-learning.

Synchronous interaction may be through the PC via text only (chatroom) or through a voice system as well as a shared web space (the virtual classroom). A sub-set that is infrequently used is a telephone voice conference and use of the same application (but not a shared workspace). Finally there is a full video conference facility.

Asynchronous interaction is usually text only (bulletin board). The use of voice mail for asynchronous communication is possible, after all, many of us use telephone message services, although this is unlikely to be used in the learning context. It is worth reflecting that video is also an asynchronous communication tool. It is appropriate in e-learning as a means of demonstrating an expert's behaviour. It may also be used to record the behaviour of a learner so that they can get feedback from an expert at a later time. This is a common technique in the classroom during role playing and also used in simulators where a learner's performance may be recorded through the system itself.

It is important to mention the role performed by real people who are adjacent to the learners. There is a correlation between the take up of e-learning and the role of local managers and pro-active administrators. The conclusion is that 'learning only becomes truly effective in a social environment'. (Hills and Francis, 1999). Given that we have this framework for interaction with others what role might any interaction have in relation to the functions? Remember that we all may perform the functions of Sensing, iNtuition, Thinking and Feeling but that two of them will be preferred and one of them will be dominant. It is the combination of our functional preferences with an inward or outward focus and a preference for new opportunities or closure that determines our personality type.

Our preference for making decisions influences the extent to which we need others as part of the learning process. The decisions we make in the learning process may be about plans and actions, they may be judgments as to how well we have done, they may be about what is true, what is important, what is related. Broadly speaking, we can say these are about content or process and they may be about ourselves or others. From this we can break down the required social interactions into:

* help in determining how we are doing (praise, peer interaction, performance coaching)
* help in planning how we will do things (performance coaching)
* help in organizing content (tutor, peer review)
* satisfaction from helping others (peer interaction).

Some people hardly need these types of interaction. Really independent learners who are inwardly focused and use objective measures to judge their progress have little, if any need for external human reference or intervention. I established a supposition at the beginning of Chapter 5 that people with this personality type may be overrepresented among e-learning professionals. However, about 60 per cent of the population use subjective human values to assess their own progress and need other people as a source of reference. Many more females than males make assessments in this way (about 75 per cent for females and 40 per cent for males). About half of the population need other people as a source of energy and motivation. So about three-quarters of us need other people to be part of the learning process in some way.

Personality and content presentation

The preferences for content presentation categorize the various personality types in a fairly simple way. Sensing types like examples and practical descriptions while iNtuition types like concepts and theory. If we present learning material in both formats then learners may chose which they prefer. Such a simple categorization does not exist for our need for other people in the learning process. We can argue that Es need people for energy and that Fs need people for help in making judgments and decisions. This help may be as individuals who receive help, for example, praise or as individuals who give help, for example, as developers of others, or as individuals who benefit from others almost as a sounding board. For example both INF types like the involvement of others because it adds meaning to their lives. They readily understand others and enjoy making use of that understanding. Learning for them carries more meaning when they can help others in that process. As another example, the EST type enjoys organizing others and being actively involved in problem-solving. Learning has meaning to them because it results in improved practical solutions. All the SF types value harmony, although not alone in this appreciation of harmonious relationships with others. Learning carries more meaning for them when it pleases other people. In terms of designing e-learning, a useable pattern is beginning to emerge. The use we make of others can be categorized into three types of interaction.

PROCESS CHECK

Is our learning well organized? Are we progressing at a rate similar to that of other people? Are we studying in the same order as others? Are we doing better or worse than those we might consider as equals? Are we doing well in the judgment of people who matter to us? Indirectly some of these questions are about content: are we right or wrong in our understanding of what we are doing? More directly these questions are a comparison with those around us, either a logical fact-based comparison or the subjective opinion of another. To put it another way, for some of us the fact that we got 9/10 in a test or are 5th in the class or cohort is important. For others, it is more important that others think we are doing well. Those of us in the latter category need other people so that we can understand what their opinion is of us.

In the e-learning context these other people may be remote or local. Their most helpful role is as a performance coach. They act as a sounding board to our plans and goals. When we achieve those goals they contribute to our sense of worth and achievement. They may be co-learners, tutors or local administrators. For those of us for whom a logical process check is important, co-learners provide a benchmark.

The tutor can provide the same type of benchmark, but with a fact-based approach. Other people are less important in this context. E-learning can provide this process check by comparing average study times. For example, the fact that most people study material for three hours over one week and then achieve a score of 95 per cent serves as a process check for a brutally objective person to measure themselves against. This type of checking is important to individuals. Some of us may remember sitting next to a pupil at school who told everyone how little time they spent revising and then proceeded to score more in every test than anyone else.

CONTENT CHECK

Have I understood everything? Have I missed anything out? Have I misunderstood anything? Which areas of my performance are good and which areas are weak? What do I do wrong? The majority of e-learning is cognitive in nature rather than behavioural. We can therefore expect that the need for a content check will be aimed at mental skills rather than interpersonal or physical skills. As such, feedback can be delivered entirely through the e-learning material. However, some of the higher order cognitive skills such as synthesis and judgment are difficult for software to assess. Human intervention in giving content feedback enables much more flexibility in what e-learning can deliver in terms of content. For many learners tutor or system feedback is only one part of the content check.

For several personality types, it is important to find out how others have organized information and what it means to them. Co-learner debate and review is an important part of the learning process. On the one hand the task of explaining to someone else what you think you know helps your understanding. On the other hand, listening or reading another person's explanation gives you a different perspective on the topic area. Both actions are beneficial in the learning process for everyone. Some personality types prefer this type of interaction more than others.

Both INT types are so independently minded that they will see little value in this. They are likely to enjoy telling others what they think but will find it hard to listen. At the opposite end of the scale the IS types will find it easy to listen but will feel less sure about putting forward their ideas. An asynchronous co-learner review process at least, means that they can consider and reflect on what they want to say before saying it. Co-learner review becomes an important part of the content review process that provides learning benefit for everyone. Some enjoy it more than others.

SENSE OF SATISFACTION

Have I been useful today? Have I achieved something? What do others think of me? What do I think of myself? Have I made progress? It is within this domain that we will find most of the emotional needs of the learning process. This may also be the area where it is most difficult for e-learning to meet these needs. Learning is not just an intellectual exercise, it has emotional connotations. Learners may derive a sense of satisfaction from helping others, praise, creating harmony, stimulating debate, being part of a joint effort and challenging others. Different personality types value these actions differently. It is apparent that some of these actions are in conflict.

Debate and harmony do not go together. A helpful supportive environment conflicts with a challenging one. In the classroom this tension is readily apparent. The experienced facilitator has methods for dealing with the personal differences arising from the different ways that people gain satisfaction from their involvement with others. Similar rules will apply to e-learning bulletin boards, collaborative sessions or chatrooms. I have concentrated on the sense of satisfaction people derive from involvement with others but we should not forget personal achievement (however measured), a new experience, solving problems, breaking up established ways of working and creating order out of chaos.

People roles in e-learning

In this section order and structure into the reasons why people find interaction an important part of e-learning will be set out. I have used an understanding of type theory and associated research to establish very clear-cut roles for people within e-learning. These are as a performance coach, a subject expert and one's peers (or co-learners).

In practical terms performance coaching will happen on a one-to-one basis either through e-mail or the telephone. Both INF types (5.5 per cent) will find this relevant only when it is highly objective and logical. Indeed they would rather measure and feedback their own performance. Most SF types (16.4 per cent) will find this relevant when based on subjective value-driven comments. Comments should emphasize praise much more. Other types respond to feedback and encouragement that is objective. The experienced performance coach will modify their style of feedback based on their understanding of the individual. For e-learning it is recommended that a performance coach or a local administrator either meets or telephones learners or requests to share an MBTI type understanding. Failing that learners can be asked to select what type of content they like, what type of feedback and the extent of their involvement with others. These answers will indicate the best way for the performance coach to interact with them. They will spend much more time with SF types than with NTs; the NTs will want objective feedback from someone who knows the topic. On the other hand SF types need a more subjective values-based approach. A performance coach concentrates on process rather than content so their skill base is in learning, how people learn, good ways of managing learning and the best ways of applying learning.

The subject coach or expert has a role in checking a learner's understanding of content. In practical terms, this can be delivered via e-mail and perhaps through a bulletin board, especially where a learning problem is shared by other learners in the same cohort. For individual learners, one-to-one feedback is appropriate although it might help them to know that others experience difficulty at the same point in a topic. This model of interaction is exactly like that of a correspondence course, the advantage of e-learning being that interaction is more frequent and of a shorter duration. Generally, tutor reports on correspondence courses are based on completed assignments and tend to be detailed and lengthy. E-learning interactions can be rapid and based much more on the learner's agenda. Tutors may respond to questions just as they do in the classroom.

Co-learner review may take place in a bulletin board or a chatroom. It involves two processes, one based on intellectual needs, the other on emotional needs. The intellectual needs are met by debate and an exchange of ideas. Some personality types (ENTJ, ESTP, INTP, ISTP, about 16 per cent) enjoy robust and challenging debate. It stimulates them and aids their understanding. Other personality types (typically the SF types with ENFJ types, 45 per cent) find debate stressful and exhausting. Two people might well describe the same interaction in very different ways, one as an argument, the other as a discussion. Within an intellectual discussion we must expect only the minority to participate. Those who enjoy debate include the independently-minded learners who might choose not to participate. There is a difficult balance to strike between harmony and debate. There are also those who enjoy helping others and these form a third group. Typically these are the NF types with the ISFP (about 23 per cent). The ISFP also seeks harmony in that relationship. The fourth group comprises those who like to organize others, typically both EST types, to some extent the NF types and the ENTJ and ESFP (about 25 per cent excluding the NF types). Again this group includes those who like to develop others and those who seek harmony as well as those who seek debate. It is possible to recognize in these differences some of the causes of interpersonal conflict and the disruptions that may occur in collaborative working.

Generally there are a large group of learners for whom interaction with other learners is an enjoyable experience, provided that the interaction matches their own need to help others, to debate, to agree and to organize. There are few learners who seek to be organized but there are many who value praise and gain reassurance when others help direct them. The majority of learners gain a sense of solidarity knowing others are engaged in the same task as themselves. People will come to a bulletin board or chatroom because it is an enjoyable experience. Enjoyment is in the judgment of the individual and people enjoy different things.

Most people have an emotional need for a sense of worth based on their interactions with each other. Bulletin boards need practical ways of allowing people to help each other. Hills (2000, p. 77) describes a method of sharing learning needs. Each member of a learning group lists three things they want help with and three topics they can coach others on. This may be posted on an e-learning bulletin board or a flipchart in the office. Everyone in the group looks at the postings and makes offers to those they may be able to help. Once a 'contract' is struck, the posting is removed and the 'contract' recorded elsewhere. Then members of the group look at the offers of help and select those they want. Again a 'contract' is struck and recorded. A precondition of this exercise is that the team is willing to share learning needs and will help each other. This technique serves two purposes, meeting the emotional needs of those who want to help others and the intellectual needs of those who need help with a particular topic either within the course or ancillary to the course.

Another emotional need individuals have is the sense of companionship that comes of being part of a joint effort. This can be met by learning projects that require learners to work together. Other techniques will include space for people to offer handy hints and tips or information about things they found interesting. People who want to argue (or debate if you prefer the term) can be portioned off in discussion threads that have a specific purpose. This will allow some people to avoid this argument and allow others to gravitate towards the debate.

This discussion on the various roles that other people fulfil in the learning process leads to a blinding glimpse of the obvious. Tutors, either e-mail tutors or local administrators, fulfil an important role for some personality types in facilitating their learning process, this is as the performance coach. Individuals may value praise, help with organizing themselves or a progress check as a comparison with an independent objective benchmark. Some individuals will have little need for such help. Interaction between learners meets a range of needs, for most it helps them organize and re-organize their thoughts. Some people gain satisfaction and fulfilment from helping others. Some people need the opinions of others to help formulate their thinking, others to feel that they are pleasing others. Some people find such interactions intrepid challenges, other thrive on and enjoy the involvement with others. Others like interactions based on the cut and thrust of debate, while some like interactions based on harmony and agreement. Tutors or facilitators have a role in ensuring that as many of these diverse needs as is possible are met. The final role of the tutor is as a subject matter expert, as an assessor of assignments and as someone to answer questions.

Action learning and e-learning

There is one final aspect of personality differences that has some relevance to e-learning. I have already mentioned that both IS-J types like to observe and reflect. There are other types (the ESTP, the ESFP and the ENTP) who have a propensity for action. Their inclination is to rush in and do something. With e-learning this is probably much less of an issue than in the classroom. By its very nature, immediate action is an oxymoron within e-learning. Even the most competent typist has to think before they rush into saying something in a chatroom. It is true that if you are studying the use of an IT application, it is possible to start work with the application and thereafter refer to the learning. This would be typical of the action-orientated individual. However, just like in the classroom, the action-orientated individual is likely to dominate discussion. They may well rush into action before finishing a piece of learning. These personality types are most suited to the byte-size learning concept. They can rush into the e-learning material, acquire a tiny bit of knowledge and then rush out to apply it. These personality types may well leave a course early. As soon as they feel they have acquired what they wanted they are off. The design solution that works for them is the work-based assignment that fits with the e-learning material. The ESTP and ESFP require this for reasons discussed earlier in the chapter. They require learning to be very practical and real. Thus, for two reasons, blending an e-learning solution with action learning in the workplace meets a need that some (but not all) individuals have in the learning process.

Planning learning and e-learning

There are individuals who like to project themselves into the future. They enjoy planning and imagining themselves at some future point. Research shows that the INTJ type does this to the greatest extent. Type theory suggests that this is more likely to occur with intuitives, that is those whose dominant function is iNtuition. Introvert intuitives are quiet and imaginative while Extrovert intuitives are those who are obviously most excited about new possibilities. Both, in different ways, will enjoy planning their future learning. The availability of a learning plan in an e-learning delivery system will appeal to these types. It gives Introvert intuitives the opportunity to quietly imagine their future success in learning, planning out what will happen week by week. The extrovert intuitives can also exercise their imagination about the future. They are likely to do this in a much more volatile way and, because of their enjoyment of new possibilities, plans will not be followed – even though the planning exercise is enjoyable.

The quiet reflective types (ISTJ and ISFJ) will also appreciate the opportunity to arrange plans. However, these types prefer present reality to future imagination. For them the advantage of planning systems is the opportunity to store facts for future use. The fact that there are lessons to be done in the future is something worth recording, so the information can be brought out and considered at that time. Since both these types also prefer order and structure, a learning plan gives the impression of an organized future existence for their learning. They will value this impression along with the other J types. The action-orientated types will abhor any planning system and are likely to reject the need for such plans, preferring to dive into action immediately.

Many e-learning systems are now sold with learning management systems (LMS) that have learning plans built-in. The previous discussion shows that about 40 per cent of a typical population will appreciate a learning plan, of whom 26 per cent do so because of the opportunity to reflect and store facts for the future rather than the opportunity to plan. Management systems have relevance to a minority of potential users of e-learning. There are other reasons for using management systems that are more relevant to the organization than the individual. In practical terms learning plans will have a strong appeal to the minority of users (about 13 per cent are dominant intuitives). There will be some appeal for the implication of an ordered world for the rest of the J types (about another 52 per cent).

The action-orientated individuals (about 16 per cent) would like the opportunity to immediately book on to a course, even more so when it is delivered to them immediately. Many organizations require an approval process before bookings can be accepted. This destroys the spontaneity which is part of the appeal of self-booking. Those who enjoy reviewing and reflecting on past achievement will appreciate the record-keeping aspects of the typical management system. This past record also gives a sense of achievement to the objectively-minded. Those who project themselves into the future will appreciate a link between future job roles, competencies required and learning available. This is sometimes available within learning management systems and yet will appeal mainly to those who enjoy imagining the future: iNtuitive types (about 25 per cent of the population). Those who are Sensing types are much more inclined to deal in 'today' facts. Therefore, as well as linking future job roles, an LMS should link the competencies required for the current job to the learning available and provide a record of what has been done or achieved in terms of acquiring the skills needed for today's job. Combining these two features broadens the appeal of LMS to all personality types.

Summary – an idealized learning model based on MBTI research

Each of the 16 personality type preferences has a characteristic approach to learning. This is extrapolated from research into their preferences for education. The research survey spans a number of years from 1985 to 1998. A plausible initial assumption might be that Introvert types will do well with e-learning; they gain energy and stimulus within themselves. However, the MBTI related educational research shows that Introverts also use other people in a number of ways to help them learn. Some Introverts need a sounding board for ideas and concepts, predominantly those Introverts who make decisions on subjective human values; the I-F-types. These types seek guidance from those around them to improve their subjective decisions. Some Introverts also need and seek motivation from others. The conclusion from the research is that, while there are some Introvert types who are very self-contained and make their decisions objectively, there are others who use other people as a source of motivation and guidance as they learn. There are also those who gain satisfaction from helping others: while this might be argued that it is not part of an individual's learning, expressing this need to help others does improve the capability for learning in some personality types.

A plausible parallel assumption to Introverts doing well in e-learning is that Extroverts will find it a difficult process as they require others to be part of the learning process. While there is a certain amount of truth in that, there are some differences between the types. Extroverts are energized by others but some like and thrive on debate, some like to organize and lead others, and there are those types who gain satisfaction from a harmonious relationship. There is a clash in learning environments between those Extroverts who enjoy the cut and thrust of debate and those Extroverts who seek harmony and consensus.

While the E/I dichotomy generates differences in learning preference, another is driven by the S/N dichotomy. Some learners need concepts and theories, other learners need examples, detail and practical reality. This difference is relatively easily catered for and many tutors would automatically move from the presentation of a concept to giving an example of its application, or alternatively working from a specific example towards a generalization. MBTI research shows that learners will have a preference for one or the other style of presenting information.

Although each of the 16 personality types is unique, it is impractical to design or implement e-learning for all personality types. If we concentrate on practical examples based in reality, we may, at best, suit the preferences of 75 per cent of the population. If we think about options in the design and base those options on MBTI functions we can significantly increase the flexibility of a course and its attractiveness to different personality types. Some redundancy is inevitable as learners will spend less time in activities appropriate to functions they do not prefer, for example their inferior functions. Exercising and using those inferior functions is likely to improve learning. Pask proved that learners who were versatile, in that they could change their strategies between holist and serialist, were more effective. The Honey and Mumford (1986) learning cycle advocates taking learners through each part of the cycle. For the same reason learners should be encouraged to exercise all their functions, although the designer must recognize that they will spend more time in, and are likely to start with, activities with which they feel comfortable. Options can be provided by the designer in a number of areas.

TYPE OF CONTENT

Where possible, learners will have an option to study concepts or examples, detail or big picture, theory or practical examples.

PRESENTATION STYLE

It can almost be taken as axiomatic that e-learning material will use sound, pictures and some type of activity, as well as text in the presentation of information.

TYPE OF INTERACTION

Interaction requires the learner to make decisions. These might be about the order to study material, whether they should study it at all, how they organize the information in their minds and what actions they take as a result of the learning. Learners will exercise their preference for making these decisions either subjectively or objectively. Computers can readily present arguments for objective decision-making and objective assessment tools. Computers can help subjective decision-making by reporting on a wide range of variables including what others concluded from the learning. It is more difficult for a computer to provide assessment feedback on subjective decisions. The best way is to present a range of answers that others have used in the past.

OPTIONS FOR LEARNERS

The options that may be built into e-learning are based on content, content presentation: whether decision-making is objective or subjective. Content will be both abstract with concrete examples, offering the big picture alongside detail. Learner interactions will require either objective or subjective decision-making. Each topic will concentrate on one of these four content styles:

- abstract
- concrete
- objective
- subjective.

Learners will have the opportunity to move between topics as they wish. Navigation interactions will provide for free-flowing navigation within a mesh structure. Each item within a mesh will have links to related topics. At each point in the mesh (at each topic), learners will have the option of moving elsewhere in the mesh, as they wish to, rather than as the designer dictates. Their choices are theory or example, objective test or subjective assessment, and visual, text, audio or activity.

THE INVOLVEMENT OF OTHERS

The fourth element of choice is that of the involvement of others as part of the learning process. The need for this is most acute where subjective decision-making and assessment is required. For Extroverts and those whose dominant or auxiliary function is Feeling, working with others is more important than using a highly interactive media-rich website. Most web designers are interested in creating this type of website, so it is likely to take priority over the areas of design such as discussion boards. This comment is based on the assumption that most web designers are introverted thinkers. This in turn is based on research findings that introverted thinkers are overrepresented in the computing industry. It is therefore dependent upon the learning designer to ensure that the communication aspects of a learning website are fully developed and appeal to those who are Extrovert and prefer making judgments based on Feeling.

The virtual classroom is an interesting sub-set of e-learning. It mimics the real classroom in that a live presenter talks while everyone listens and watches a screen that may display slides or another computer application. It might be assumed that Extroverts would find this a way of tapping into others and gaining energy from the interaction. While there is a certain amount of truth in this, there are also significant challenges in using a virtual classroom. There are as many differences between Extroverts as there are similarities. The most apparent difference is the need for harmony contrasted with the need for debate. If you need harmony you may find debate stressful, if you need debate you may find harmony boring, although you might like other people being nice to you.

Learners benefit from a sense of achievement. For objective decision-makers this sense is based in facts. The computer element of e-learning can provide these facts based on progress, test scores, scenario results and by comparison with others. For subjective decision-makers this sense of achievement is based in opinions as much as in facts. This highlights the importance of praise for those who make subjective decisions about themselves.

The roles that others take in the learning process may be grouped into four types:

(1) Giving help in determining how we are doing.
(2) Giving help in planning how we would do things.
(3) Help in organizing and understanding content.
(4) Gaining satisfaction from helping others.

Of these, the first two are both concerned with the process of learning, so we can refine the role of others in relation to the learning process into three areas, help with the process of learning, organizing the content and gaining satisfaction from the involvement of others. We may map these four activities into three human roles.

Performance coach

The amount of time individuals require from someone in this role varies with personality. The communication aspect of e-learning enables a performance coach to interact with learners more frequently than they can do with other forms of distance learning (or self-study learning). Some learners may need more praise and others may thrive on more challenge, but the role of a performance coach is fundamentally the same whatever the medium that is being used for learning.

Tutor

This role varies from being someone who answers questions to someone who provides feedback and ideas presented by learners. The tutor must pay attention to providing both subjective and objective feedback. As they become familiar with the personality of the learner they will bias the type of feedback to suit the individual. This is something most tutors will do relatively easily in the face-to-face learning environment. It is a greater challenge to vary the style and sensitivity of the feedback when your only channel of communication is e-mail or the telephone. Tutors should also provide examples and concepts when answering questions from learners. Again, this will be biased according to the personality of the learner. It is usually much simpler to bias this feedback because intuitives will ask questions about concepts and those who prefer Sensing will ask questions about examples.

Learner to learner review and interaction

It is in this area that learners who value the opinions of others gain their sense of achievement. The risk is that those who thrive on debate will dominate any electronic collaborative space and that they will deter those who seek harmony in their relations with each other. Learners have a need to interact with others, to help others, to debate, to agree and to organize. These needs are not entirely mutually inclusive. The role of the on-line tutor is to ensure that discussion boards are used in a balanced way. It may be that alternative media is used, for example telephone conferencing, to meet the needs of those who find an electronic collaborative space lacking in opportunities to either agree, to organize or to help others.

Another difference between learners is based on an individual's need for forward planning, typical of a J type personality. Many P type personalities also forward plan, although they are less likely to stick to the plan than J type personalities. Learning management systems may be valued by any learner for their capability of providing individual learning plans.

The need for activity is another difference between personality types with ESTP, ESFP and ENTP types expressing that need strongly. Taking immediate action within e-learning is difficult. Jumping up and interrupting a discussion is not something that can be done within an e-learning course or discussion group. Moving directly to a test is one way of satisfying this need to 'do something'. One clear advantage of e-learning for the activity-biased learner is the capability of booking and receiving a course immediately. Another may be to move from the learning material straight into an activity, this is easy to do when learning about a computer application as the learning and the job use the same tool.

7 *From Theory to Practice*

Theoretical basis for a functional learning model

The three preceding chapters are a survey of MBTI theory and the experimental observations or Pask, Carroll and (briefly) Kolb. As such it is interesting, but not necessarily in a form that is of immediate use to an e-learning designer. Those engaged in producing e-learning require immediate and practical ideas for producing material that makes some allowances for the different preferences individuals have. The fact that these preferences are based on personality means that we can apply some order and structure to these differences. This order and structure makes it practical to design e-learning material that makes allowances for individuals. I am not considering the individual differences that arise out of prior knowledge. Current ideas around pre-course testing and menu systems provide excellent ways of assessing prior knowledge and making recommendations for content selection by an individual learner. A comprehensive menu system hands control to the learner. This may also allow them to exercise a preference for gaining an overview or studying the detail first, provided that option has been built into the design: many good on-line courses are designed to hand this type of control to the learner. I propose going one step further and designing specifically for personality differences. It is surprisingly simple to do given the existing framework of the MBTI functions. My purpose in this chapter is to present some simple and practical ideas that can be used by designers and to back that up with a couple of hypothetical examples of how specific pieces of design might be implemented.

The typical paradigm for technology-delivered learning is similar to that which we find in a lecture room. A lecturer or designer represents the expert and they display the information for the learner to absorb. In the lecture hall the lecturer stands at the front and pontificates, perhaps with some minor involvement from the audience. The audience receives the information and may choose to omit certain parts of it by losing interest, or even falling asleep. Likewise in on-line material the e-learning designer will include information in the course content and present it to the learner. In one sense authors are no different and this book is a serial presentation of a sequence of ideas and examples. The reader may structure the work as they see fit reading it in any order they like. Although chapter summaries occur at the end of each chapter they may be used by the reader to decide which bits of a chapter to read or whether to read the chapter at all.

For on-line material the designer structures the course, perhaps in accordance with a systematic model of training. Thought goes into the sequencing and the design of the best route for the learner to take. If there is a pre-course test or assessment, the system may advise the learner which bits of the course they should do and in what order. Yet previous observations shows us that learners know best and wish to access material and apply meaning to it in ways that they prefer. For the learner, a book has an advantage in that they can flick over parts that they are not interested in and annotate and label parts that they are. They can bring added meaning to a book by interacting with it. This interaction allows a reader to exercise subjective or objective judgment as well as reading about examples and theories. This may not be the case with e-learning. The designer may constrain the path learners will take through the material. Perhaps interaction is only allowed at certain points in the course. Whereas a book is a book and all books have much the same physical structure, each piece of e-learning is distinctive with special features and a style of interaction and navigation not shared with other courses. Opportunities for the learner to interact with the material have to be built in by the designer. Interactions may be specific constraining the learner with limited choices. This is the age-old paradigm of the teacher teaching. Learners feel patronized and will lose control over that which they are learning. This is accepted perhaps by a child, but will be resented by an adult, who would much rather be in a position of controlling his or her own learning.

E-learning gives us the advantage of placing that control with the learner and then the designer can concentrate on providing support and content, rather than controlling the actions that the learner takes. The drawback for each and every e-learning designer is that they cannot observe the reactions of the learners in time to respond by changing the product. Face-to-face training allows the tutor to respond to these changes and attitudes of the learner at the point of delivery. The functional model of learning that I proposed in Chapter 6 makes it possible, by considering the preferences people have, both for topics and for their learning preferences, for the learner to exercise those preferences while the material is being delivered. Although some duplication is inevitable, offering learning choices that match the personality type dichotomies allows the designer to build in change that responds to a learner's personality. That response will be by personal choice. The starting point is to break away from linear design. Linear solutions remain the easiest way for designers to think about and structure material. After all, a designer cannot bend time and has to work through the design as a linear process. Although a designer has to think as a serial action they must create their design to be inherently flexible. The first step in designing for this flexibility is for a designer to have a model, or paradigm, for design. The approach suggested is based on topic charts. For e-learning each topic chart is self-contained.

Both Pask and Carroll in their own way constructed topic charts that were self-contained bits of learning material. The current jargon phrase is 'learning objects' although different interpretations and definitions exist as to what a learning object actually is. For Carroll they would be no more than five minutes of learning to help people through a specific task. For the UK National Learning Network that supports e-learning in schools, a learning object is a 20-minute piece of training with objectives and a review and assessment process. Pask laid down no such criteria when he constructed learning in this segmented way. I will use the phrase topic chart to avoid confusion with existing definitions of learning objects. As you will see later an item in a topic chart is not only self contained it is internally homogeneous for functional activity. Judgment is either objective or subjective and content is either concrete or abstract. Ideally the cognitive level will be homogeneous. A topic item will use different presentation styles, diagrammatic, text, aural and allow movement. Because Pask's work predated PCs each topic was delivered in one media; text, workshop session tutor discussions, for example. Carroll on the other hand discovered that due to the almost random way in which learners access material it was necessary to have each chunk self-contained. Pask emphasized the need to understand the nature of a topic and its interrelationships with other topics. Because the topic sessions, described by Pask as conversations, were each in different media and this tended to classify the topics. The work of Bloom in developing taxonomy for cognitive skills gives one method of classifying topics. The topic might require knowledge, comprehension, application, analysis, synthesis or evaluation.

A FUNCTIONAL TAXONOMY

The early research work of Kolb and subsequent work on MBTI preferences indicate that there are topics that appeal to the different personality types. I propose a further taxonomy based on these MBTI functions. These topics have been categorized as Sensing, iNtuition, Thinking or Feeling. For example, a Thinking topic would be objective, demonstrate cause and effect and indicate that there was a correct answer. It would be a closed topic in the sense that it leads to closure. It might require any level of cognitive skill from knowledge to evaluation, but is more likely to require higher order skills. A Sensing topic would be very real and practical and detailed. It would be an open topic in that it presents information for the learner, draws no conclusions and leads to further investigation. An iNtuition topic would be theoretical and abstract, probably bringing in interrelationships between facts and theory. It would be open leading to further investigation. A Feeling topic would be subjective and have a number of different conclusions. It would be closed. All these topics might include cognitive or interpersonal skills at any level.

Having established a topic chart, Pask proposed drawing links between them and this, of course, is a process any good e-learning designer will work through. This gives them a means of presenting a storyboard with multiple relationships. I propose that the designer should go one step further and define each topic as example, detail, big picture or theoretical. Other ways of describing the differences might be abstract or concrete. Other topics, which require the learner to make decisions, would be characterized as objective or subjective. There should be no topics that go from experience to subjective conclusion within the topic, or any that move from abstract to a conclusion of cause and effect. Individual learners may chose to move from topic to topic in those ways, or they may chose not to. Breaking the compulsory link allows the learner to exercise their preferences. Constructing a topic chart in this way we can begin to define e-learning material in relation to MBTI functions and by extension, personality types as well as in terms of taxonomy of cognitive or interpersonal skills.

We still have the situation that 16 types are too many to design for. I am not proposing that we should design just for an ISTJ or an ENTP, I am proposing that we can construct material in such a way that those different personality types will find a route through the material that is comfortable for them. The designer does not have to consider all 16 types provided he or she provides choices that match the MBTI dichotomies.

The two functional dimensions are most significant in relation to the content. That is the Sensing/iNtuition dichotomy and the Thinking/Feeling dichotomy. Any example of on-line learning material should have activities appropriate to these functions in roughly equal measure. There will be some redundancy in that the same task will be included in different ways. For example, rules will be demonstrated and also explained and learners may access the demonstration or the explanation in either order.

EXERCISING PREFERENCES FOR THE INVOLVEMENT OF OTHERS

The next step is to consider the other MBTI dimensions. These represent preferences for the style of activities rather than the activities themselves. For example, is it with others or by one self; can the learner go off at a tangent, or work through the material thoroughly one step at a time? The E/I dichotomy is relevant to the involvement of others in any interactions. An assumption frequently made is that Extroverts do less well in e-learning because they need the involvement of others as a source of energy. A close study of MBTI-related research shows that Introverts need others as well and that there is a pattern to the need for others, for both Introverts and Extroverts.

Four needs for other people in learning may be identified:

(1) to lead, organize and develop others,
(2) to create harmony and agreement,
(3) to generate debate and discussion, either to help formulate one's own ideas or as a source of energy,
(4) to gain a feeling of solidarity; a reinforcement that what I am learning is valuable because others are learning the same.

In Chapter 6 I described the 'people roles' involved as performance coach, tutor and co-learner groups. These needs are a somewhat simplified version of the research summary that are shown in Table 7.1. Table 7.1 shows the need for the involvement of others that each MBTI type has, and is indicative in the sense that it implies a sharp cut-off between each type for such involvement. For example, we all appreciate praise but some of us need it more than others. Table 7.1 indicates where a need for others is a major influence on the personality.

Table 7.1 Need for involvement of others in the learning process for each MBTI type

MBTI type	Praise needed	Formulating ideas with others	Debate needed	Need to organize others	Harmony appreciated	Need for role models	Developers of others
ISTJ						Yes	
ISFJ		Support	Yes		Yes	Yes	
INFJ	Some			Yes			Yes
INTJ							
ISTP							
ISFP	Yes	Support			Yes		Yes
INFP				Yes			Yes
INTP							
ESTP	Some	Challenge	Yes	Yes			
ESFP	Some	Support		Yes	Yes		
ENFP	Some						Yes
ENTP							
ESTJ				Yes			
ESFJ	Yes	Support			Yes		
ENFJ	Yes	Support		Yes	Yes		Yes
ENTJ		Challenge		Yes			

Simplifying these needs further as shown in the list above makes it apparent that we have two types of involvement with others, social as indicated by items 1, 2 and 4 and help in stimulating and organizing ideas as described at item 3. Items 1 and 4 are complimentary, if some people want to lead and help others then some people want that help and leadership. Virtual action learning sets provide a simple way of combining those needs, while recognizing that learners must not be asked to contribute equally. Virtual learning sets imply the existence of a tutor to facilitate those sets.

The second simplification is to recognize that 2 and 3 are opposites. Vigorous debate may stimulate some learners, and worry and exhaust others. This is pushing the boundary somewhat but then the same constraint applies to any learning process done in collaboration with others. Using sub-sets of learners in virtual sets so that some sets debate and argue and others spend their time agreeing may solve this potential source of conflict. It may be that designing for these characteristics becomes too difficult; how would people know which learning set to chose for example. Briefly virtual action learning sets should be designed into e-learning, not everyone has to participate, those that do will determine their own level of involvement. The tutor or coach will spot those that do not contribute and, for those put off by either debate or lack or it will generate alternative ways of interacting. Those who have little need for others in the learning process will continue on their own.

BALANCING THE NEED TO EXPLORE OR CONCLUDE LEARNING

The Perceiving/Judging dichotomy is relevant to the closed or open nature of the learning material. This may be paraphrased as 'give me answers' or 'give me ideas', hence the need to conclude learning or explore a topic further. The nature of the design task is to give people answers, after all that is what tutors do in a classroom, or do they? Undoubtedly some tutors do and some do not. Uniquely, e-learning can give answers for those who want it and leave others with ideas.

PUTTING IT TOGETHER

I propose that choices for all these four dichotomies can be built into an e-learning design. The designer will not hand over total control to the learner, after all they would not do so in a classroom and the tutor-learner relationship is one of mutual balance. As well as presenting choices a good designer will take a learner through a learning process. There are a number of models that might be used.

The Honey and Mumford learning process is perhaps the most well known, with its learning cycle from pragmatism to activist or to activity, to review, to theory. E-learning design may be built around this model: present an abstract theory; give practical examples of that theory; ask learners to put into practice some of those examples; ask them to review what they did and then move to refine the theory.

Another model is that of drill and practice: watch an expert; listen to the expert explain; practice step-by-step with feedback from the expert; and practice the full task. Drill and practice is a learning model that has been around for a few centuries.

I am proposing another model that is deliberately divorced from a cycle or any suggestion of progression. A model that relates to the individual's preferences may be based on the MBTI functions.

The functional learning cycle

In the process of learning, individuals must gather data and information about the world around them. They then make inferences from that data in relation to their prior knowledge, and progress to making decisions about that data and organizing it in ways that make sense to them. They may enter this model at any point, perhaps making decisions about their perceptions of the information that will be offered before they gather it. Those with strong Judging preferences may chose to place what they will learn into a box in their mind before they have learnt it. For example they may decide that the topic is 'not for them', or that it is an extension of a previous idea, not something really new to them. Those with strong perceiving preferences will prefer collecting information and consider it a natural activity. The learning model has four possible entry points but only two exit points (see Figure 5.5 on page 112). At some point, perceiving types have to be content with the fact that all the relevant information they need to learn a new skill has been given to them and what is now needed is an understood structure in their minds.

This learning model is based on the four functions described by the MBTI type theory. I introduced this as an example of an idealized model in chapter 5 (see Figure 5.4 on page 111). We know from the theoretical research that each of us will have a preference for the abstract or the concrete. We will have a preference for detailed examples or theoretical explanations. This is the first dichotomy the e-learning designer has to consider and they can make allowances for these preferences by giving learners a choice in the way in which they work through material. You may exercise that choice now, in this paper, by skipping to a description of the design examples occurring later. Or you may choose to continue to read this theoretical explanation.

The functional learning cycle initially allows learners to exercise a choice between concrete and abstract presentations. They may select to read a theoretical explanation, to look at diagrams describing relationships or be tested on the abstract concepts. Alternatively they may choose to read about examples, observe role models or study the detailed steps in a process or procedure. Both topics cover the same ground but from different perspectives.

The challenge for the designer may be to explain an abstract concept by the presentation of concrete examples. The learner should, of course, be free to move from one topic style of presentation to another as they see fit. The first part of the material helps the learner absorb information, the second stage enables them to make decisions and organize that information in a way that is meaningful. They may choose to do this by the exercise of cause and effect and an objective analysis, or they may choose to do this through a subjective assessment based on values rather than facts. Helping learners organize information is done with interactions and questions. At each stage the learner has to make a decision based on the concrete information that they have gathered, or the abstract information that they have inferred. The presentation of the learning material should enable people to move from either the concrete presentation or the abstract presentation, to either the objective analysis and testing or the subjective values-based assessment. The possible routes through the material are shown in Figure 5.5. Each cycle might be quite short, bearing in mind that when learners interact with the material they move to decision-making. The diagram shows a multiplicity of routes through the material, the assumption being that learners will complete both the examples and theoretical sections before moving to the testing and assessment, it does not have to be like this.

Learners may move between all four elements to suit their preferences. The ideal and natural preference for every type will be to take one route through the material that moves from their dominant or auxiliary function in the data presentation sections (examples and theory), through to the judging sections (objective testing or subjective assessment). This would require some types to start with their auxiliary function rather than their dominant one. It would mean that all learners could confine themselves to exercising the functions that they most prefer: their dominant and their auxiliary. It would also limit the range of activities that learners use. The designer may introduce constraints to either encourage or force learners to exercise activities that they do not prefer. For example, if a learner only looks at examples then the programme may encourage or coerce the learner to study theory, not as much as is used by the avid theorist, but enough. The justification for this constraint is supported by Pask's research, where he found that the versatile learner who combined the strategies of holist and serialist was more effective than one who used only one strategy.

All the theories of learning cycles indicate that learning works best when learners exercise activities that are not their preferred style. And it is at this point that the designer may exercise some degree of control over the learner. Those who move from the example sections towards the testing section, for example, should be encouraged to study the theory before moving into a judging phase. This will be challenging for learners, as they will be exercising activities that are appropriate to one of their least preferred functions. Having presented a theoretical model of how a learning cycle might work by the presentation of choices let me move to an example of how it might work in practice.

Example of interpersonal skills training in interviewing

Sheila is a bubbly and lively trainer of interpersonal skills. She likes the interaction in the syndicate room. She is very empathetic with people and listens well. Her enthusiasm and energy rub off on the learners. As a result she carries them with her and creates motivation by her presence in the classroom.

She now has to design some on-line material in interviewing skills. This is required to increase the availability of this training within the organization for which she works and to achieve some reduction in travel costs. The topic is interviewing candidates for job roles as part of a restructuring within the organization. When she does this face-to-face she concentrates on the people issues, asking participants to play roles. These roles are simple at first and then become more complex. She would tend to launch straight into practice, giving good quality and well-received feedback to participants. They had an opportunity to practice in a safe environment and learn by their mistakes. There were always participants who wanted to know about the structure of an interview and have techniques explained to them before trying them out. Sheila would use her personality to try out ideas first and encourage those participants to practice and then ask them what it was they had learnt. She knows she cannot do this through on-line learning. Sheila has a friend who is very objective, perhaps a bit unfeeling. She talks to him about the interview process and the points that need to come out and gets his help to structure the topic. The interview by nature is linear, although techniques for evaluating one's own performance and preparation for the next are not. Assessment of an interpersonal skill is subjective and carries emotional connotations. Sheila splits the topic into emotional approaches to assessment and those that are purely intellectual.

Intellectual evaluation is about whether the aims were achieved, was all the information transferred, was there good quality communication and was this checked, did both parties understand what the other was trying to achieve. Emotional evaluation is

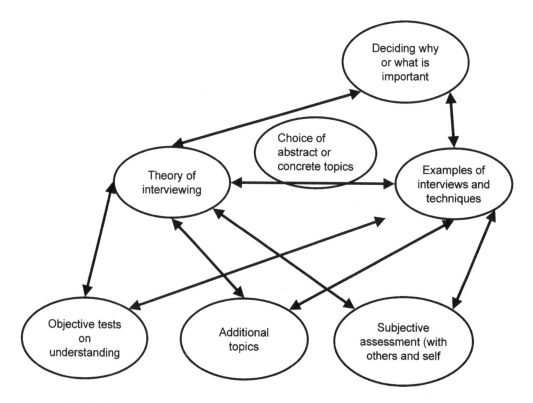

Figure 7.1   A design structure for interviewing skills

about whether the interviewer and interviewee felt comfortable. Did the interview flow with no awkward pauses and did the two participants establish rapport. The techniques associated with interviews include questioning. Getting questioning right is about choosing questions correctly, and hearing and listening to the response in a meaningful way. For the other party it is about hearing and understanding the question and testing to see whether the answers provided are matching the interviewer's needs. The e-learning course must cover preparation and evaluation of the interview, as well as the interview itself.

There are four main parts to the design (see Figure 7.1).

(1) The core of the topic which is presented in a number of stages each of which is either concrete or abstract (centre of Figure 7.1)
(2) A decision making part (testing or assessment) (bottom corners of Figure 7.1).
(3) Additional topics for learners to explore at will.
(4) Topics that help learners put the material into context or decide what is important to them.

I have expanded the basic design diagram in Figure 7.2. There is a basic linear sequence, which represents the interview with its stages. Within each stage there is an alternative presentation of concept or practical example. This meets the need of those whose dominant or auxiliary function is either iNtuition or Sensing. From each and every stage it is possible to select any one of a range of techniques used within the interview process. This will meet the needs of perceivers, who like to explore related topics. Parallel to the interview sequence

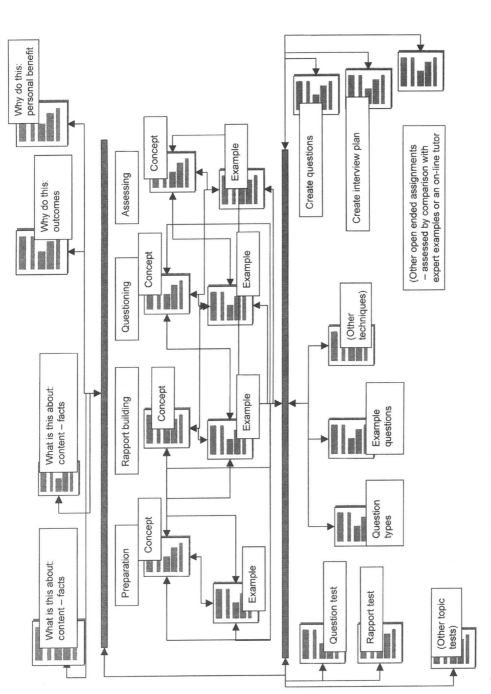

Figure 7.2 A design mesh for interviewing skills

and within the subject core are modules about emotional and intellectual preparation and emotional and intellectual evaluation. These are not shown in Figure 7.2 but will follow a similar pattern of allowing learners to choose modules. Emotional preparation will include such issues as how the interviewer might control their own responses to an aggressive outburst from the interviewee. This is perhaps less likely in the scenario described but will be relevant for disciplinary and appraisal interviews.

The testing and assessment material is both subjective and objective. Rather than think of this as tests it may be more helpful to recognize that these modules help learners organize and structure their learning: they help decision-making either subjectively or objectively. Again learners will choose what they do and in what order. Many learners will start here. It is likely to split so that the sections about intellectual content require objective evaluation; categorize questions as open or closed, identify any closed questions you used in a previous interview, list the stages of an interview for example. The modules on emotional issues are more likely to be subjective, how did you feel at the start of the interview and how did you think the other person felt: how well did you do in building rapport. The interview sequence, that is the subject core, includes demonstrations of role models and the preparation and evaluation sections are scattered with questions and interactions.

There are also modules to help learners make decisions about learning before they start. This will allow learners to use their dominant Judging function to make objective or subjective decisions about why they should study, in what order, for what benefit, how much effort they will make and for how long. Perhaps only about half the learners will use this before settling down to learn the subject core but it gives them the option of having a plan. All topics will use a full range of visual cues as well as text. Audio and video will be available where the technology allows.

The design is sign-posted as to whether the section is talking about theory or using concrete examples. Learners may move through the material in whatever route seems appropriate to them. I have simplified the design into major blocks of material and shown this in Figure 7.3. This provides a template for structuring topics. Another test of the design is to draw up the topic list and see how well balanced it is in relation to the four functions, the cognitive skill level and the style of presentation. This is useful even if the type of proposed design structure is not used. Balancing concrete, abstract, subjective and objective material is used so that every learner will find something that appeals to them.

TOPIC CHART FOR E-LEARNING

One of the proposals I make is that activities within e-learning are characterized in accordance with MBTI functions that is as concrete or abstract but open, or leading to a subjective or objective closure. We can then ensure that material is available to the learner in all these forms. If the learner can access these under their own control this will make due allowance for individual preferences. This does rely on being able to characterize topics in this way? Let us see if this will work with the topic of interviewing.

Interviewing requires planning, an atmosphere conducive to open and honest two-way communication, question techniques and a positive experience for both parties (at least positive in the sense that everyone feels they are treated equally whatever the outcome). I have listed some of the topics that we might expect to find in an on-line course on interviewing.

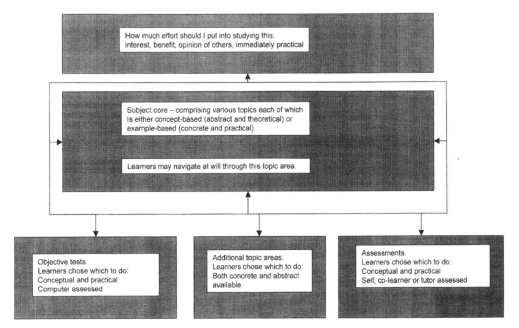

Figure 7.3 Simplified design mesh for interviewing skills

- An example of an interview plan.
  This is a concrete topic giving an example of the plan of a specific interview. It presents information without asking for any decisions. As with any example it is relevant only to the type of interview that it demonstrates. Examples of plans for different interviews may be needed.
- Items to consider when developing an interview plan.
  This is an abstract topic presenting a global view that would apply to more than one interview type. Some elements of it could be presented diagrammatically. The topic would include reasons as to why items are included in a plan. This is an open topic but capable of being converted or readily linked to a decision topic.
- Select items to be included in the plan for your interview.
  This is an objective decision-making topic that leads on directly from the previous topic. Some learners may wish to do them in reverse order. They may prefer to make the decision and then seek justification for it by reviewing the previous topic. This reinforces the mesh-like nature of topics within e-learning. There is no right or wrong order in which to study topics. This topic may be turned into one requiring subjective reasoning, but only in the situation where there are no 'right' answers.
- Watch an interview.
  This is a concrete example. It might be presented as a role model with an example of excellence, in which case, it is an open topic requiring observation and memory, rather than judgment. It can be turned into a topic requiring subjective reasoning, where it is presented as a less than perfect interview. In this case the learner should provide a critique of the interview. Such a critique is likely to have many 'right' answers and learners may compare and contrast their feedback and critique with that of others. The others with whom they compare their answers might be co-learners or tutor-derived examples.

- List the actions that are taken before conducting the interview.
  This is an abstract topic. It will include things like room presentation and what information an interviewee should be supplied with.
- Show examples of background information used in a selection interview.
  This is a concrete topic and, as with previous concrete topics, will vary depending on the requirements of the interview, for example, recruitment, disciplinary or appraisal. If the learner is given a list, or examples, of background information and is asked to select the material that is relevant then this topic will require objective decision-making.
- Self-assessment checklist.
  This is certainly a topic that requires decision-making. It may be presented in ways that are subjective or objective. Typically an objective assessment would deliver yes or no type answers; for example, 'did you ask the interviewee if they had any questions?' It might be described in ways that are subjective; for example, 'how well did you establish a rapport with the interviewee?'
- Select or amend questions for use in an interview.
  This requires objective reasoning on the assumption that questions are assessed against clear criteria. It is relatively easy to develop these criteria and the difference between open and closed questions is one of syntax measurement. It is possible for a computer program to provide some of this assessment.
- Describe the types of questions and what they achieve.
  This is an abstract topic. The topic would explain the syntax of open and closed questions. The various types of closed questions would be described with typical answers that might be expected.
- Give examples of questions used in an interview and the results achieved.
  This is a concrete topic. Learners either read or listen to what was said in an interview and the reply achieved.

I have summarized this topic chart in Table 7.2. It is apparent that this list of possible on-line learning material is rather short on subjective judgment exercises. Of the two examples that are given one is based on self-assessment and the other on a video (or practical work-based) exercise, where learners observe and make judgments based on these observations. These judgments are then compared with those from other learners, or examples given by a tutor. Using a computer for subjective reasoning has inherent difficulties. It is this fact that provides the most convincing argument for the involvement of real people within the learning process, it may be a reason why different personality types are drawn to different topics. If you like objective judgment, mathematics is more likely to appeal than a career in sales. If you like subjective judgment then mathematics is unlikely to appeal. A preference for subjective reasoning may also cause a learner to dislike e-learning. Those whose dominant function is Feeling will find little in pure on-line learning that stimulates that function. What there is, has to be presented as input from other people; that is from co-learners. There is no reason why these co-learners should not be hypothetical, that is, examples of people whose comments are created by the designer.

MEETING THE NEEDS OF EXTROVERTS

It is apparent from the previous example that subjective judging needs input from other people. Working with others in virtual (or real) learning groups is one way to achieve this.

Table 7.2 Topic list for interviewing subjects

Topic	Concept	Example	Subjective interaction	Objective interaction
Interview plan example		Yes		
Items in a plan	Yes			
Select items for a plan				Yes
Watch an interview		Yes		
Assess another's interview			Yes	
List what to do before an interview	Yes			Yes (if tested)
See examples of background information needed		Yes		Yes (if the learner is asked to select what is used
Self assessment checklist			Yes if open ended	Yes if closed: single right answers
Select questions to use (or amend questions)				Yes
Describe questions to use and what for	Yes			
Examples of questions used and what answers were given		Yes		

Note: This list shows topics categorised in accordance with activities appropriate to MBTI functions.

Other ways include tutor input and the use of personal comment from previous learners. A designer might create such input as part of the learning material, in other words, make it up. This is not enough for everyone. It makes insufficient allowance for those who gain energy from interaction with others.

Although the e-learning designed by Sheila includes self-assessment on a subjective basis this needs to be shared with other people. The first addition she makes is that each participant has a 15-minute telephone conversation with her about their preparation for an interview. This will occur at an early stage of their on-line study time, and must occur before they do their first real interview. Before the telephone conversation with Sheila they will send her their preparation for the interview in accordance with the on-line section on planning. During the conversation, Sheila gives feedback on this preparation and talks about their emotional preparedness as well. They have an opportunity to share concerns with her. This is a challenge for a telephone interview, as it requires a high level of trust to be established very quickly. Participants then complete the rest of the on-line material and conduct their first interview, ideally in company with a colleague. The colleague should be aware of the content of the course, as well as having previously conducted interviews of this type. After the interview the participants send Sheila notes that they have made and have another 15-minute telephone conversation.

An option, which is available for some, is for two participants to get together and observe each other's interview. It may be possible to do an audio or video recording of the interview, in which case this can also be sent to Sheila. Part of the study material includes videos of ideal interviews and participants can elect to see these. Given a broadband connection or a CD-ROM delivery, this video material can be included with the on-line material. This combination gives participants theory, examples and role models. They can gain energy from the telephone conversations and, where possible, by interacting with another participant. The recording of an interview and reflecting that back to the virtual tutor encourages the judging process. However, this needs to be enhanced by a reflective review with others to produce a subjective assessment and an objective analysis of a successful interview.

Getting two people together to share the interview process encourages subjective assessment, based on another person's view. This will suit the preference of those who make judgments based on empathy with others. An objective analysis of what actually happened in the interview will help those who make judgments based on logic. During the feedback telephone conversation it will help Sheila if she knows the type preferences of the particular participant she is talking to. An objective analysis is still needed and Sheila decides on a simple test. She presents participants with examples of questions they might ask. Learners categorize the questions in two ways: first, at what stage in the interview they would use this question type; and second, the likely response from the interviewee.

The on-line material provides knowledge about the structure and techniques to be used in the interview process. The first practice session is in the real environment, and while this is a major challenge for some, the individual can be supported in this process by the virtual tutor. The design makes allowances for different personal preferences and the way information is presented. There is a presentation of knowledge, both in detail and demonstrations of examples. There is also a presentation of the theoretical structure and an analytical explanation of question technique. This is both a pragmatic and a theoretical explanation and the benefit of this approach is justified, both by an understanding of personality type and by the Honey and Mumford learning cycle. The presentation of knowledge is followed by an opportunity to practise with a review process. The review process is both subjective, based on interactions with others, and objective based on interactions with a test system. This process exercises all the MBTI functions so that there is something in the course that appeals to everyone.

Example of training for project management

I have given one example of how the design and learning ideas based on an understanding of MBTI type preferences may be used. Here is another. George wants to make good use of an e-learning program during project management training. The course available is already used by many project managers. Learners who progress through this course finish as competent in all the organizational and technical skills appropriate to the project management role. However, those who complete the course say they have difficulty with resolving conflict and recognizing when project teams are about to get into delays and difficulties. A training needs analysis that George conducts reveals that project teams feel project managers are detached and concentrate too much on charts and reports. Project managers' bosses say they do not have a feel for a project, although when asked to describe what 'feel' means they have difficulty articulating it. The behaviours they see are that project managers do not give quick answers about the state of the project, or do not seem to know the views of others outside the project.

An analysis of the e-learning course shows that it covers all the technical details of the resource management, planning, tools, communicating, quality assurance and implementation. The course is very logical: uses periods of practice and review as well as providing content. Mock plans are created from case studies and reviewed against ideal model answers. There is a wealth of detail and clear descriptions of the theoretical background, the life cycle of a project, stakeholder management and quality standards. There is practice with mock plans and scenarios in various parts of a project life cycle. This is an ideal e-learning product dealing with cognitive skills and an opportunity to practice. In presentation terms the content is available in both a practical and theoretical form, appealing to both S & N type personalities. The opportunities to practise, the self-tests and the competency tests all help learners to structure the information objectively based on cause and effect. There is no subjective assessment, so those who like to make decisions about their own learning on Feeling criteria are not supported.

George talks to the existing senior project managers who have completed the e-learning course. On the basis of their comments he sees that the course encourages a view that project management is about a logical sequence of tasks. This is presented so that each task follows a previous task in a cause and effect chain. It includes all the issues of people management and provides vignettes of teams interacting. The skills of team leadership, communication, collaborative working and influencing others are described. The e-learning presents both role models, training and interactive sessions on these topics. The implementation concept implicit in the design is that learners will work through the e-learning and then be equipped with all the knowledge to be project managers. Review and assessment are built-in to the product but this is focused on the learning rather than the performance. Any assessment of interpersonal skills is based on the cognitive understanding of those skills, rather than the skills themselves.

Like many technology-based training products developed over the years, the design assumes learning is self-centred: that is the learning takes place with the learning material. In practice we know that this is not true. Learning is completed as the information is organized and structured by learners in ways that make sense to them. George knows that people need to do that in two ways, objectively and subjectively. Ideally everyone needs to do it in both ways but different individuals will prefer one approach or the other. A web-based course makes it difficult for subjective decision-making. It encourages a view that there is one way to be a good project manager. The course presents a role model. Allowance is made for those who prefer concrete examples and those who prefer abstract theory, but the testing and assessment and the interactive sessions assume there is always one objectively-measured answer. There is no allowance for subjective decision-making with a multiplicity of answers. There is too little emphasis on the vagaries of human nature.

George believes that an opportunity can be given for structuring material subjectively by establishing an action learning set and bringing new project managers together where they can talk about their learning and seek the views of others. However, the overriding business rationale for the e-learning course was to eliminate travel costs. A virtual learning set, based on a discussion board and e-mail, might work. A high level of trust is needed for this work. This implies that learners have a willingness to share knowledge about themselves.

George's first aim is to ask those who undertake the course to create a presentation about themselves as people rather than as project managers. This they share with each other half way through the existing course as a means of building trust. As they apply the learning they use the virtual learning set to share problems. George encourages this and develops an error-welcoming atmosphere. He deliberately praises the volunteering of mistakes, especially those associated with the problem areas identified by project teams and by project sponsors. These were that teams felt they were not listened to and sponsors felt project managers did not know the views of others outside the project. George also adds a module on listening skills and influencing. These topics are also discussed in the virtual learning set. Learners put forward many different solutions to the same sort of problem. Each time the attitude adopted by George as the facilitator is, 'if it works for you then it's okay'. A certain amount of care is needed with this response as once learners come to expect it from George then its effectiveness is destroyed. Inevitably some learners adopt best practice from each other. Not all learners are truly comfortable in the virtual learning set. Some highly objective learners prefer to rely on their own objective assessment, but at least they are exposed to alternative views. Some highly private learners have difficulty presenting their problems to the set. A key part of George's role is to recognize both situations and take appropriate action. Clearly those who are highly objective need objective feedback from those around them.

For the others George holds one-to-one sessions. For these particular learners George also endeavours to develop a 'buddy' system simply so that people are able to share their concerns with at least one other in a similar type of role. The learning solution introduced by George of both the virtual learning set and the module on influencing skills highlights the subjective aspect of project management. Seeking the views of others makes for a subjective assessment and review of learning. This is preferred by those whose dominant function is that of Feeling. It will be useful for all learners. George's assessment of both the existing course and the nature of the problem led him to determine that there was too great an emphasis on objective decision-making and insufficient attention paid to the interpersonal interactions that are required within the project management environment.

In describing these two examples I have tried to provide something for those whose dominant function is Sensing and prefer concrete examples to theory. The other purpose of the examples is to show that applying the functional model to e-learning design is very practical. It may be designed into every e-learning programme and the inherent hypertext linking in web browsers makes it easy to provide a learner with a course that uniquely suites their own preferences for learning.

Conclusion

In this book, I have set out a view that e-learning will be successful not because it is superior to other forms of learning but because there are significant changes in society. Given that supposition, then e-learning design must be improved so that it is superior to other forms of learning. The best hope for that is in designing a unique experience for each learner that takes account of their preferences. The functional learning model I propose provides a framework in which an e-learning designer and an on-line tutor can, together, achieve that. I present here an encapsulated view of my arguments.

Training and development is constantly evolving. A brief scan of the changes over time shows that, although efforts are made to plan and manage that evolution, in practice personal differences and human nature twist it. The changes that remain are those originally driven by major forces outside the control of individuals. Revolutions and wars have played their part in driving the change in training methods. The way people learn has to be considered in the context of the changing nature of society. E-learning is just another way of presenting material – another way of training. It is both less capable and more capable than methods used previously. In that sense it is no different than any other technical development in the past.

The Internet is with us and the amount of use made of it is increasing. Its growth will not be as rapid as many thought, but it will grow. Part of that growth will be in its use as a learning medium, but we can expect major changes in people's attitudes to learning material. The Internet already provides free e-learning as an add-on to other services. There is learning from the manufacturer of products, particularly in the computing industry, learning from professional institutes, learning from unions and the wide availability of a wealth of material in academic websites. The value of all this free material will exceed that from traditional academic approaches and from employers. The individual will have more choice. I expect the greatest growth of e-learning to come from courses leading to qualifications that are studied by groups of people in cohorts.

The criticism levelled against e-learning is that it lacks social aspects. It is true that social aspects are a major factor in people's attitudes to learning. Learners like to be with others and this is not entirely for the learning benefit that others bring. In a corporate environment a face-to-face training event is important for who you meet as much as for what you learn. Networking in large organizations is one of the means by which people progress and get promoted. If we consider the learning input we get from other people then this can be categorized into a number of discreet functions. These are: acting as role models, providing sources of information in response to questions, giving feedback on performance, giving praise, encouraging a sense of community and solidarity, someone to debate with and, in the case of a charismatic tutor, someone who acts as a source of inspiration. Our need for others to perform these various roles varies with our personality.

Many of these functions can be replicated in e-learning, especially with a broad definition of e-learning that includes a virtual learning set. The exceptions may well be the provision of a source of inspiration. The charismatic tutor generates enthusiasm and excitement in the learner. To some extent it may be possible to replicate this with highly interactive media-rich learning material. The drawback is that, like all forms of learning, different personality types vary in the extent to which this appeals to them; some learners like media-rich interactive content more than others. Praise may also be difficult to deliver electronically. The value we place on praise depends on our opinion of the giver as well as on the content. It almost goes without saying that someone with whom we interact electronically is likely to be less important than someone we see day-to-day in the workplace.

If we actually look at what learners do when using technology then we can see a number of common features they:

- have an unrealistic expectation of e-learning
- interrupt the delivery of the material in ways that are unexpected by the designer
- do not follow instructions
- acquire erroneous concepts and hang on to them even when proved wrong more than once, and
- are impatient with learning material and want to 'get on with the job'.

If we monitor the way learners manage their way through learning material two distinct strategies emerge. Learners fall into two groups of holist and serialist learners. They either like the big picture and will pursue several learning goals at once, or they like detail and will pursue one learning goal at a time, completing it thoroughly. Another way of looking at the differences between learners that is based on observation is as accommodators, convergers, assimilators or divergers.

- Accommodators will try out new actions and get things done. They may be considered to be people-centred and are overrepresented in the sales and care professions.
- Convergers will work from a theory and then get something done about it. They may be considered to be ideas-centred and are overrepresented in technical and managerial job roles.
- Assimilators like to reflect and construct a theory. They are ideas-centred and are overrepresented in research and academia.
- Divergers think up new ideas based on practical experience. They may be considered as people-centred and are overrepresented among those who innovate and seek change.

This categorization of learners is based on the work of Kolb who also indicated that there was a correlation between these learning preferences and personality types. This link is also reinforced by the fact that certain personality types are overrepresented in certain professions. There is evidence from the work of Kolb that specific personality types are attracted to specific learning strategies. The conclusion is that personality drives preferences for learning activity as well as career choice.

One well-respected personality model in existence since the 1940s is the MBTI. This is based on the psychological type theory developed by Jung in the 1920s. The fact that this model is based on four dimensions, each of which is a dichotomy, means that it may be possible to create, economically, e-learning that matches preferences for each type. There is also a substantial amount of research into the way in which different MBTI personality types approach learning. We can draw on this research to make inferences about the use of e-learning.

An understanding of each dimension reveals that two of them can be used to construct a model of human activity, specifically in this case, a model of learning activity. The dimensions are those of perceiving, the S/N dichotomy and judging, the T/F dichotomy. We all need to perceive and judge. This is part of everyday activity and we all do this as part of the learning process. Each of us prefers to do this in different ways depending on our personality preferences. Given that there are only four basic types of activities it is possible for e-learning to provide learners with activities appropriate to all four choices. Each of us will have a preference for just one of these activity types, with a second type supporting it. If the dominant activity preferred is a perceiving activity it will be supported by a judging activity and vice versa. However, in much the same way that Pask found that learners who switched between holist and serialist strategies were better learners than those who used only one strategy, so learning will be improved if all the MBTI activities are exercised. Because the functional model of learning is based on the four MBTI functions of Sensing, iNtuition, Feeling and Thinking, it can also be related to the nature of learning topics. The functions may be described as:

S   perceive what is real and immediate focusing on practical details
N   perceive ideas and concepts focusing on relationships and the large-scale nature of topics
F   judge subjectively, weighing many factors in the balance, both quantifiable facts and non-quantifiable opinions
T   judge objectively relying on cause and effect and paying attention to facts only.

Learning activities may be designed that exercise these functions. E-learning gives us the advantage in that the activities may be separated and learners can choose the order in which they study topics. Most people spend time in just two of these activities, as previously mentioned, one perceiving and one judging. Few pay attention to all four activities. An analysis of MBTI personality types, based on research, shows each type with a preference for a limited range of activities in relation to learning material. The bulk of this research is based in traditional educational environments, but we can draw a number of inferences that are applicable to e-learning. We can analyse the common features across personality types. Introverts gain energy from being by themselves but need others to discuss ideas with and as a source of motivation and guidance. Extroverts find solitary learning more tiring than Introverts and need others as sources of energy, as well as someone to discuss ideas with and sources of motivation and guidance. Some personality types like to help or organize others and can gain satisfaction from applying this to the learning process.

- Those who perceive by iNtuition like concepts and ideas.
- Those who perceive by Sensing like the real and immediate and practical detail.
- Those who judge by Feeling like to seek the opinions of others and organize their thoughts subjectively.
- Those who make judgments by Thinking make objective decisions, relying on cause and effect.

We can design material for each one of these activities. MBTI research enables us to predict how many people like practical topics (74 per cent), how many like ideas and concepts (25 per cent), how many make subjective decisions (57 per cent) and how many make objective decisions (42 per cent). There is a gender difference with more females than males making subjective decisions and more males making objective decisions. Subjective decision-making usually requires input from other people. We can replicate that in e-learning by ensuring that material is provided from others, either as part of the course or as input from co-learners.

We can establish patterns in the learning preferences of the various personality types and use these patterns to design e-learning content and e-learning interactions with other people. Navigation should be flexible with users moving, at their choice, through a mesh of topics (learning objects). Learning objects will be constructed like sentences, one idea, self-contained and in accordance with grammatical rules. Long sentences must be crafted more carefully than short sentences; so it is with learning objects. Each learning object, or topic, will include only one type of functional activity, concrete presentation, abstract presentation, objective judgment or subjective judgment.

Every module or course of learning objects will have a balance of functional types. Subjective judging requires opinions and is more difficult to do without the involvement of others in the learning process. This involvement is best achieved through the role of performance coach, tutor and learning communities (virtual learning sets). Participants in virtual learning sets may thrive on debate or on agreement. This introduces a conflict, which must be managed by a facilitator. Other differences are that some participants will be very active and some, who are more reflective, may observe rather than taking part. An experienced facilitator will determine the reason for either over involvement or under involvement in a learning set and take appropriate action. There is a significant challenge in understanding people in a virtual environment and it would be unfair for someone who seeks harmony to be dragged into a vigorous conflicting debate that others find stimulating. Ideally every e-learning course will use some type of learning set.

This involvement can be implemented in a number of different ways. Depending on the corporate culture and the personalities of the learners, a purely electronic solution may be possible. In other cases a workplace group may be needed. The desired management role of coach fits perfectly alongside e-learning. Not only does the manager provide the opportunity for learners to put into practice what they have learnt, the manager may also provide an environment in which some learners may organize their thoughts and ideas based on what is happening around them, as much as on what they have learnt in the course.

So what happened to Hurry and Steady and do they prefer the new maze designed along functional principles? Hurry is a bit of a holist and now finds some rooms with tiny morsels of the best cheese early on. Each morsel is tied to a room full of more of the same cheese so he can find his way to what interests him easily. The conceptual cheese that he prefers is scattered about with example cheese that he stumbles across and briefly samples before hurrying on to the next morsel of conceptual cheese. Steady finds his example cheeses neatly laid out with all the same type together with a bit of concept cheese at the end. He finishes all of one type of cheese before moving on. Both of them have to complete a maze before leaving the rooms. They have to place a little piece of cheese in the right place in the maze and that helps them to remember the taste of the various cheeses. Two friends of Hurry and Steady usually start with the challenge of the maze first so that when they find the cheeses later on they already know where it fits in the maze. They are very happy to make lots of mistakes when they first go into the maze. Each animal learns and eats differently, just like their human counterparts.

References and Other Reading

Addison, P. (1995), *Now the War is Over*, London: Pimlico.

Angharad, G. and Cooper, C. (2001), *Employers' Use and Awareness of Vocational Learning Approaches*, London: Department for Education and Employment.

Bloom, B. S. (ed.) (1956) *Taxonomy of Educational Objectives: The Classification of Educational Goals: Handbook I, Cognitive Domain*. New York, Toronto: Longmans, Green.

Buzan, T (1989) *Use Your Head*, London: BBC.

Carroll, J, (1990), *The Nurnberg Funnel*, Cambridge MA.: the MIT Press.

Culturegram'98 Italy, (1997), Provo, UT.: David M. Kennedy Center for International Studies, Brigham Young University (also available at www.culturegrams.com).

Culturegram'98 Sweden, (1997), Provo, UT: David M. Kennedy Center for International Studies, Brigham Young University (also available at www.culturegrams.com).

Dewey, J. (1902), *The Child and the Curriculum* (University of Chicago Contributions to Education, No. V), Chicago: University of Chicago, reproduced in *The Collected Works of John Dewey – The Middle Works*, edited by J. A. Boydston, Carbondale and Edwardsville, Ill: South Illinois University Press, 1969–1991.

Eisenberger, R., Cummings, J., Armeli, S. and Lynch, P. (1997), 'Perceived Organizational Support', *Journal of Applied Psychology* 82, 5, pp. 812–820.

E-Mori technology tracker (2003), http://www.mori.com/emori/tracker.shtml.

Evans, E. J. (1983) *The Forging of the Modern State – Early Industrial Britain*, New York: Longman.

Gagne, R. M. (1965), *The Conditions of Learning*, New York: Holt, Rhinehart and Winston.

Gagne, R .M. and Briggs, L. J. (1979), *Principles of Instructional Design*, 3rd edition, New York: Holt, Rhinehart and Winston.

Haber, R. (1970), 'How We Remember What We See', *Scientific American*, May, p. 105.

Hedges, P. (1993), *Understanding your Personality*, London: Sheldon Press.

Hills, H. (2001), *Team-based Learning*, Aldershot: Gower.

Hills, H. and Francis P. (1999), 'Interaction Learning', *People Management* 15 July, pp. 48–49.

Honey, P. and Mumford, A. (1986), *The Manual of Learning Styles*, Maidenhead: Peter Honey Publications.

Jewell, H. M. (1998), *Education in Early Modern England*, London: Macmillan.

Kendall, E. (1998), *MBTI Manual Supplement*, Oxford: Oxford Psychologists Press.

Kolb, D. A. (1984), *Experiential Learning*. New Jersey: Prentice Hall Inc.

Lloyds Bank Staff Journal, (1948), *The Dark Horse*, June, London: Lloyds Bank.

Lowe, N. (1998), *Mastering Modern British History*, London: Macmillan.

Mager, R. F. (1972), *Goal Analysis*, California: David. S. Lake.

Marsick V. J. and Watkins K. (1990), *Informal and Incidental Learning in the Work Place*, London: Routledge.

Myers, I., Briggs, M., McCaulley, H., Querk, N. L. and Mammer, A. L. (1998), *MBTI Manual* 3rd Edition, Palo Alto, CA.: Consulting Psychologists Press.

Negroponte, N. (1995), *Being Digital*, London: Coronet Books.

Office of National Statistics (2003), http://www.statistics.gov.uk/pdfdir/int0403.pdf.

OFTEL (2003), Consumers' Use of Internet Oftel Residential Survey, http://www.oftel.gov.uk/publications/index.htm.

Pask, G. (1976a), 'Conversational Techniques in the study and practice of Education', *British Journal of Educational Psychology*, 46, pp. 12–25.

Pask, G. (1976b), 'Styles and Strategies of Learning', *British Journal of Educational Psychology*, 46, pp. 128–148).

Pask, G. (1988), 'Learning Strategies, Teaching strategies, and Conceptual or Learning Style' in R. R. Schmeck (ed), *Learning Strategies and Learning Styles*, New York: Plenum.

Pedler, M. (1997), *Action Learning in Practice*, Aldershot: Gower.

Pipe, P. and Mager, R. F. M. (1999), *Analyzing Performance Problems: Or You Really Oughta Wanna*, 3rd revision edition, Atlanta, GA: The Center for Effective Performance.

Rengger, R. E. and Turner, M. C. R. (1988), *Evaluation of the Lloyds Bank CBT/IV Workstation*, Teddington: National Physical Laboratory.

Rose, C. and Nicholl, M. J. (1997), *Accelerated Learning for the 21st Century*, London: Judy Piatkus.

Russell, P. (1979), *The Brain Book*, London: Routledge and Kegan Paul.

Skinner, B. F. (1968), *The Technology of Teaching*, New York: Appleton-Century-Crofts.

Stevens, W. B. (1998), *Education in Britain 1750–1914*, London: Macmillan.

Stroud, Dick (1998), *Internet Strategies*, London: Macmillan.

Taylor, AJ.P. (1992), *English Social History 1914–1945*, Oxford: Oxford University Press.

The Learning Age, (1998), London: The Stationery Office.

Trevelyan, G. M. (2000), *English Social History*, London: Penguin.

Turing, A. M. (1950), Computing Machinery and Intelligence, *Mind*, 49, pp. 433–460.

White House Press Release (2001), http://clinton5.nara.gov/library/hot_releases/January_16_2001_3.html)

Winton, J. R. (1982), *Lloyds Bank 1918–1969*, Oxford: Oxford University Press, p. 152.

Index